BRIAN AZZARELLO
WRITER

JIM LEE
PENCILLER

SCOTT WILLIAMS
INKER

ALEX SINCLAIR
COLORIST

ROB LEIGH
NICK J. NAPOLITANO
LETTERERS

SUPERMAN CREATED BY
JERRY SIEGEL & JOE SHUSTER

# SUPERMAN
## FOR TOMORROW

VOLUME ONE

## SUPERMAN: FOR TOMORROW VOLUME ONE

Published by DC Comics.
Cover, introduction and compilation
copyright © 2005 DC Comics.
All Rights Reserved.

Originally published in single
magazine form in SUPERMAN
#204-209. Copyright © 2004
DC Comics. All Rights Reserved.
All characters, their distinctive
likenesses and related elements
featured in this publication are
trademarks of DC Comics. The
stories, characters and incidents
featured in this publication are
entirely fictional. DC Comics does
not read or accept unsolicited sub-
missions of ideas, stories or artwork.

DC Comics, 1700 Broadway,
New York, NY 10019
A Warner Bros. Entertainment Company
Printed in Canada. First Printing.
ISBN: 1-4012-0351-5

Cover art by Jim Lee &
Scott Williams with
Alex Sinclair

"ARE YOU OUT OF YOUR MIND?"
That was my response to a question only a lunatic
would ask me: "Do you want to write SUPERMAN for a
year?" The lunatic, though, was Jim Lee, a monstrous-
ly talented artist and the most powerfully loved man in
all of comic land — not to mention a blind brute
lunatic, who always, always answered his own questions before they were asked. I'd spent some time with
him socially, and seen him in action — he was a mas-
ter of both Snake and Crane. I quietly hung up the
phone, and pushed some projects off my desk. I was
writing SUPERMAN for a year.

I was writing Superman.

"Are you out of your mind?" That's the question
Will Dennis, my handler, asked me when I told him I
was writing Superman. He not only knew, but facilitated
my living, which was trafficking in little people's big
mistakes, and Superman was not up that alley. "It's a
done deal, pal. The ducks are in the pond — Jimmy
Lee asked me if I wanted to." The silence on the other
end of the receiver screamed he understood. "I think
he's going to ask you to ride shotgun," I added. More
silence. Will was a young turk; already a marked man
at DC. This gig would make him a friendless one.

A few nights later we were sitting at a table in a
real tony San Franciscan restaurant. Jim had sent his
private jet for us, as he has an unnatural distrust of
commercial airline travel. Also at the table were Scott
Williams, Jim's "fixer," and Alex Sinclair, the weird
muscle of the group. Besides being insane, talented,
and loved, Jim was a legendary gourmand and only
dined in five-star establishments. His crew had the
same tastes. Will and I were clearly out of our league,
being cut more from a "hotdog and a beer" kind of
cloth. I figured Jim brought us all together for dinner to
hash Superman, but he was more interested in trying to
get a Korean showgirl who'd joined us earlier to tell him
the truth. That was just as well, as I was mulling over
how a grifter had taken me for five bucks outside the
restaurant. *How did he know what city I got my shoes in?*

Just as dessert was being served, Jim lost inter-
est in the showgirl. He stuck his spoon in Scott's panna
cotta and said, "Let's talk Superman." Nobody said a
word. We were all waiting for Jim to do the telling. ➡

# INTRODUCTION

BY BRIAN AZZARELLO

"Mmmm… that's good," he said, licking his lips. "Not what I expected." Reaching across the table, he dragged his finger across the top of Sinclair's chocolate torte, cutting a deep canal. He held the finger to his nose, and breathed deeply. "This smells fresh to me." With a fluid grace usually exhibited only by figure skaters, he snatched Will's mousse out of the waitress's hand before it hit the table, and with a tongue that would make Gene Simmons blanch, licked the plate clean. "Is that olive oil and basil I taste? *Très innovative!*" He then looked in my direction. His brow furrowed when all he saw was a cup of black coffee. "Aren't you having dessert?" he asked — which I knew meant, "What are you having for dessert?"

This was it. The moment of truth. I looked Jim in the eye. "I don't like sweets. Never have."

"Are you out of your mind!?" Alex, Will, and Scott twitched at once, like some spastic Greek chorus.

The walk back to the hotel is a blur. Jim and his boys had peeled off at a tiny Gelato stand along the way, leaving just me and my handler to the enormity of our situation. We both knew this was gut check time, but for some reason we were happy about it.

Outside the Hyatt, Dan Didio, The VP of DC, was waiting for us. With him was Superman's pal, Eddie Berganza. Eddie's purple plaid bow tie was hanging from his collar, and his trademark green jacket — which he referred to as the "symbol of his individuality and belief in personal freedom" — was drenched in sweat. Dan was pacing back and forth, and Eddie was trying to stay out of his way, which is impossible, as there is no clear pattern to Dan's pacing. The fat Cuban in his mouth billowing a rich and fragrant cloud over his head — he was nervous, and rightly so. Dan knew I didn't like sweets, having wined and dined me countless times on the company tab. "How'd it go?" he demanded, clearly expecting the worst.

Will and I looked at each other. "Say Dan, I bet you five bucks I can tell you what city you got your shoes in," I said to him.

"Are you out of your mind?" he responded, taking the bait.

**BRIAN AZZARELLO**
**Chicago, 2005**

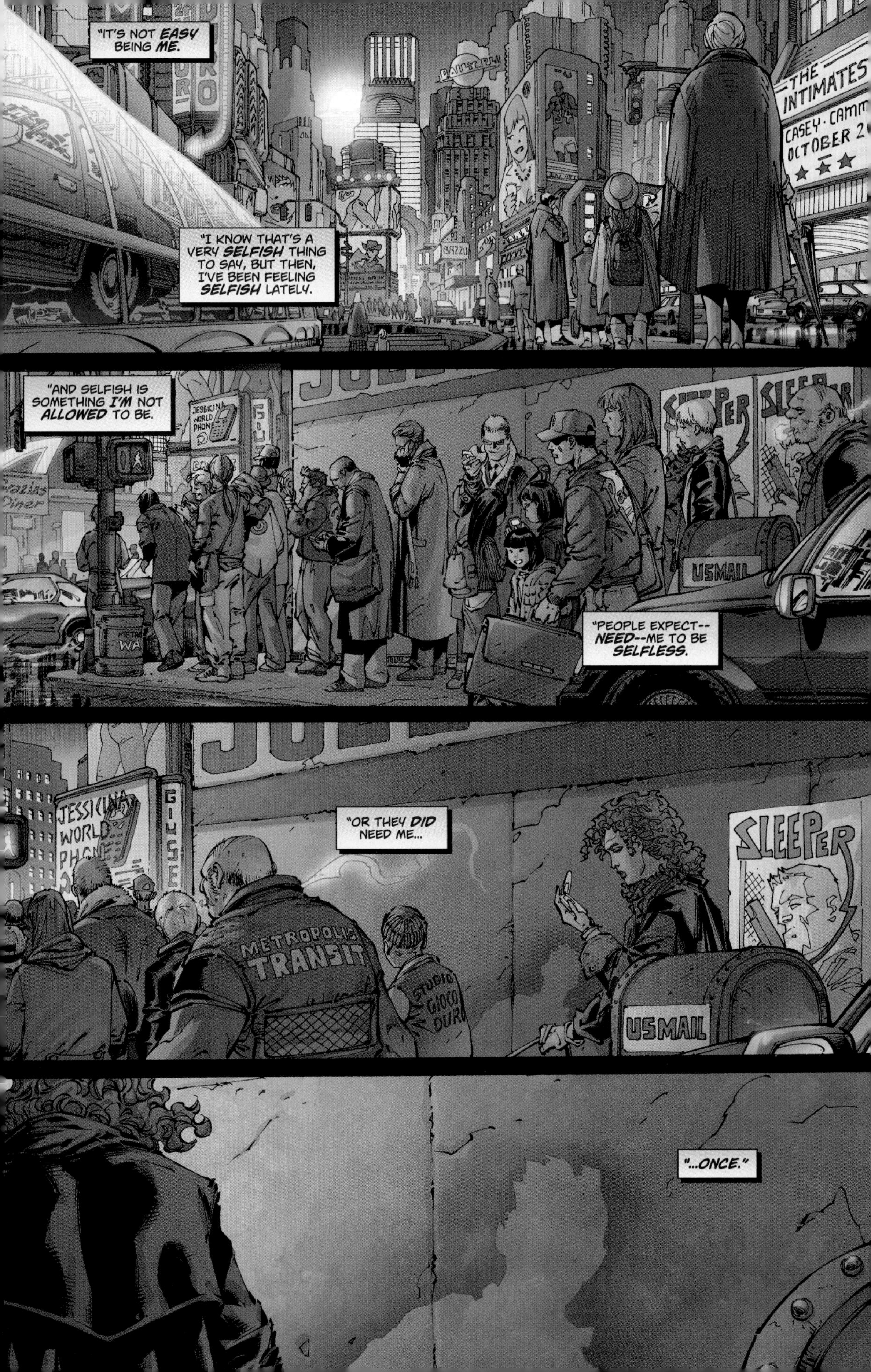
"IT'S NOT EASY BEING ME.
THE INTIMATES
"I KNOW THAT'S A VERY SELFISH THING TO SAY, BUT THEN, I'VE BEEN FEELING SELFISH LATELY.
"AND SELFISH IS SOMETHING I'M NOT ALLOWED TO BE.
JESSICINA WORLD PHONE
SLEEPER
US MAIL
"PEOPLE EXPECT--NEED--ME TO BE SELFLESS.
"OR THEY DID NEED ME...
SLEEPER
METROPOLIS TRANSIT
US MAIL
"...ONCE."

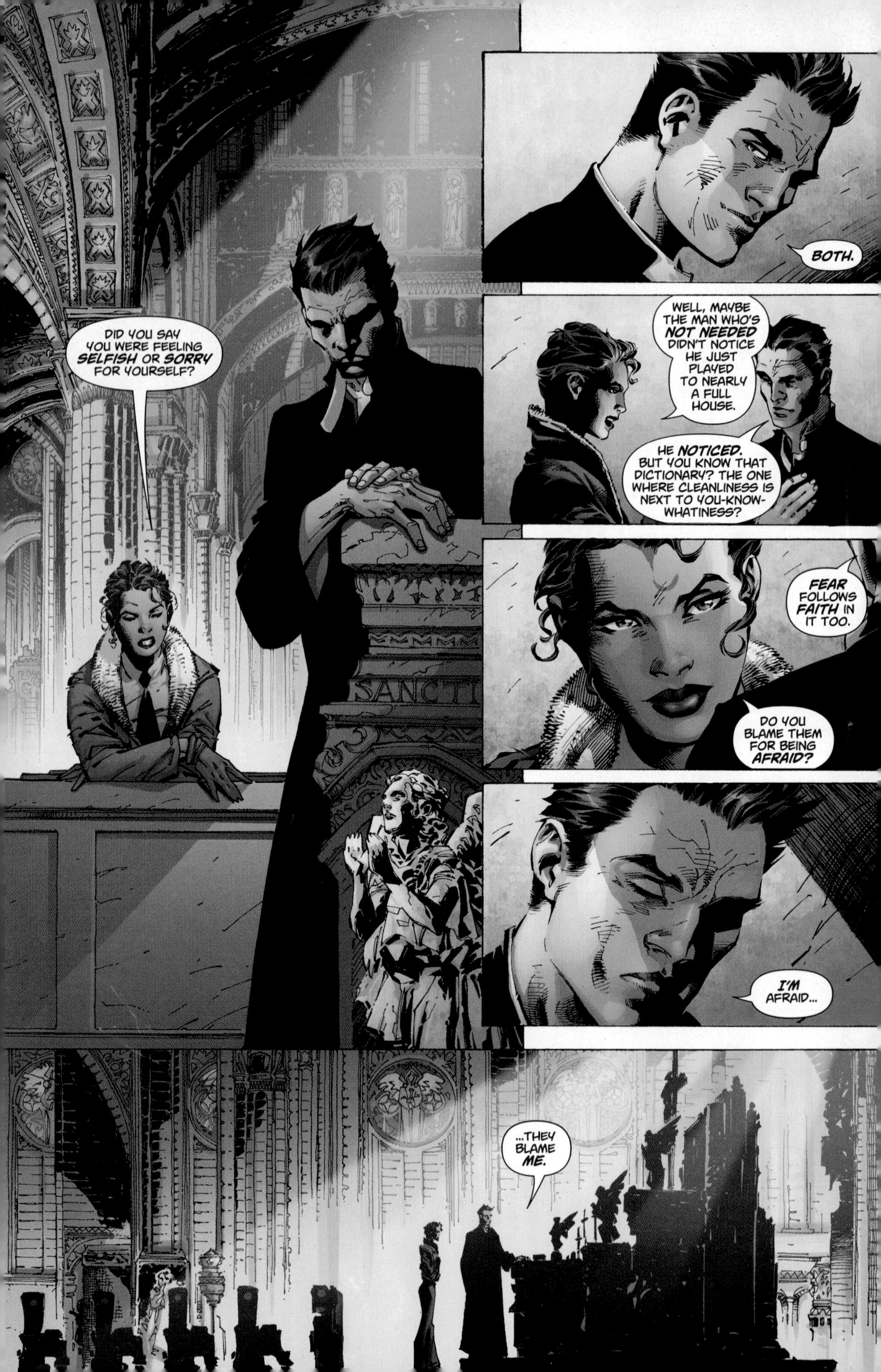
DID YOU SAY YOU WERE FEELING SELFISH OR SORRY FOR YOURSELF?
BOTH.
WELL, MAYBE THE MAN WHO'S NOT NEEDED DIDN'T NOTICE HE JUST PLAYED TO NEARLY A FULL HOUSE.
HE NOTICED. BUT YOU KNOW THAT DICTIONARY? THE ONE WHERE CLEANLINESS IS NEXT TO YOU-KNOW-WHATINESS?
FEAR FOLLOWS FAITH IN IT TOO.
DO YOU BLAME THEM FOR BEING AFRAID?
I'M AFRAID...
...THEY BLAME ME.

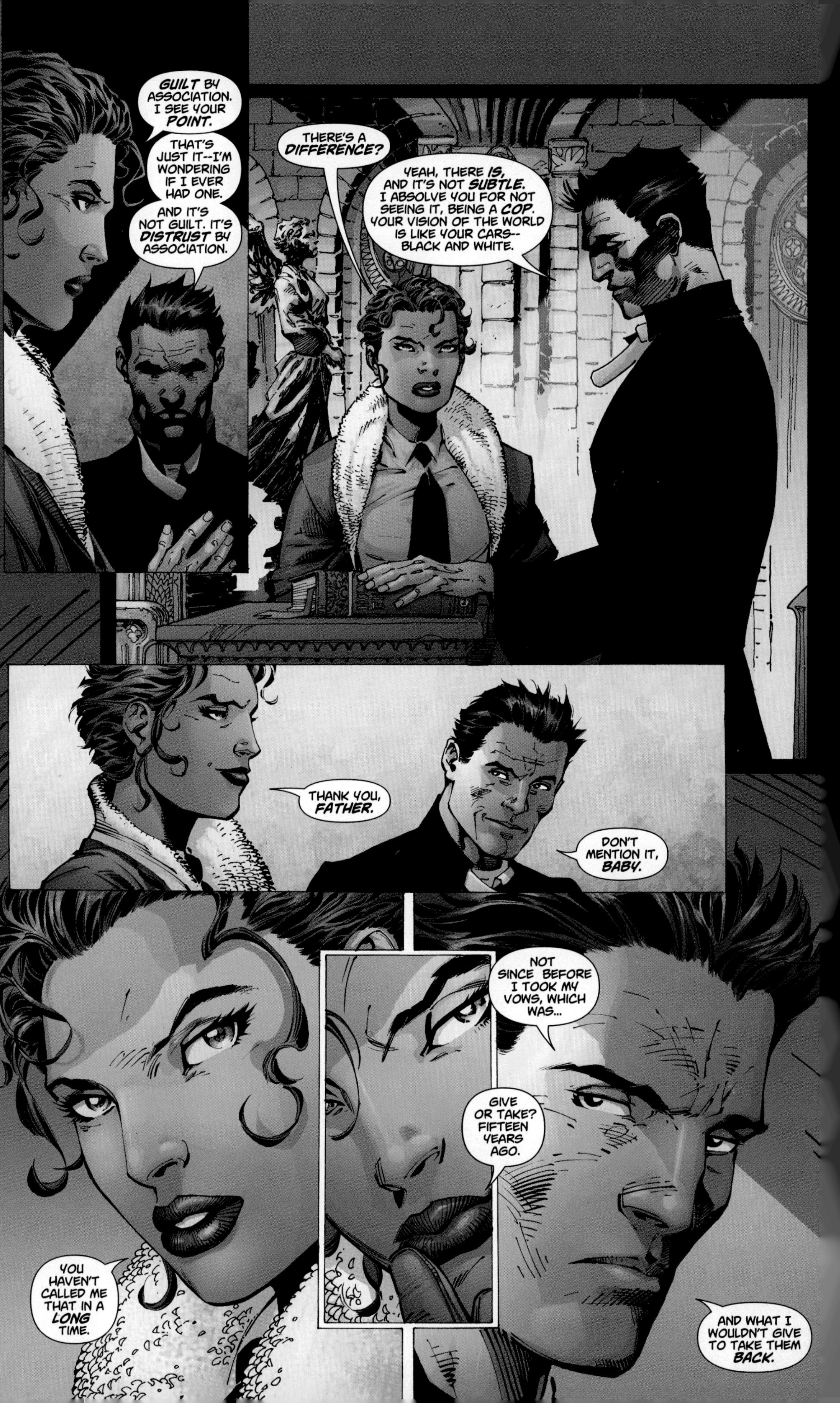
GUILT BY ASSOCIATION. I SEE YOUR POINT.
THAT'S JUST IT--I'M WONDERING IF I EVER HAD ONE.
AND IT'S NOT GUILT. IT'S DISTRUST BY ASSOCIATION.
THERE'S A DIFFERENCE?
YEAH, THERE IS, AND IT'S NOT SUBTLE. I ABSOLVE YOU FOR NOT SEEING IT, BEING A COP. YOUR VISION OF THE WORLD IS LIKE YOUR CARS-- BLACK AND WHITE.
THANK YOU, FATHER.
DON'T MENTION IT, BABY.
YOU HAVEN'T CALLED ME THAT IN A LONG TIME.
NOT SINCE BEFORE I TOOK MY VOWS, WHICH WAS...
GIVE OR TAKE? FIFTEEN YEARS AGO.
AND WHAT I WOULDN'T GIVE TO TAKE THEM BACK.

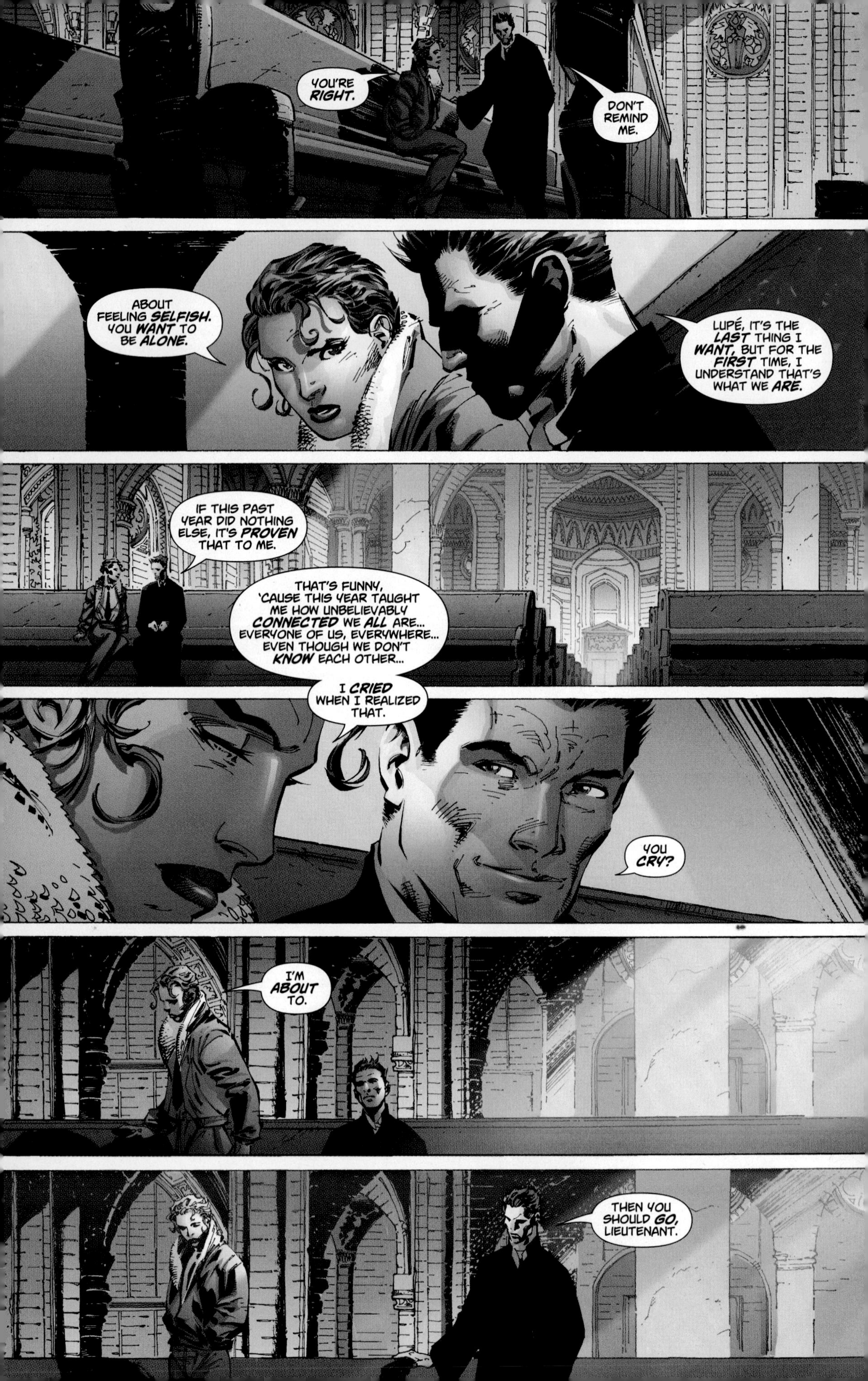
YOU'RE RIGHT.
DON'T REMIND ME.
ABOUT FEELING SELFISH. YOU WANT TO BE ALONE.
LUPÉ, IT'S THE LAST THING I WANT, BUT FOR THE FIRST TIME, I UNDERSTAND THAT'S WHAT WE ARE.
IF THIS PAST YEAR DID NOTHING ELSE, IT'S PROVEN THAT TO ME.
THAT'S FUNNY, 'CAUSE THIS YEAR TAUGHT ME HOW UNBELIEVABLY CONNECTED WE ALL ARE... EVERYONE OF US, EVERYWHERE... EVEN THOUGH WE DON'T KNOW EACH OTHER...
I CRIED WHEN I REALIZED THAT.
YOU CRY?
I'M ABOUT TO.
THEN YOU SHOULD GO, LIEUTENANT.

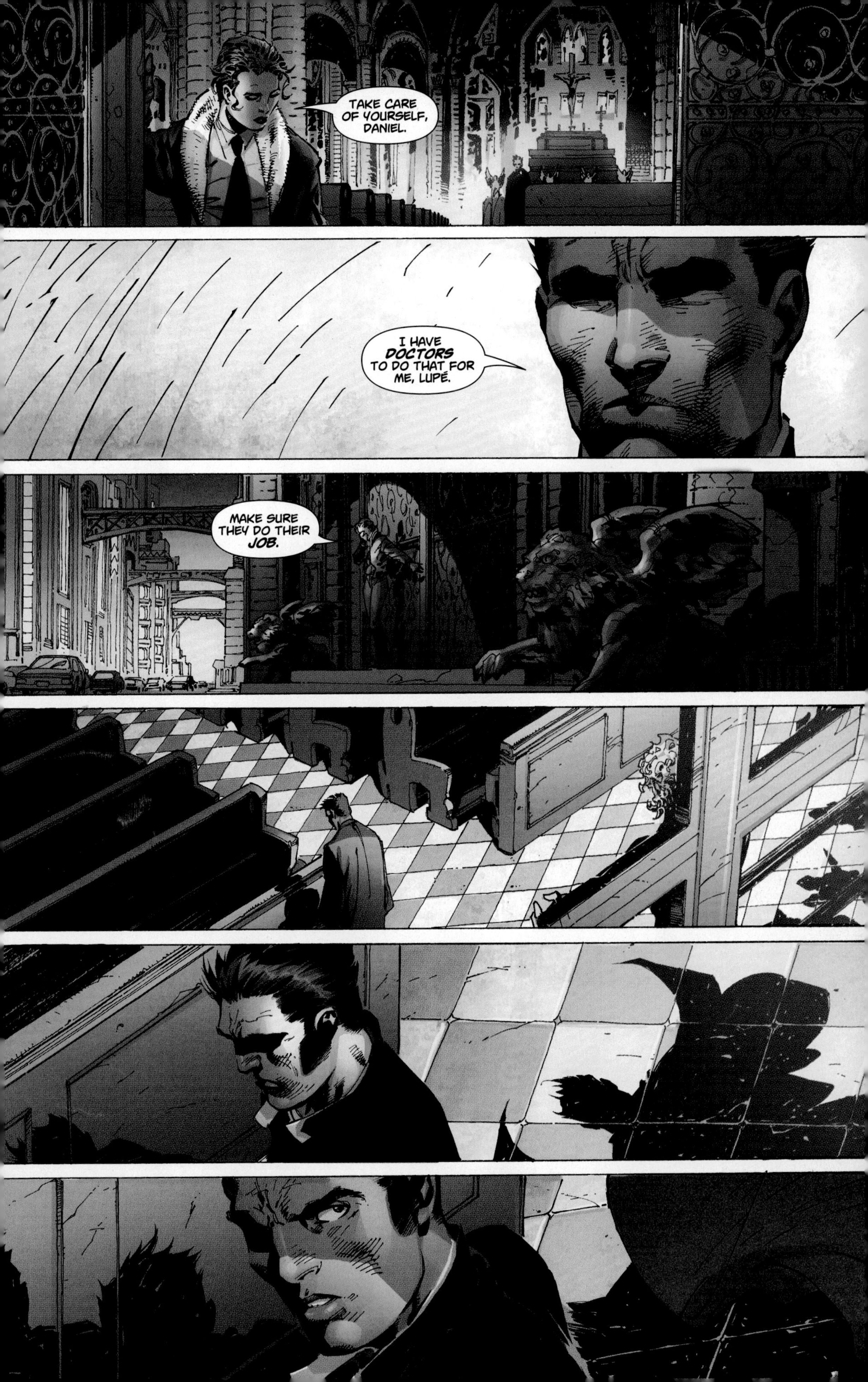
TAKE CARE OF YOURSELF, DANIEL.
I HAVE DOCTORS TO DO THAT FOR ME, LUPÉ.
MAKE SURE THEY DO THEIR JOB.

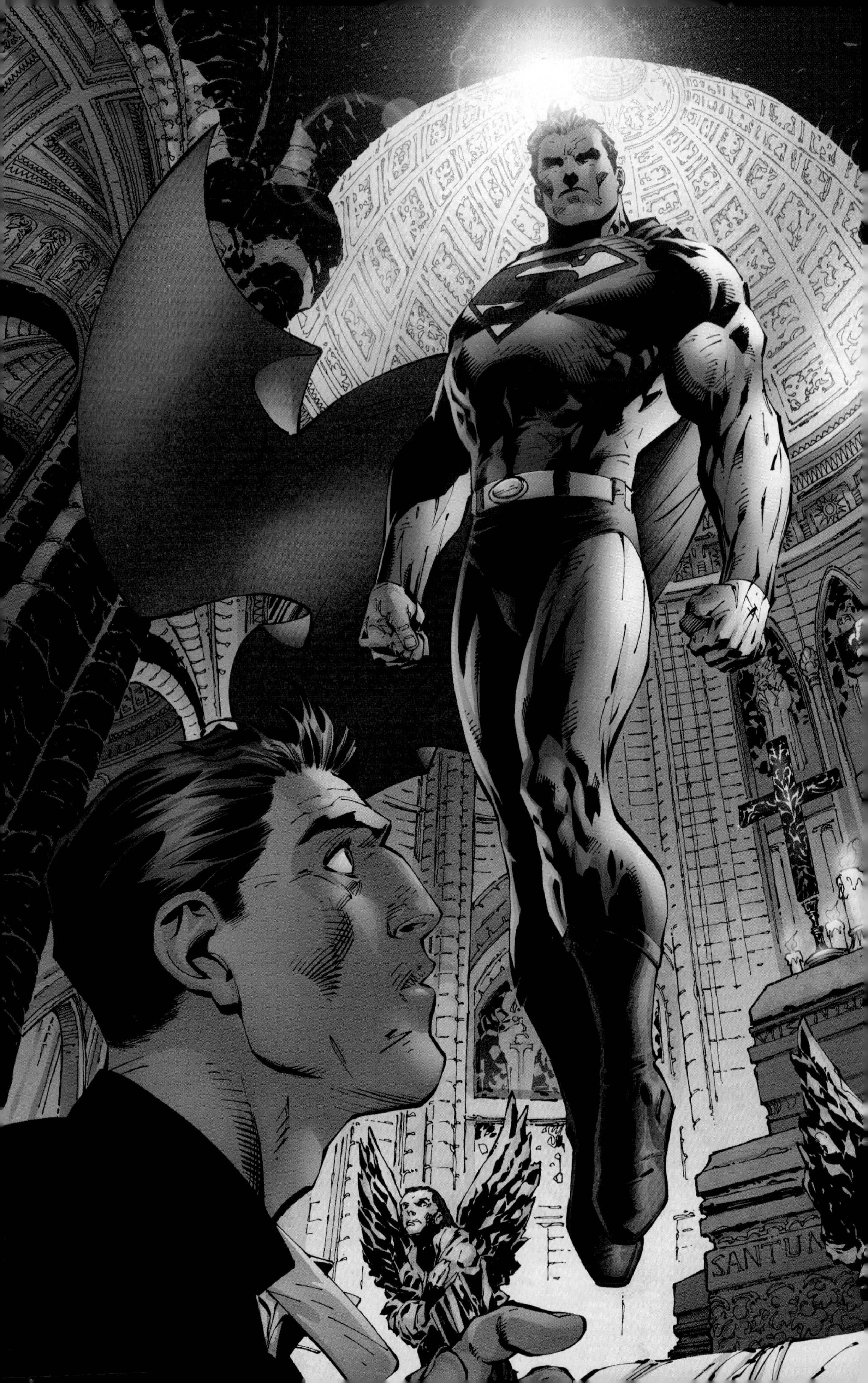

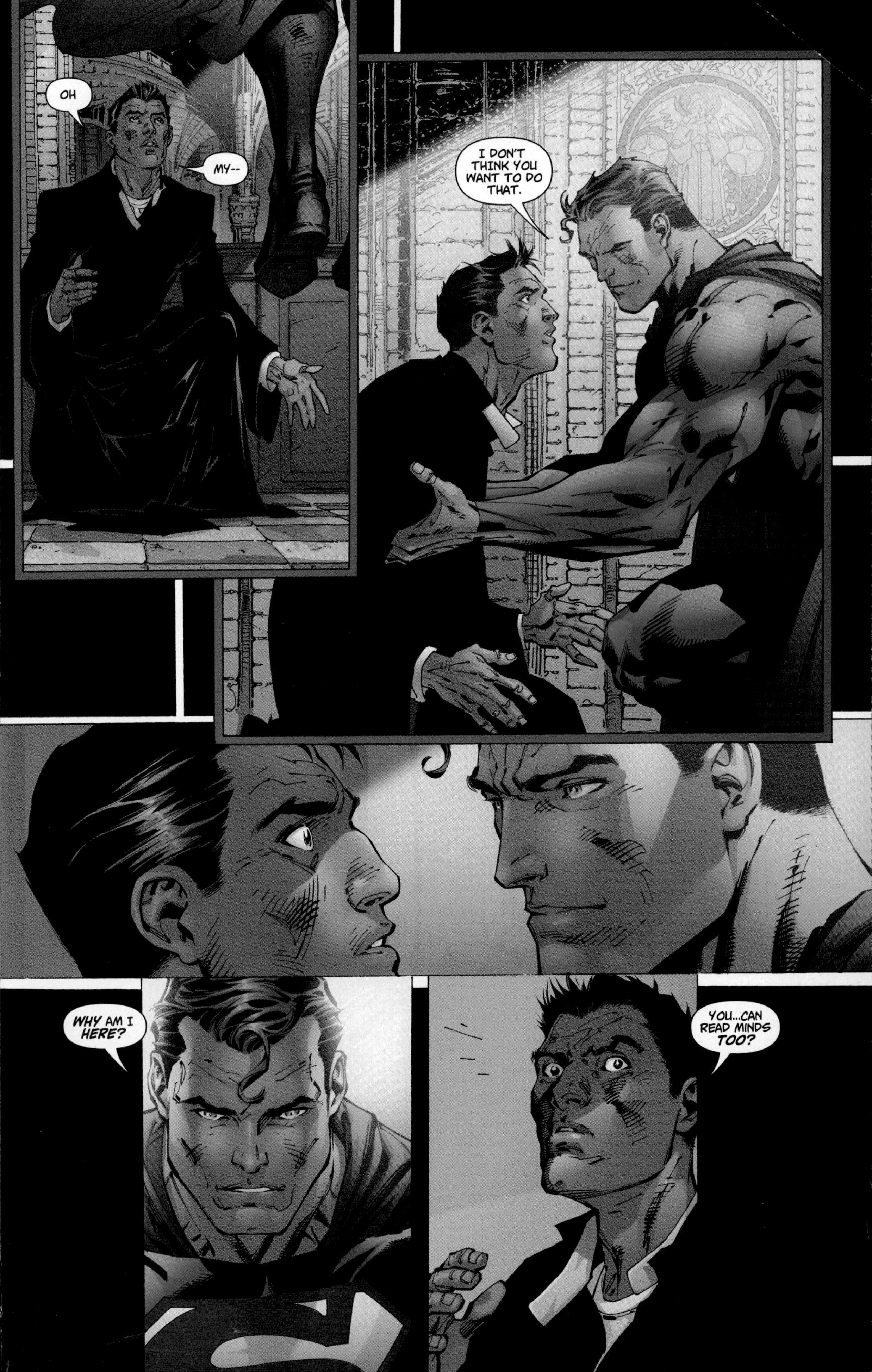
OH
MY--
I DON'T THINK YOU WANT TO DO THAT.
WHY AM I HERE?
YOU...CAN READ MINDS TOO?

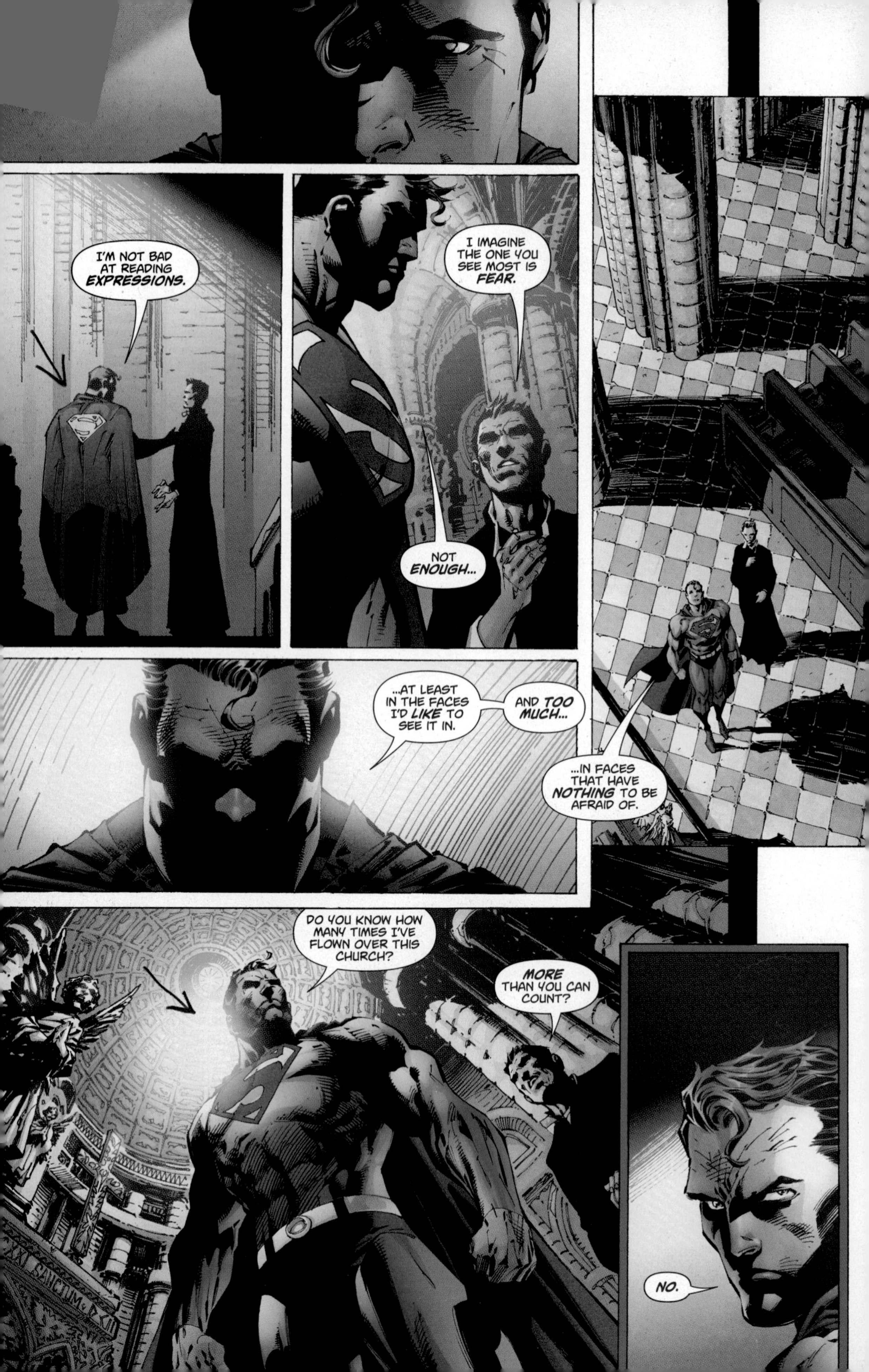
I'M NOT BAD AT READING EXPRESSIONS.
I IMAGINE THE ONE YOU SEE MOST IS FEAR.
NOT ENOUGH...
...AT LEAST IN THE FACES I'D LIKE TO SEE IT IN.
AND TOO MUCH...
...IN FACES THAT HAVE NOTHING TO BE AFRAID OF.
DO YOU KNOW HOW MANY TIMES I'VE FLOWN OVER THIS CHURCH?
MORE THAN YOU CAN COUNT?
NO.

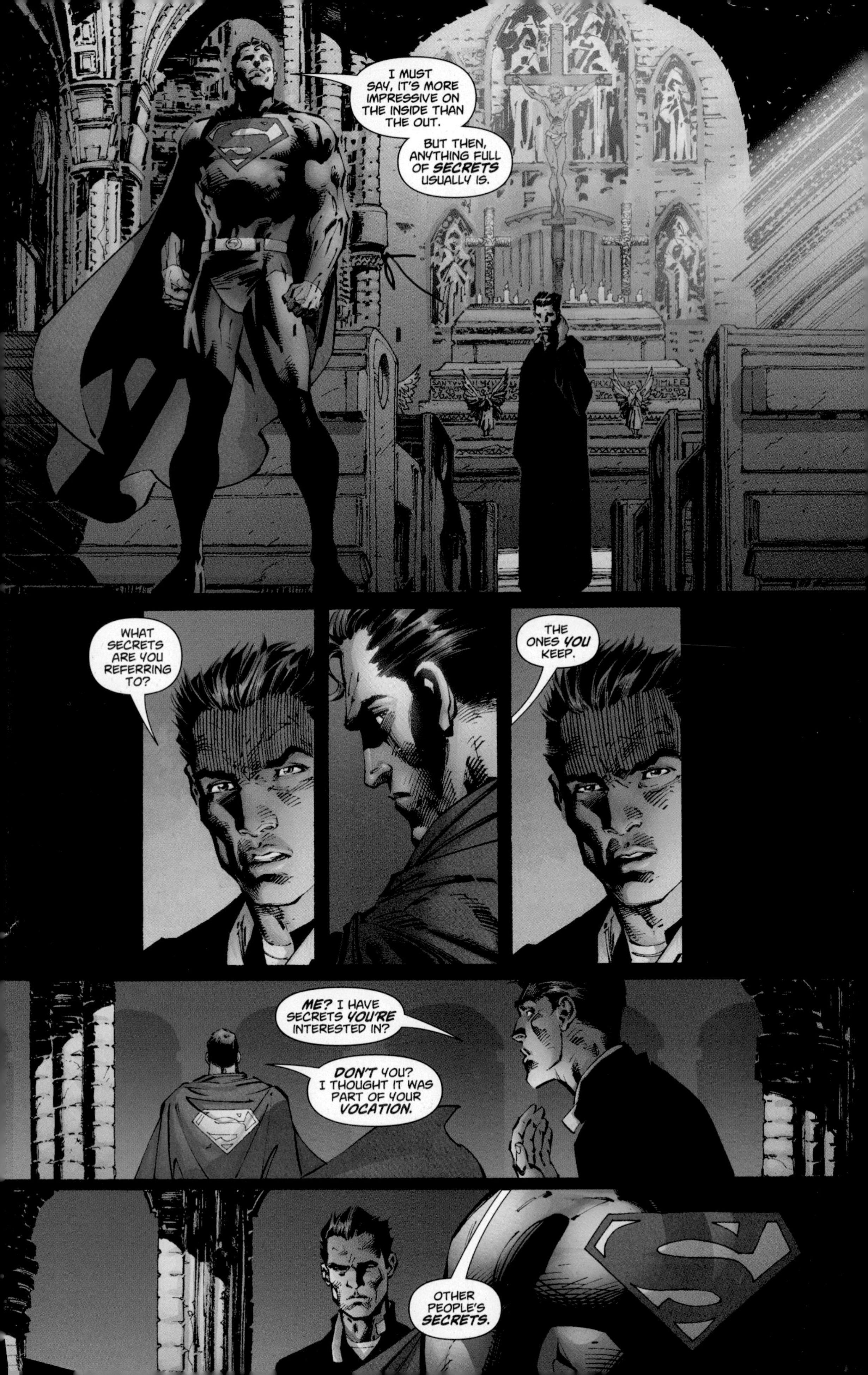
I MUST SAY, IT'S MORE IMPRESSIVE ON THE INSIDE THAN THE OUT.
BUT THEN, ANYTHING FULL OF SECRETS USUALLY IS.
WHAT SECRETS ARE YOU REFERRING TO?
THE ONES YOU KEEP.
ME? I HAVE SECRETS YOU'RE INTERESTED IN?
DON'T YOU? I THOUGHT IT WAS PART OF YOUR VOCATION.
OTHER PEOPLE'S SECRETS.

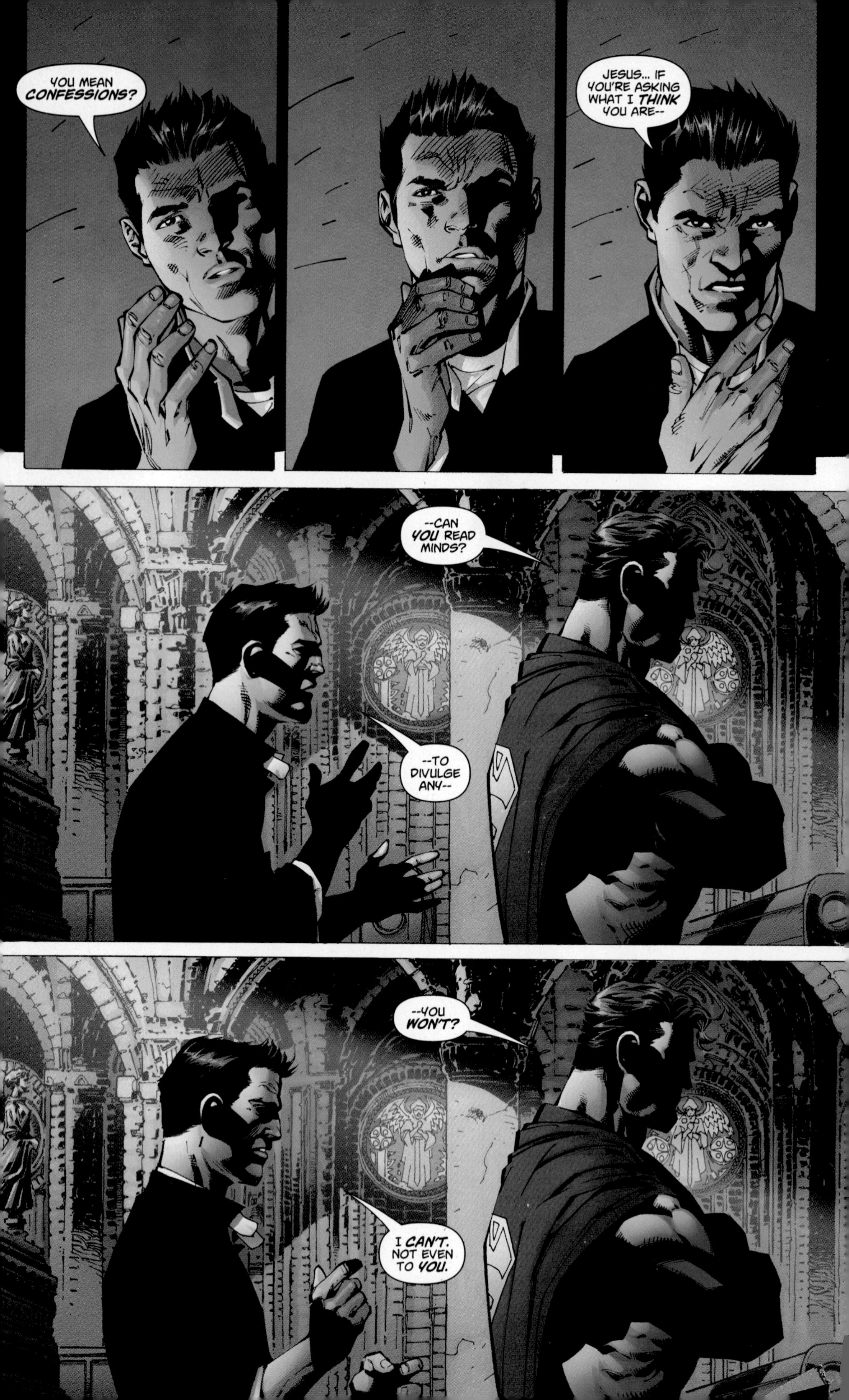
YOU MEAN CONFESSIONS?
JESUS... IF YOU'RE ASKING WHAT I THINK YOU ARE--
--CAN YOU READ MINDS?
--TO DIVULGE ANY--
--YOU WON'T?
I CAN'T. NOT EVEN TO YOU.

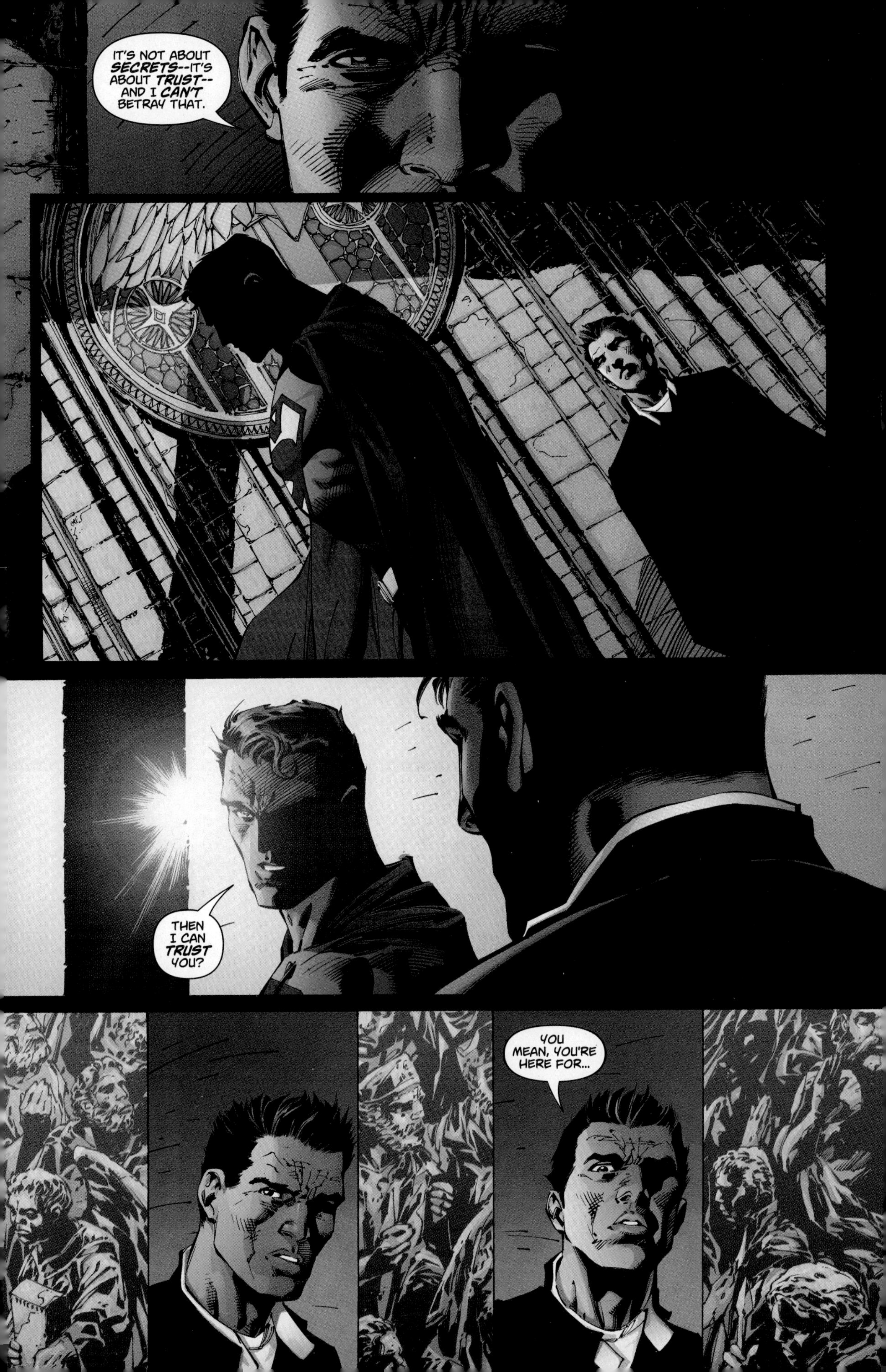
IT'S NOT ABOUT SECRETS--IT'S ABOUT TRUST--AND I CAN'T BETRAY THAT.
THEN I CAN TRUST YOU?
YOU MEAN, YOU'RE HERE FOR...

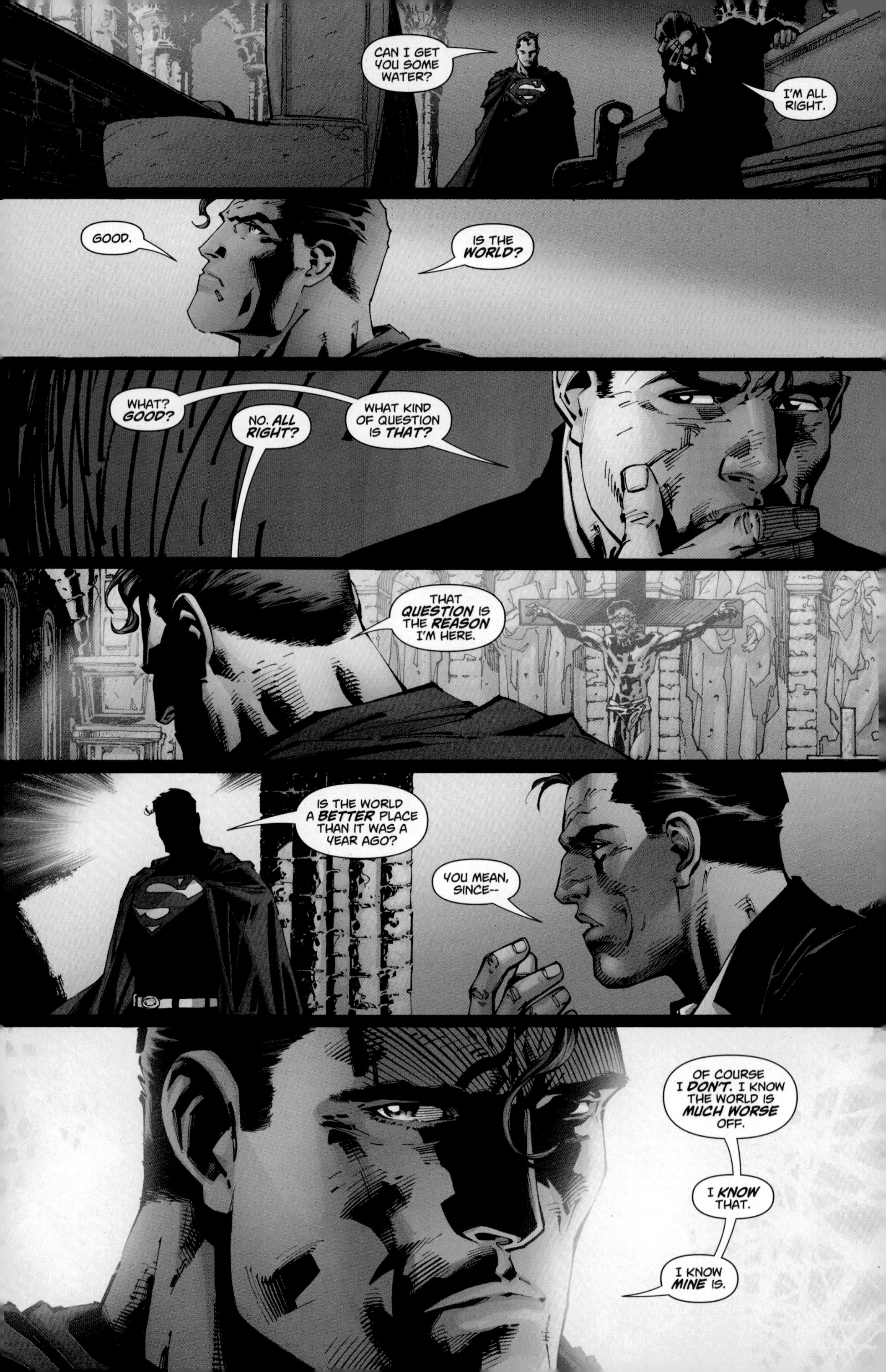
CAN I GET YOU SOME WATER?
I'M ALL RIGHT.
GOOD.
IS THE WORLD?
WHAT? GOOD?
NO. ALL RIGHT?
WHAT KIND OF QUESTION IS THAT?
THAT QUESTION IS THE REASON I'M HERE.
IS THE WORLD A BETTER PLACE THAN IT WAS A YEAR AGO?
YOU MEAN, SINCE--
OF COURSE I DON'T. I KNOW THE WORLD IS MUCH WORSE OFF.
I KNOW THAT.
I KNOW MINE IS.

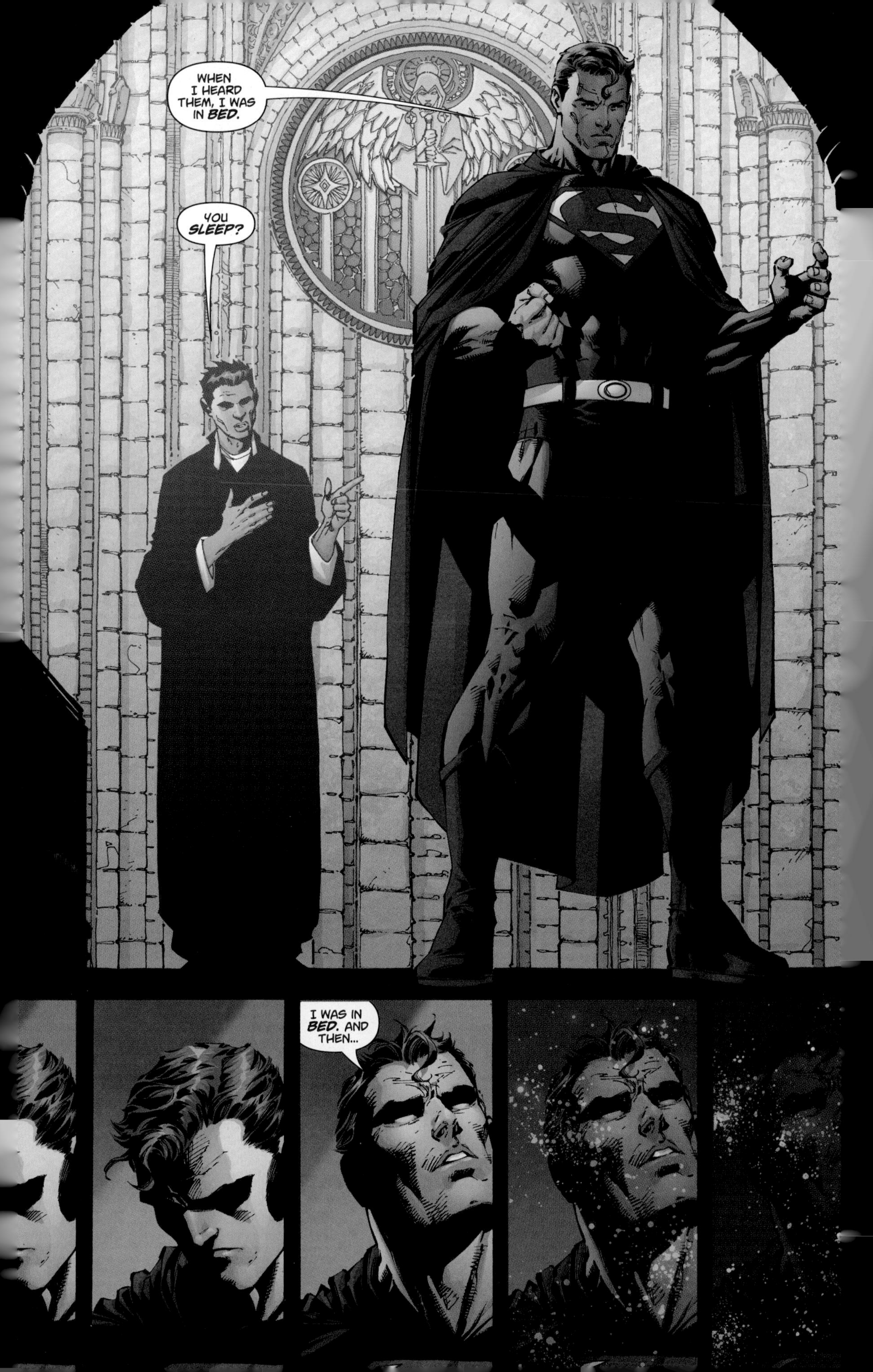
WHEN I HEARD THEM, I WAS IN BED.
YOU SLEEP?
I WAS IN BED. AND THEN...

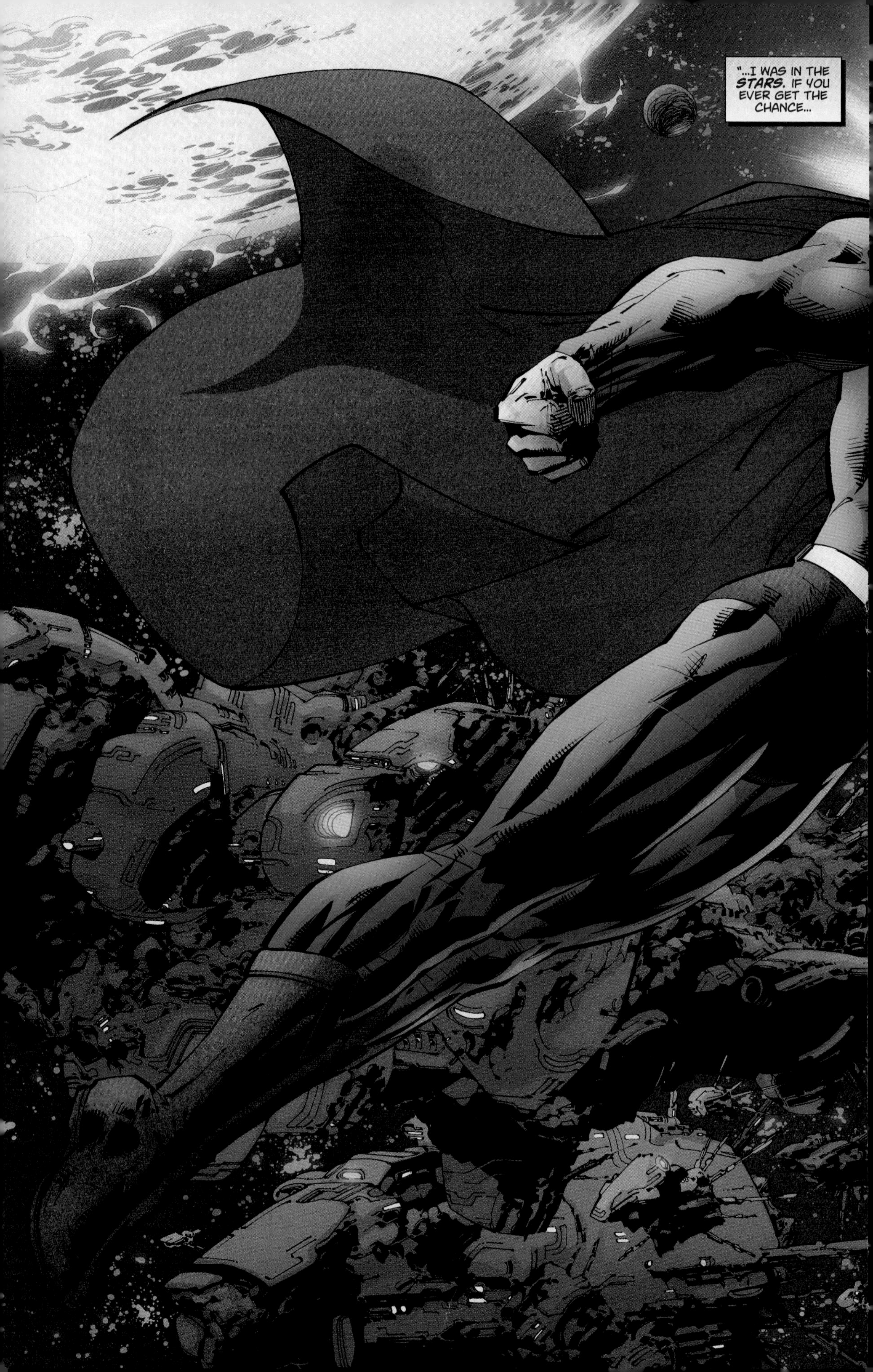
"...I WAS IN THE STARS. IF YOU EVER GET THE CHANCE...

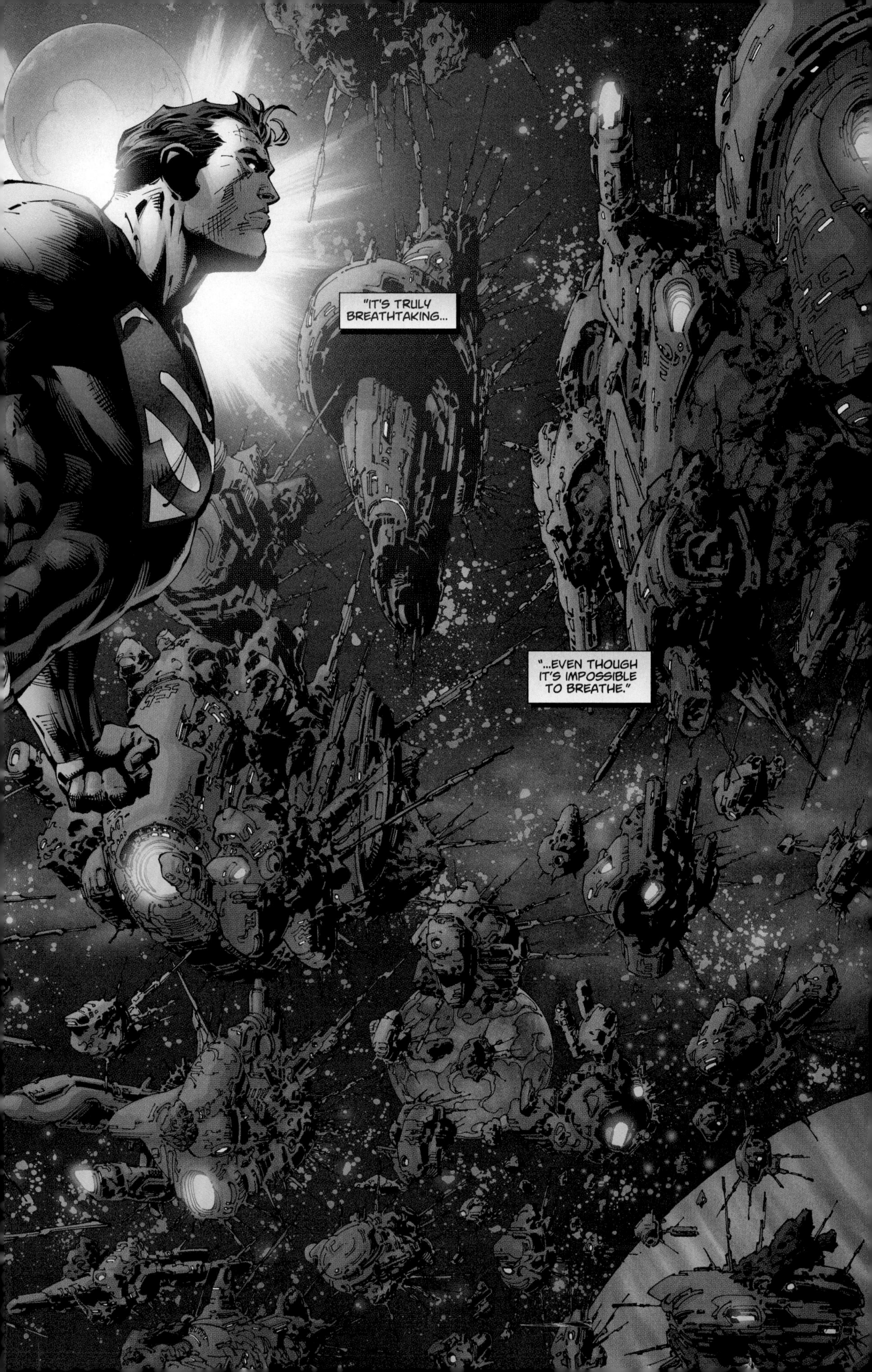
"IT'S TRULY BREATHTAKING...
"...EVEN THOUGH IT'S IMPOSSIBLE TO BREATHE."

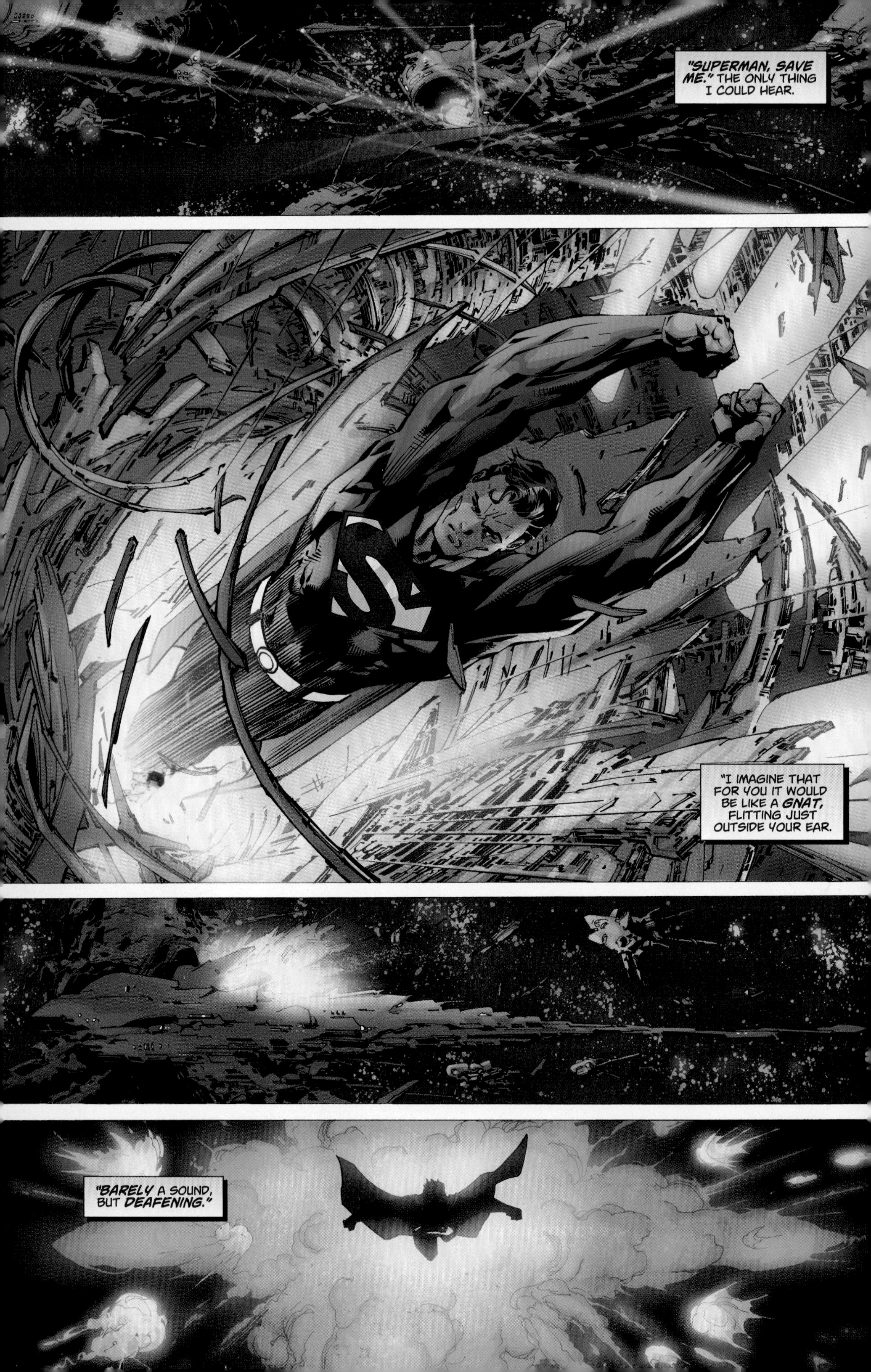
"SUPERMAN, SAVE ME." THE ONLY THING I COULD HEAR.
"I IMAGINE THAT FOR YOU IT WOULD BE LIKE A GNAT, FLITTING JUST OUTSIDE YOUR EAR.
"BARELY A SOUND, BUT DEAFENING."

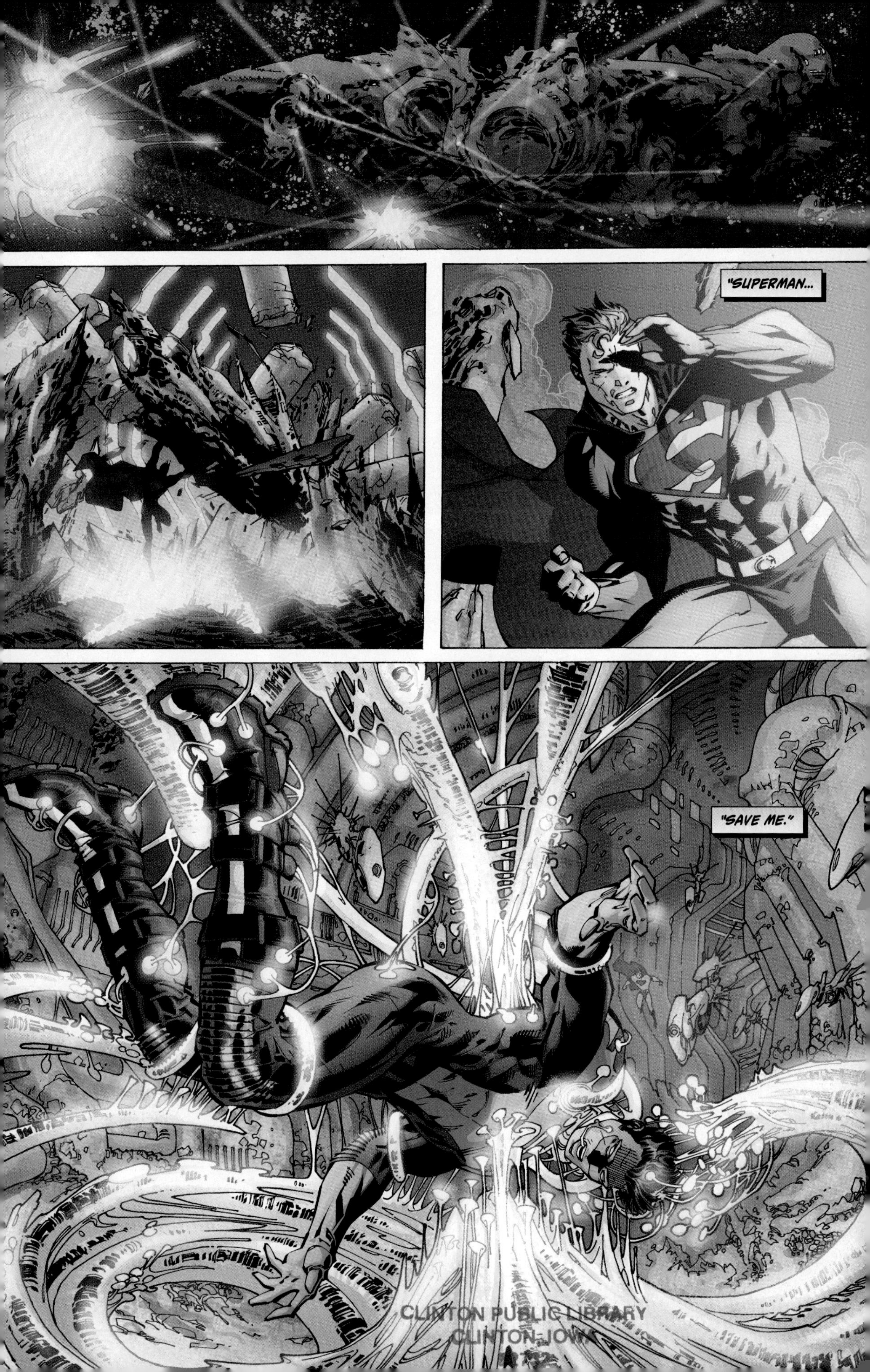
"SUPERMAN...
"SAVE ME."

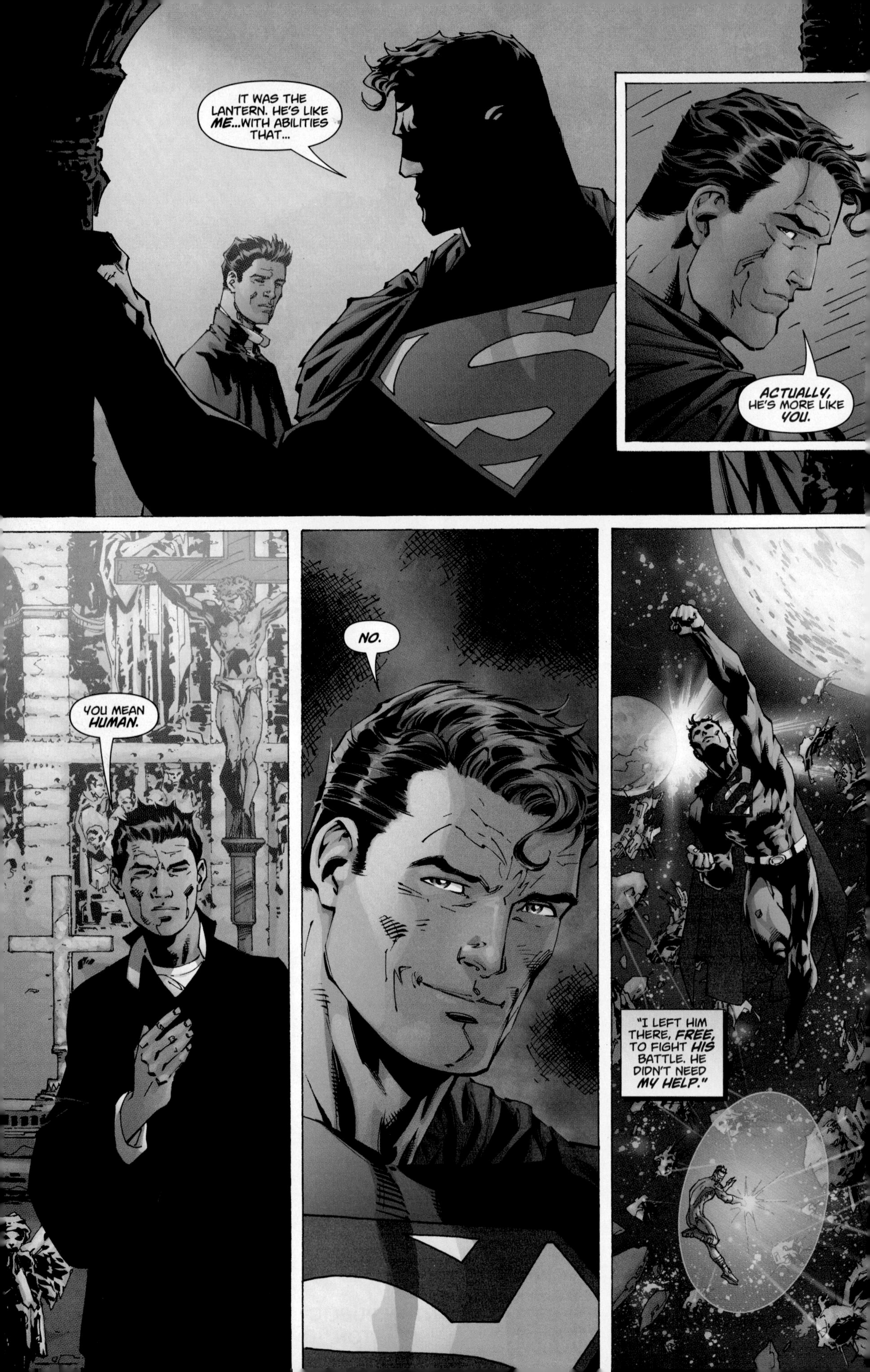
IT WAS THE LANTERN. HE'S LIKE ME...WITH ABILITIES THAT...
ACTUALLY, HE'S MORE LIKE YOU.
YOU MEAN HUMAN.
NO.
"I LEFT HIM THERE, FREE, TO FIGHT HIS BATTLE. HE DIDN'T NEED MY HELP."

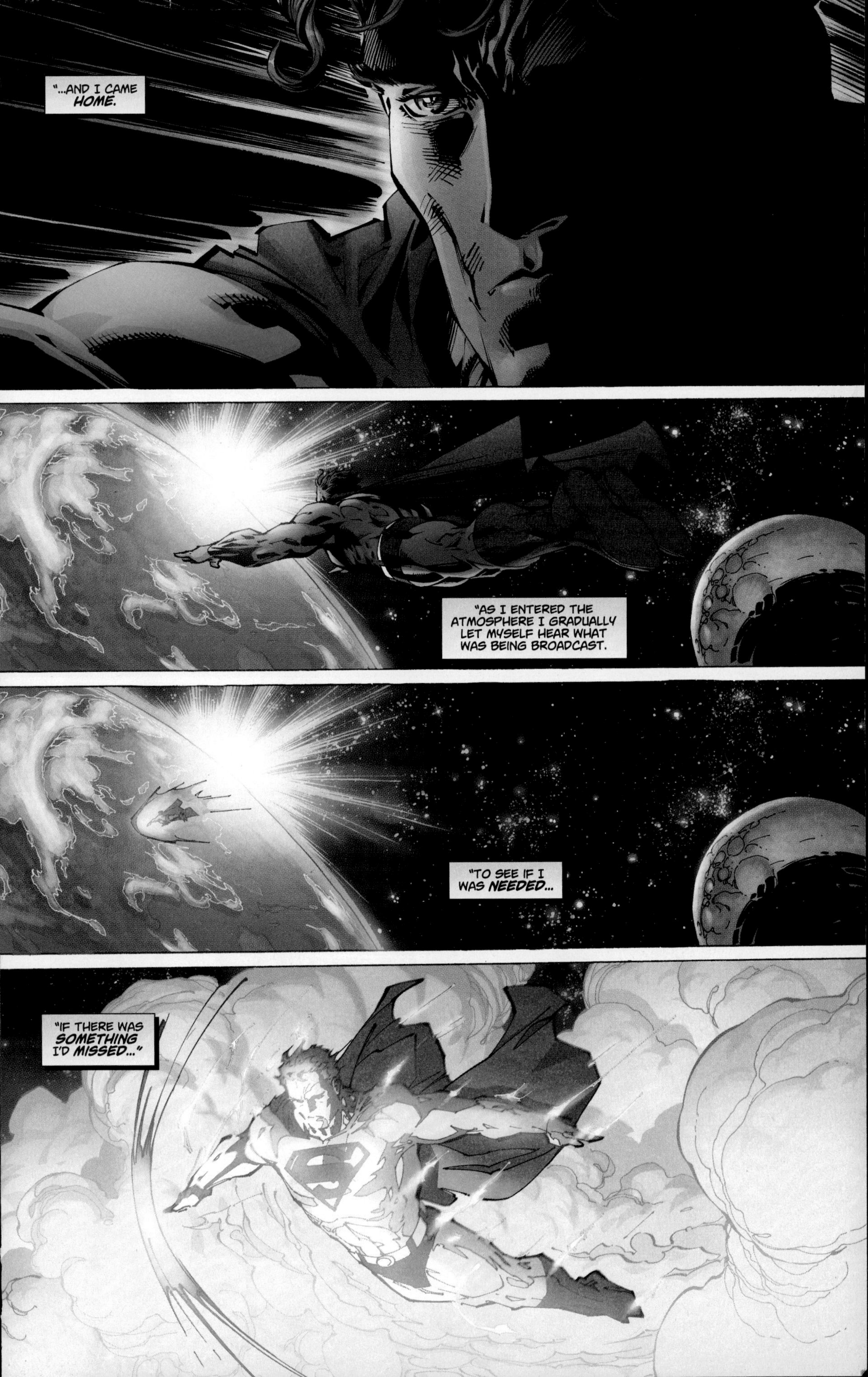
"...AND I CAME HOME.
"AS I ENTERED THE ATMOSPHERE I GRADUALLY LET MYSELF HEAR WHAT WAS BEING BROADCAST.
"TO SEE IF I WAS NEEDED...
"IF THERE WAS SOMETHING I'D MISSED..."

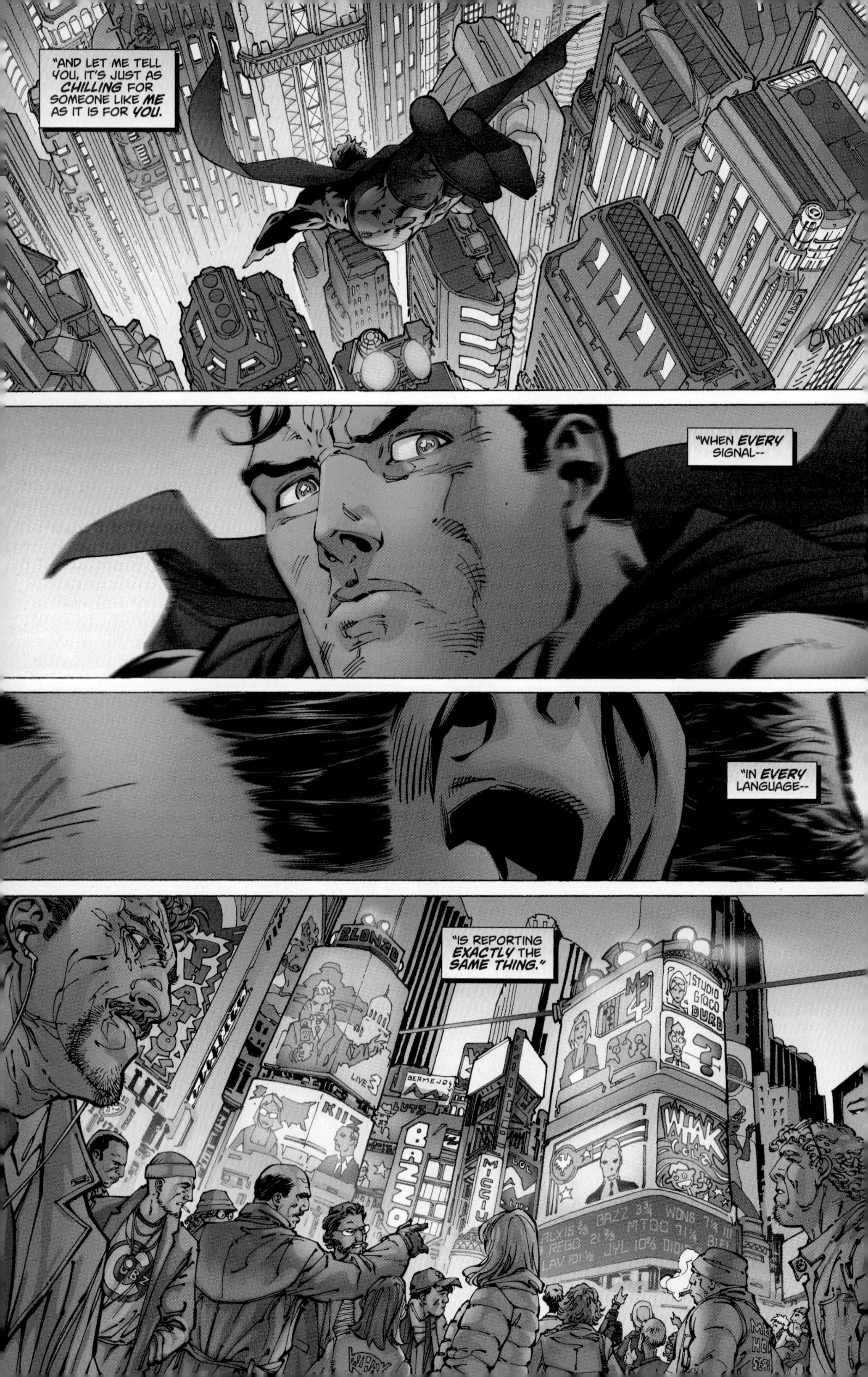
"AND LET ME TELL YOU, IT'S JUST AS CHILLING FOR SOMEONE LIKE ME AS IT IS FOR YOU.
"WHEN EVERY SIGNAL--
"IN EVERY LANGUAGE--
"IS REPORTING EXACTLY THE SAME THING."

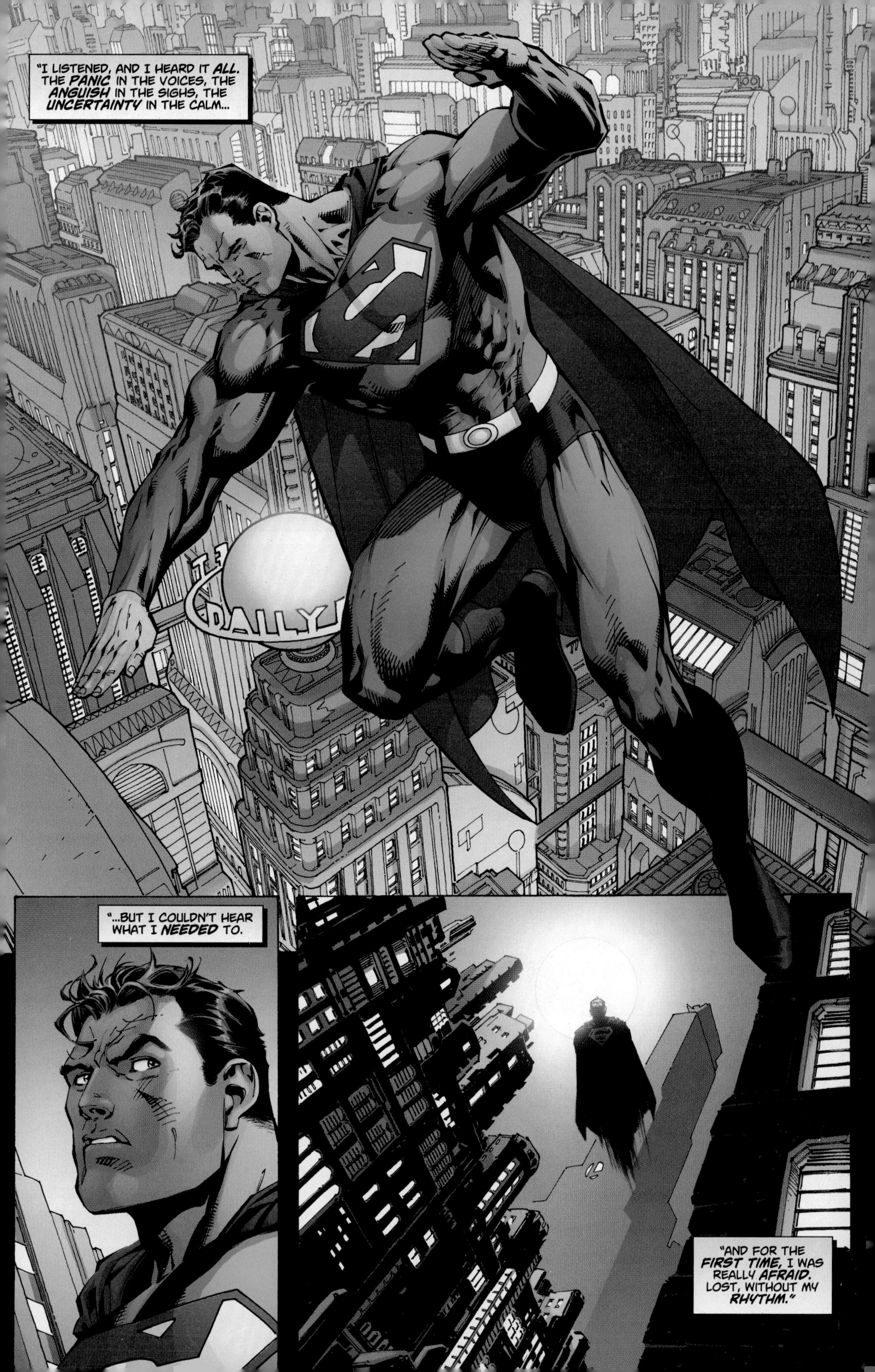
"I LISTENED, AND I HEARD IT ALL. THE PANIC IN THE VOICES, THE ANGUISH IN THE SIGHS, THE UNCERTAINTY IN THE CALM...
"...BUT I COULDN'T HEAR WHAT I NEEDED TO.
"AND FOR THE FIRST TIME, I WAS REALLY AFRAID. LOST, WITHOUT MY RHYTHM."

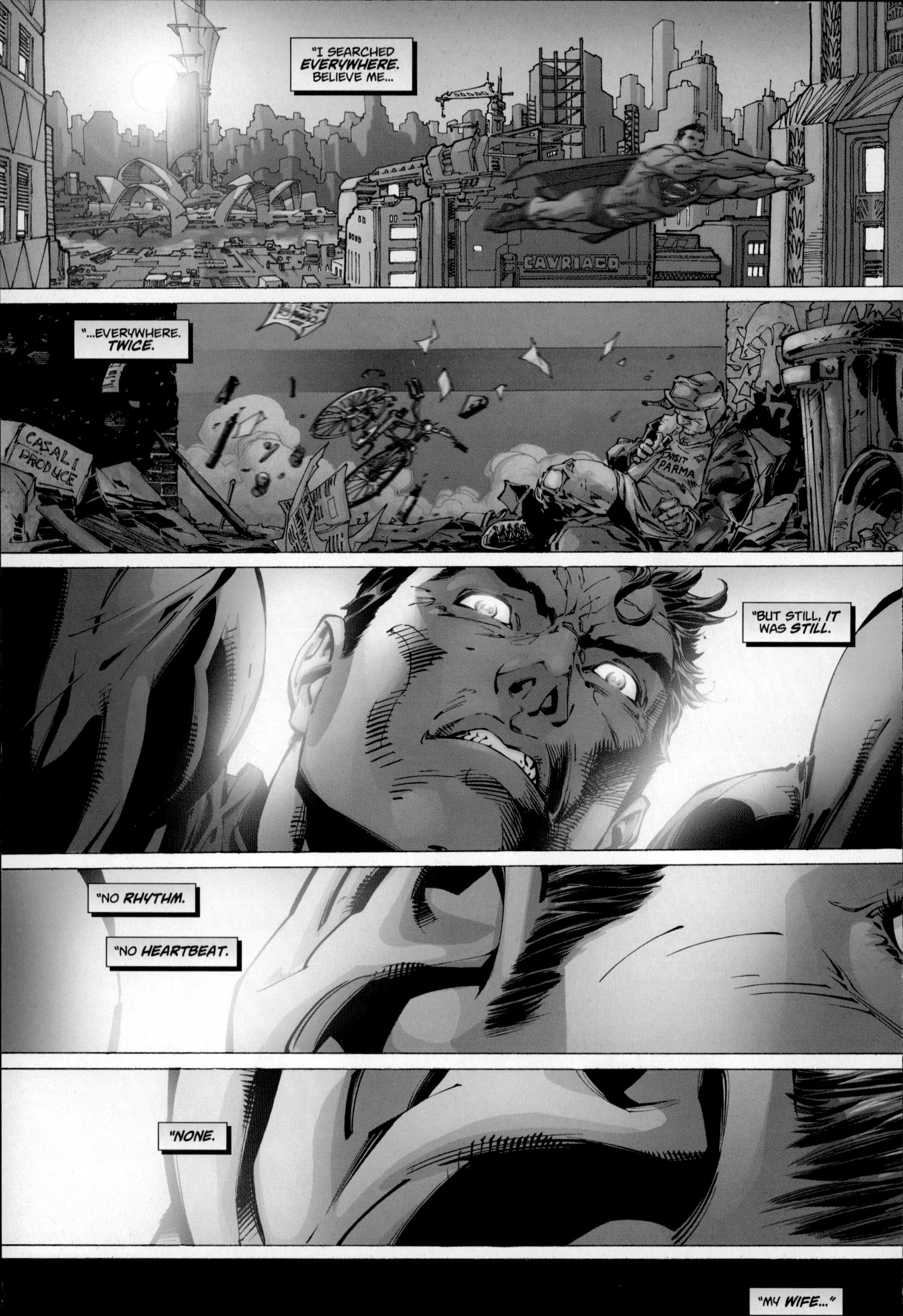
"I SEARCHED EVERYWHERE. BELIEVE ME...
CAVRIACO
"...EVERYWHERE. TWICE.
CASALI PRODUCE
VISIT PARMA
"BUT STILL, IT WAS STILL.
"NO RHYTHM.
"NO HEARTBEAT.
"NONE.
"MY WIFE..."

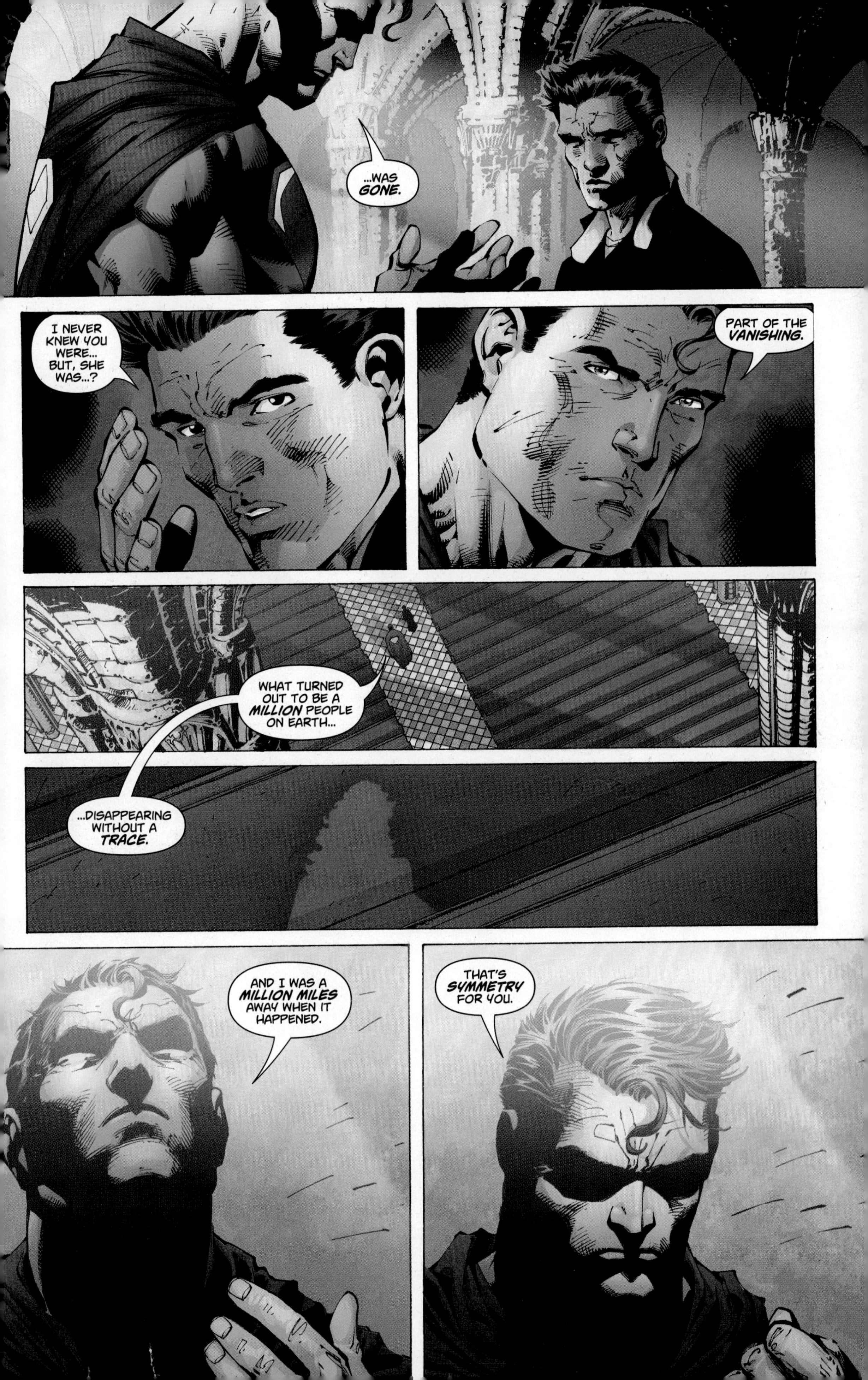
...WAS GONE.
I NEVER KNEW YOU WERE... BUT, SHE WAS...?
PART OF THE VANISHING.
WHAT TURNED OUT TO BE A MILLION PEOPLE ON EARTH...
...DISAPPEARING WITHOUT A TRACE.
AND I WAS A MILLION MILES AWAY WHEN IT HAPPENED.
THAT'S SYMMETRY FOR YOU.

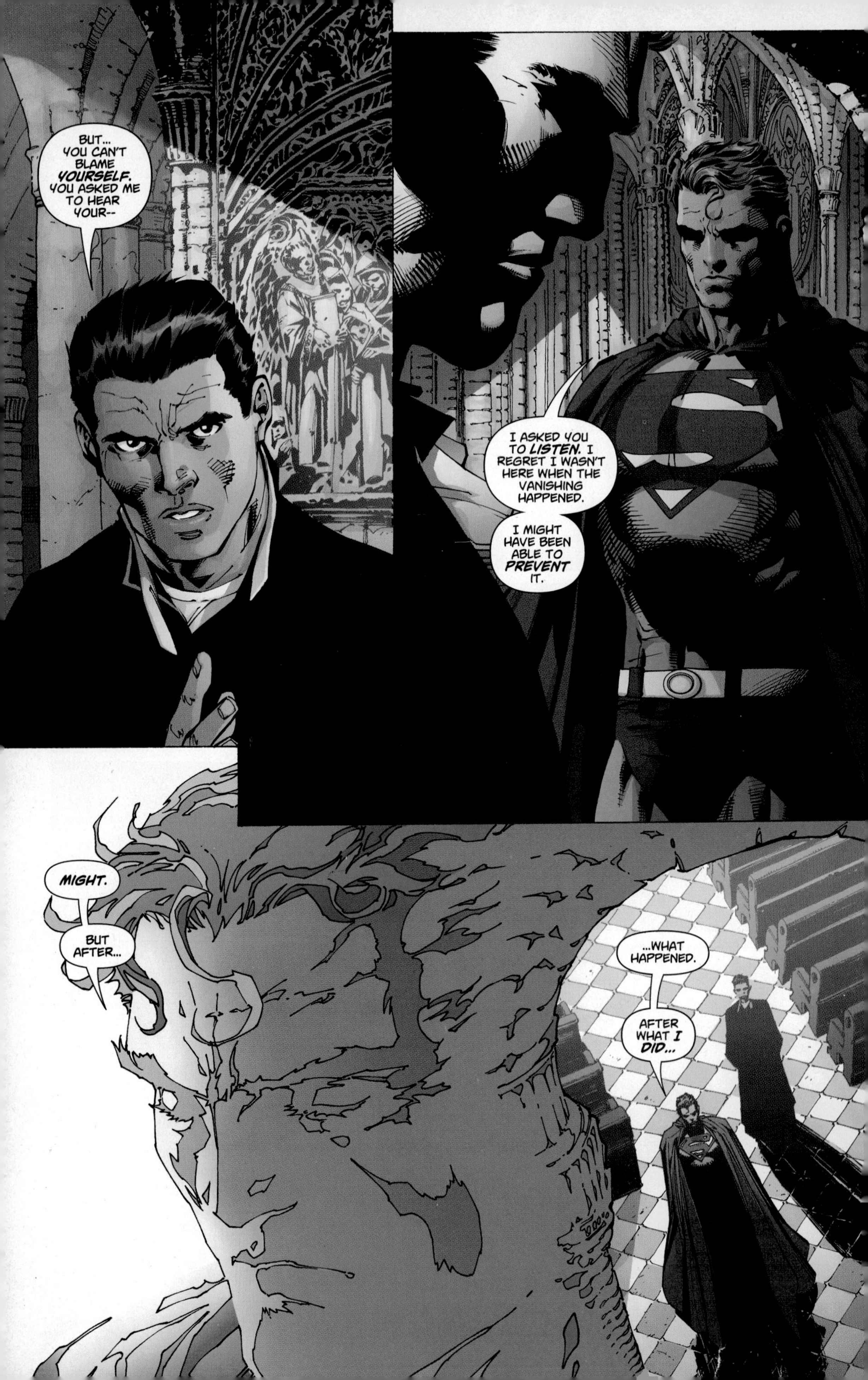
BUT... YOU CAN'T BLAME YOURSELF. YOU ASKED ME TO HEAR YOUR--
I ASKED YOU TO LISTEN. I REGRET I WASN'T HERE WHEN THE VANISHING HAPPENED.
I MIGHT HAVE BEEN ABLE TO PREVENT IT.
MIGHT.
BUT AFTER...
...WHAT HAPPENED.
AFTER WHAT I DID...

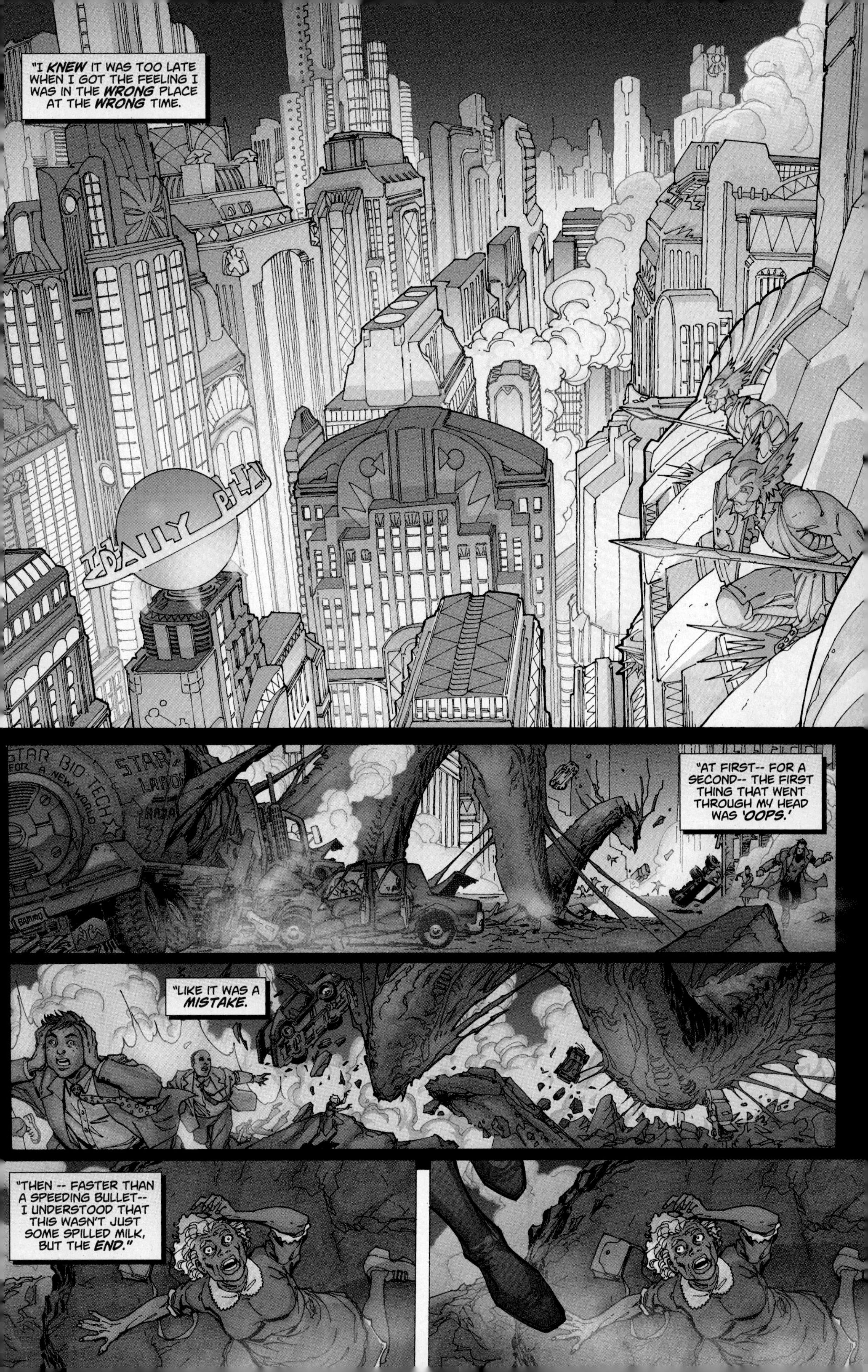
"I KNEW IT WAS TOO LATE WHEN I GOT THE FEELING I WAS IN THE WRONG PLACE AT THE WRONG TIME.
STAR BIO TECH
FOR A NEW WORLD
STAR
"AT FIRST-- FOR A SECOND-- THE FIRST THING THAT WENT THROUGH MY HEAD WAS 'OOPS.'
"LIKE IT WAS A MISTAKE.
"THEN -- FASTER THAN A SPEEDING BULLET-- I UNDERSTOOD THAT THIS WASN'T JUST SOME SPILLED MILK, BUT THE END."

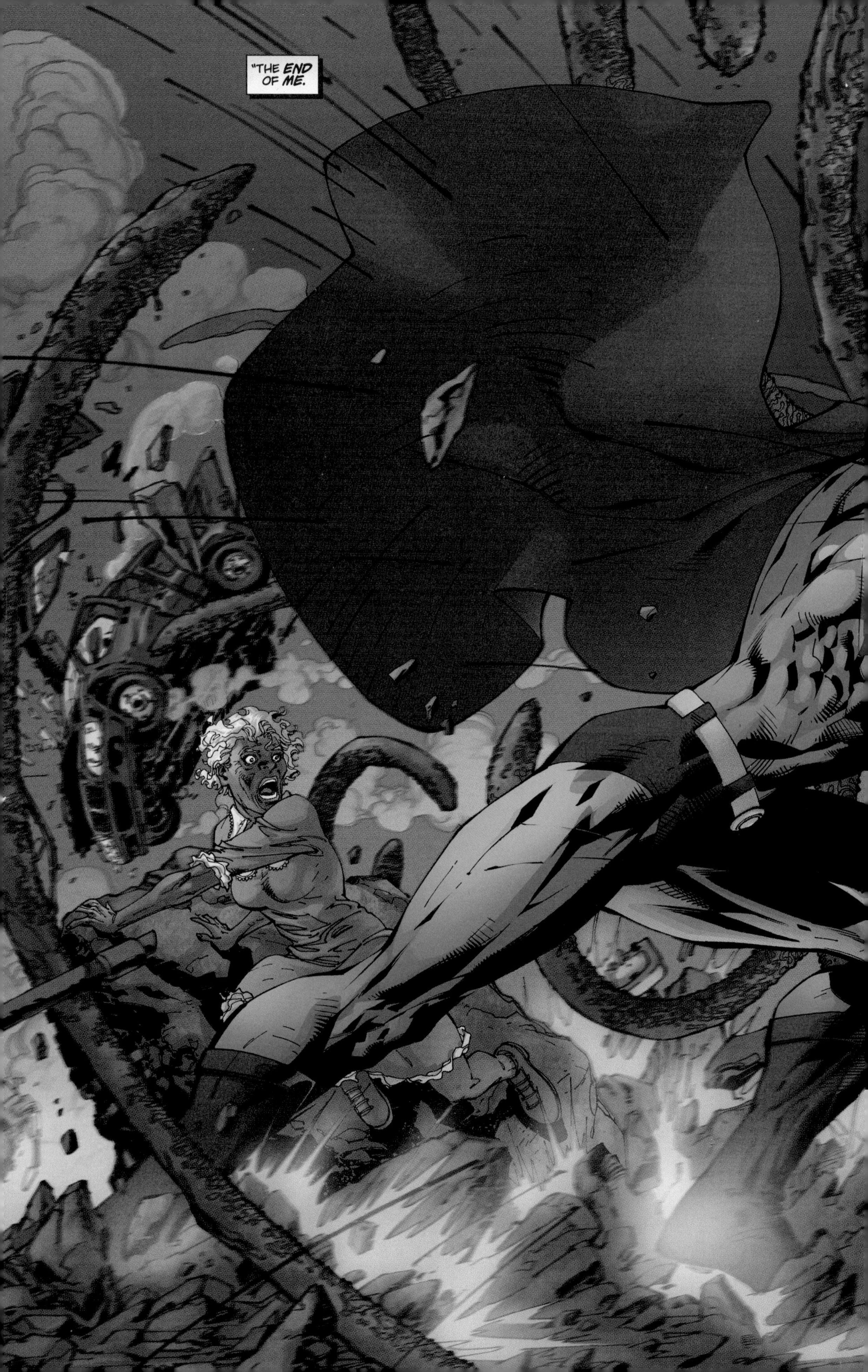
"THE END OF ME.

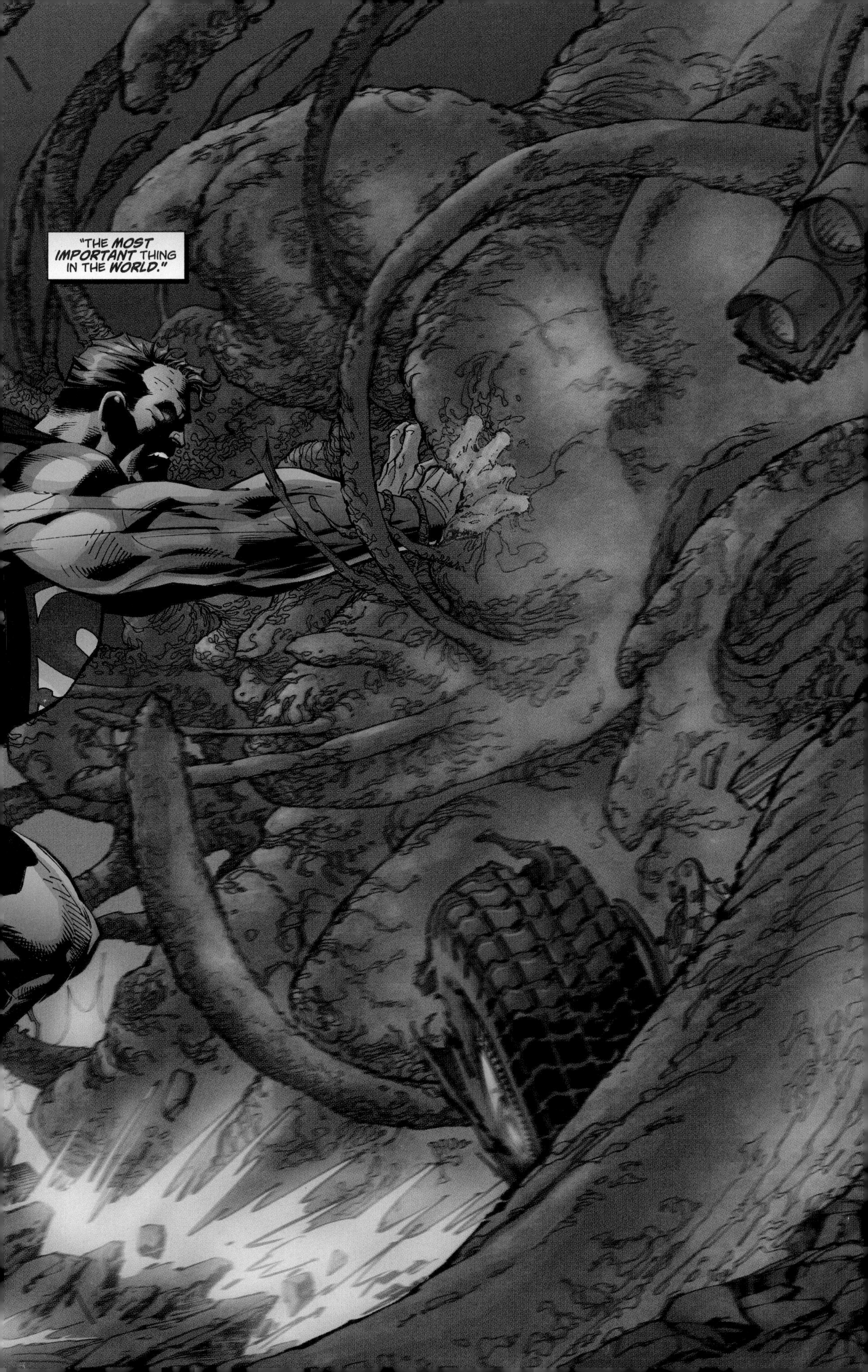
"THE MOST IMPORTANT THING IN THE WORLD."

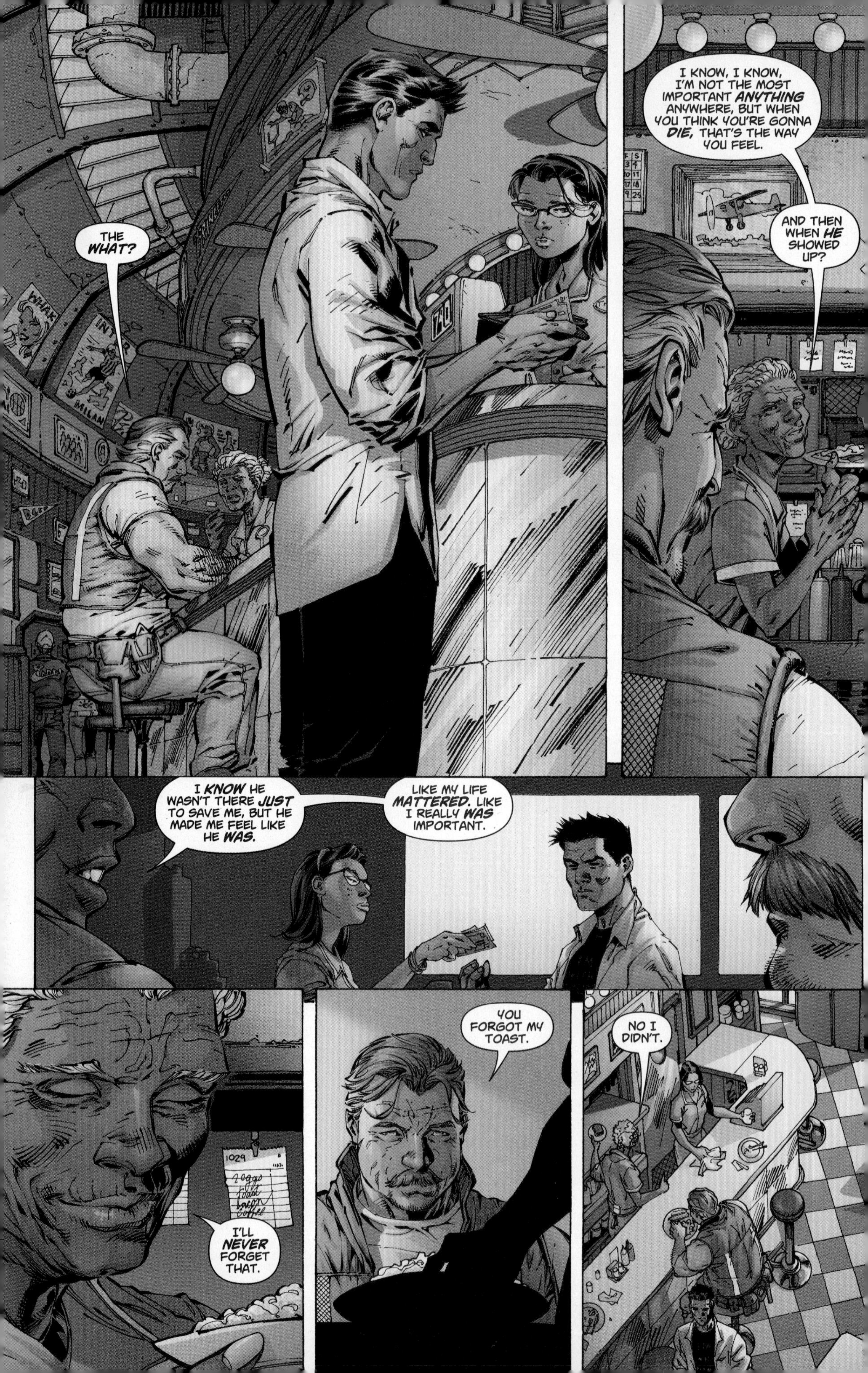
THE WHAT?
I KNOW, I KNOW, I'M NOT THE MOST IMPORTANT ANYTHING ANYWHERE, BUT WHEN YOU THINK YOU'RE GONNA DIE, THAT'S THE WAY YOU FEEL.
AND THEN WHEN HE SHOWED UP?
I KNOW HE WASN'T THERE JUST TO SAVE ME, BUT HE MADE ME FEEL LIKE HE WAS.
LIKE MY LIFE MATTERED. LIKE I REALLY WAS IMPORTANT.
I'LL NEVER FORGET THAT.
YOU FORGOT MY TOAST.
NO I DIDN'T.

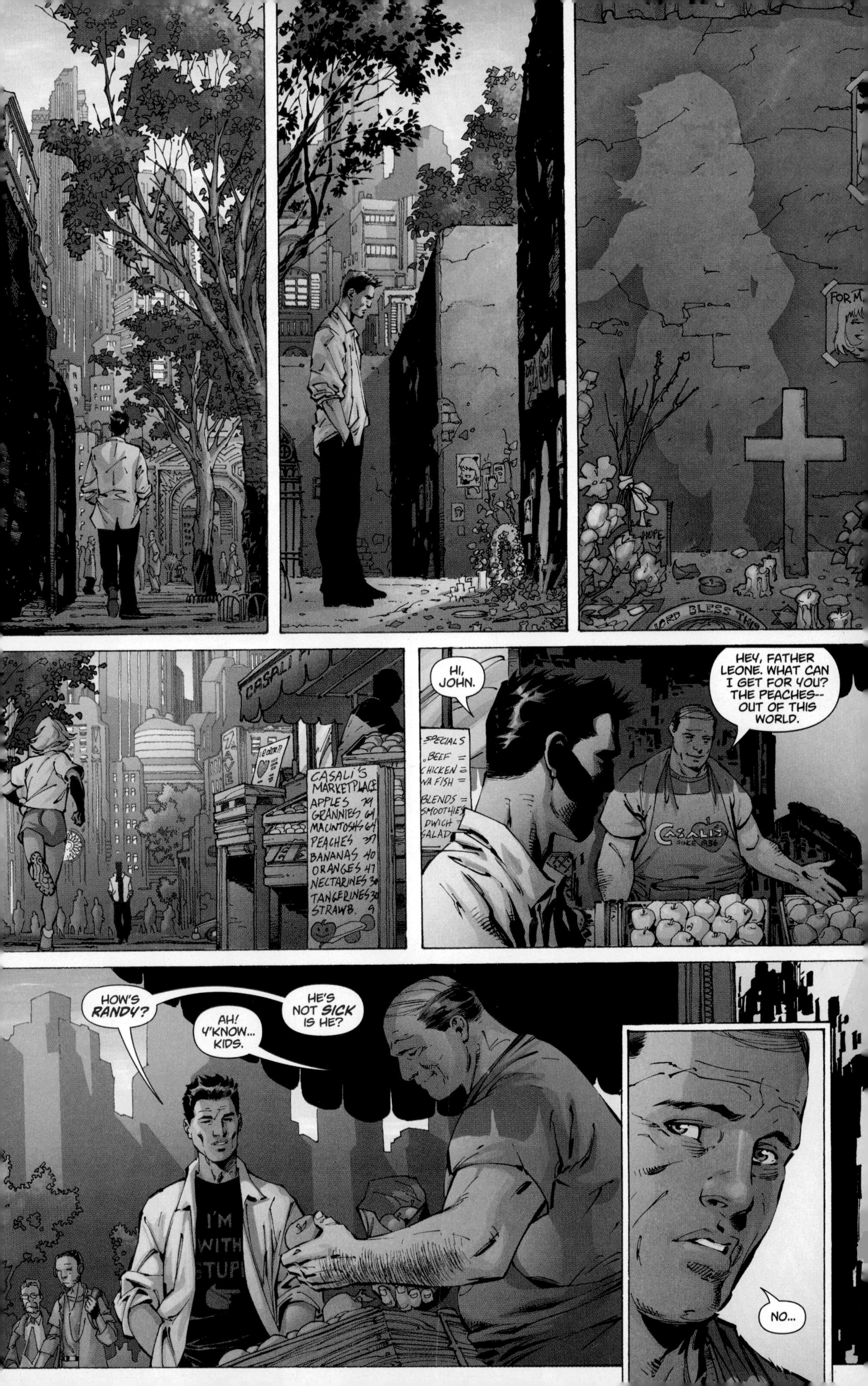
HOPE
CASALI'S MARKETPLACE
APPLES 79
GRANNIES 64
MACINTOSHES 64
PEACHES 37
BANANAS 40
ORANGES 47
NECTARINES 30
TANGERINES 30
STRAWB. 9
HI, JOHN.
HEY, FATHER LEONE. WHAT CAN I GET FOR YOU? THE PEACHES-- OUT OF THIS WORLD.
CASALI'S SINCE 1936
HOW'S RANDY?
AH! Y'KNOW... KIDS.
HE'S NOT SICK IS HE?
NO...

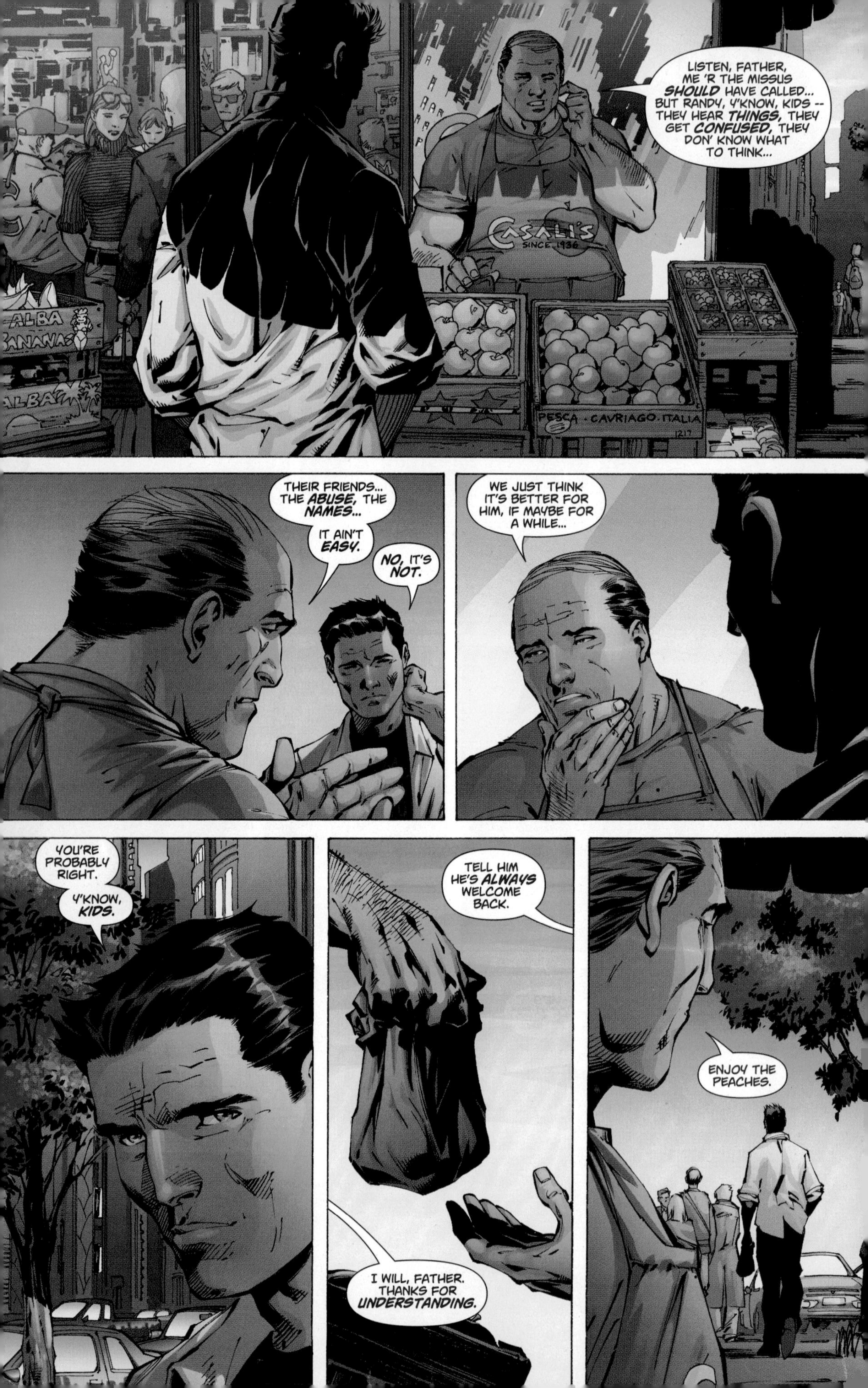
LISTEN, FATHER, ME 'R THE MISSUS SHOULD HAVE CALLED... BUT RANDY, Y'KNOW, KIDS -- THEY HEAR THINGS, THEY GET CONFUSED, THEY DON' KNOW WHAT TO THINK...
CASALI'S SINCE 1936
ALBA BANANAS
ALBA
PESCA · CAVRIAGO · ITALIA
THEIR FRIENDS... THE ABUSE, THE NAMES...
IT AIN'T EASY.
NO, IT'S NOT.
WE JUST THINK IT'S BETTER FOR HIM, IF MAYBE FOR A WHILE...
YOU'RE PROBABLY RIGHT.
Y'KNOW, KIDS.
TELL HIM HE'S ALWAYS WELCOME BACK.
I WILL, FATHER. THANKS FOR UNDERSTANDING.
ENJOY THE PEACHES.

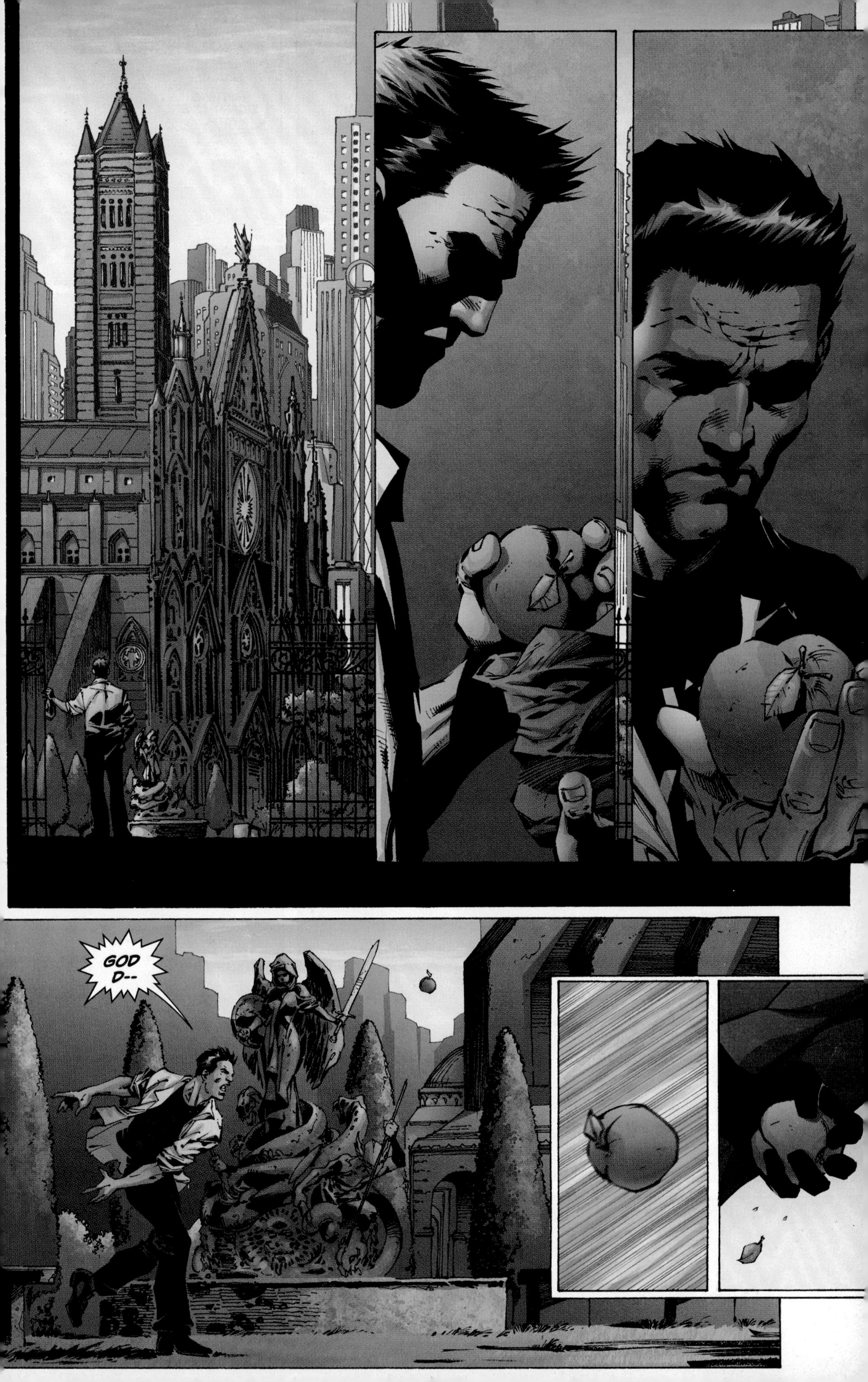
GOD D--

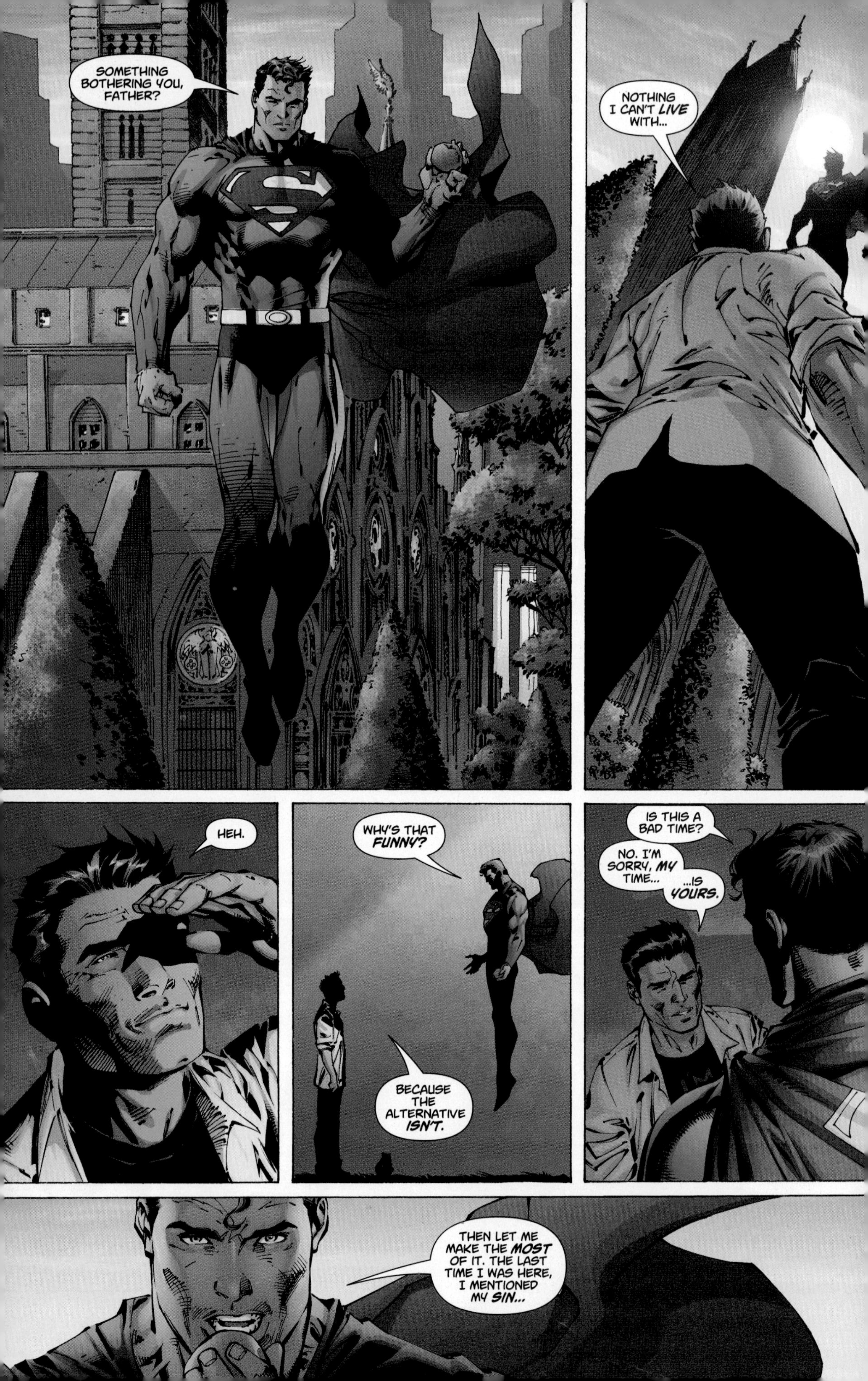
SOMETHING BOTHERING YOU, FATHER?
NOTHING I CAN'T LIVE WITH...
HEH.
WHY'S THAT FUNNY?
BECAUSE THE ALTERNATIVE ISN'T.
IS THIS A BAD TIME?
NO. I'M SORRY, MY TIME...
...IS YOURS.
THEN LET ME MAKE THE MOST OF IT. THE LAST TIME I WAS HERE, I MENTIONED MY SIN...

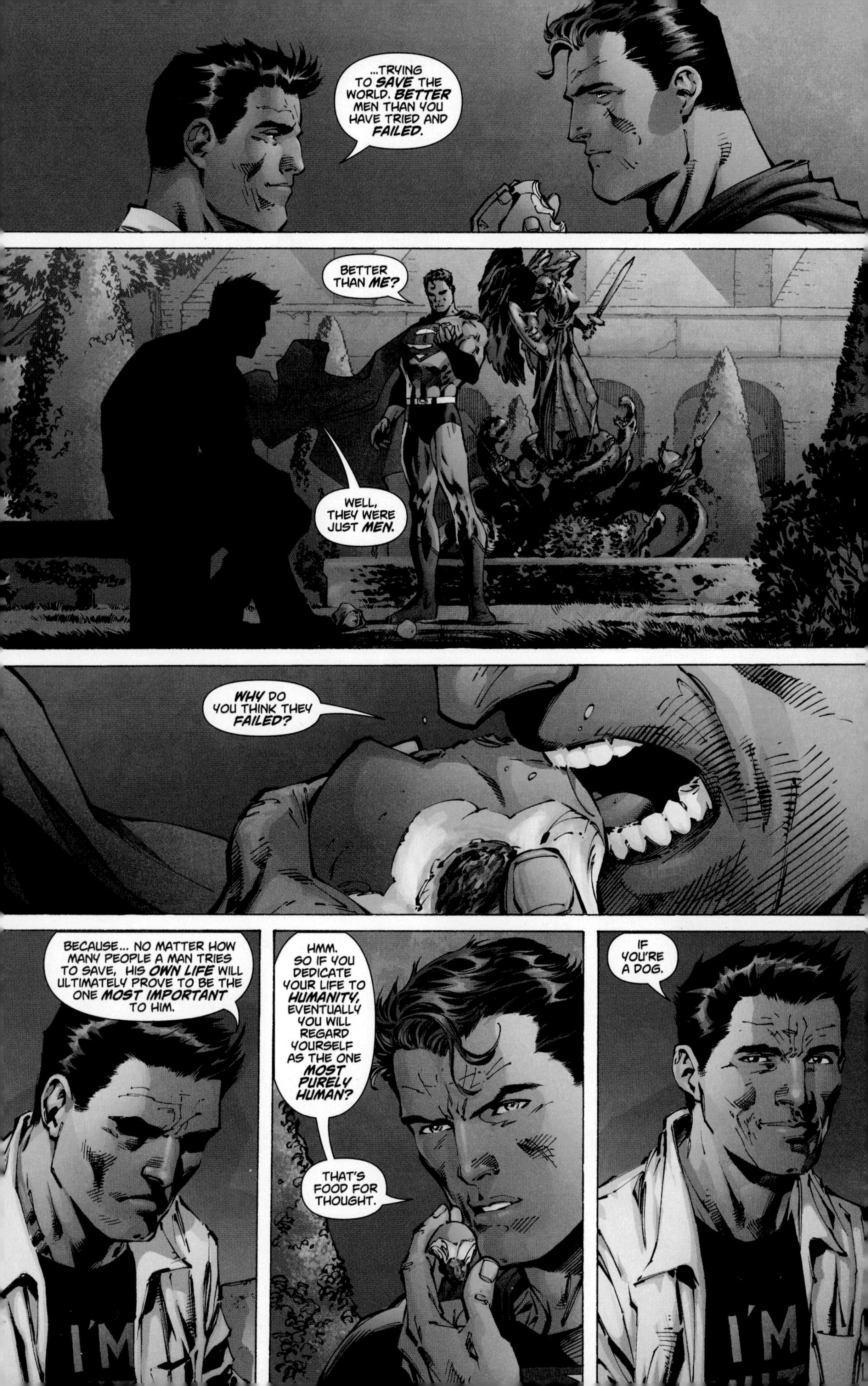
...TRYING TO SAVE THE WORLD. BETTER MEN THAN YOU HAVE TRIED AND FAILED.
BETTER THAN ME?
WELL, THEY WERE JUST MEN.
WHY DO YOU THINK THEY FAILED?
BECAUSE... NO MATTER HOW MANY PEOPLE A MAN TRIES TO SAVE, HIS OWN LIFE WILL ULTIMATELY PROVE TO BE THE ONE MOST IMPORTANT TO HIM.
HMM. SO IF YOU DEDICATE YOUR LIFE TO HUMANITY, EVENTUALLY YOU WILL REGARD YOURSELF AS THE ONE MOST PURELY HUMAN?
THAT'S FOOD FOR THOUGHT.
IF YOU'RE A DOG.
I'M
I'M

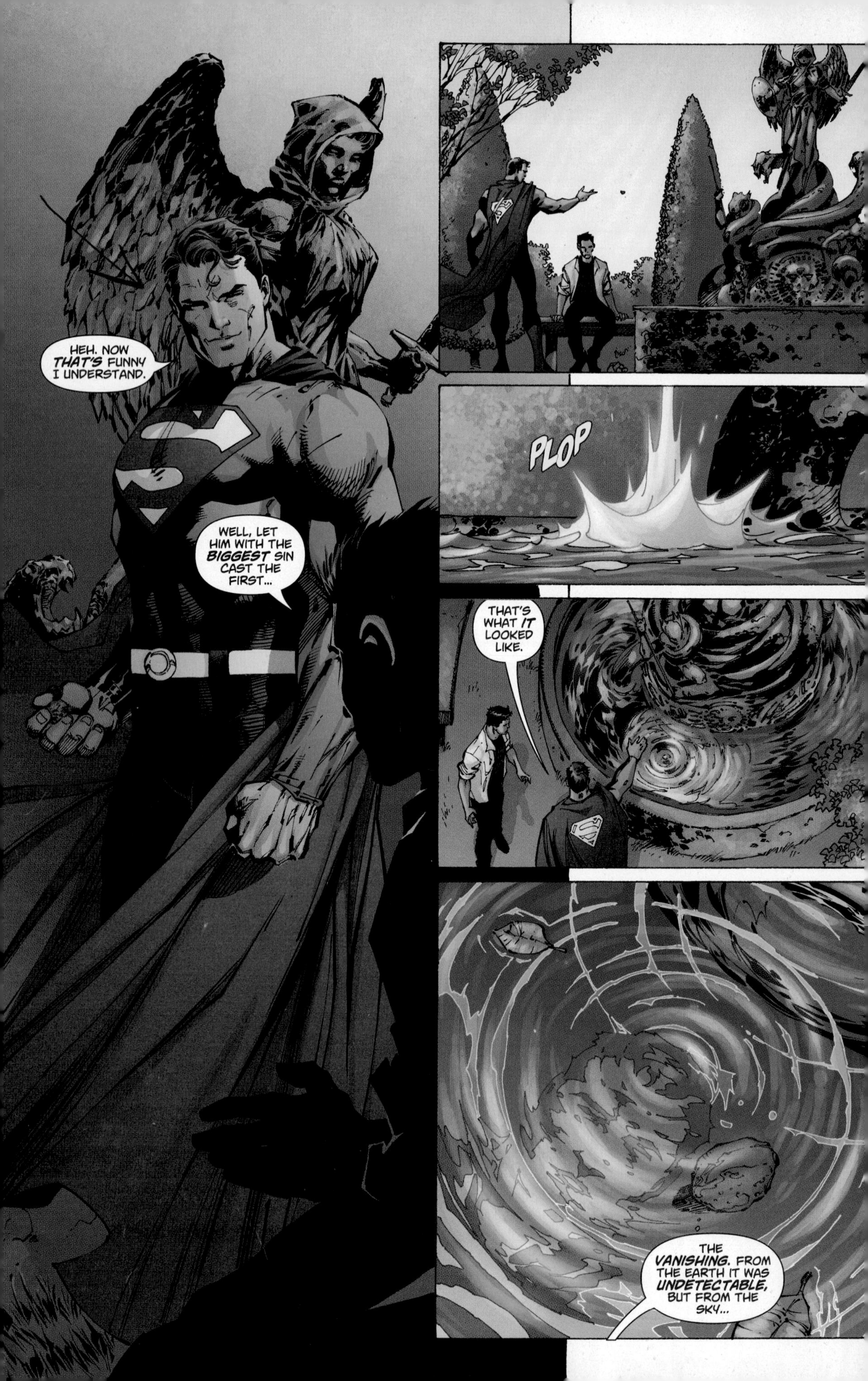
HEH. NOW THAT'S FUNNY I UNDERSTAND.
WELL, LET HIM WITH THE BIGGEST SIN CAST THE FIRST...
PLOP
THAT'S WHAT IT LOOKED LIKE.
THE VANISHING. FROM THE EARTH IT WAS UNDETECTABLE, BUT FROM THE SKY...

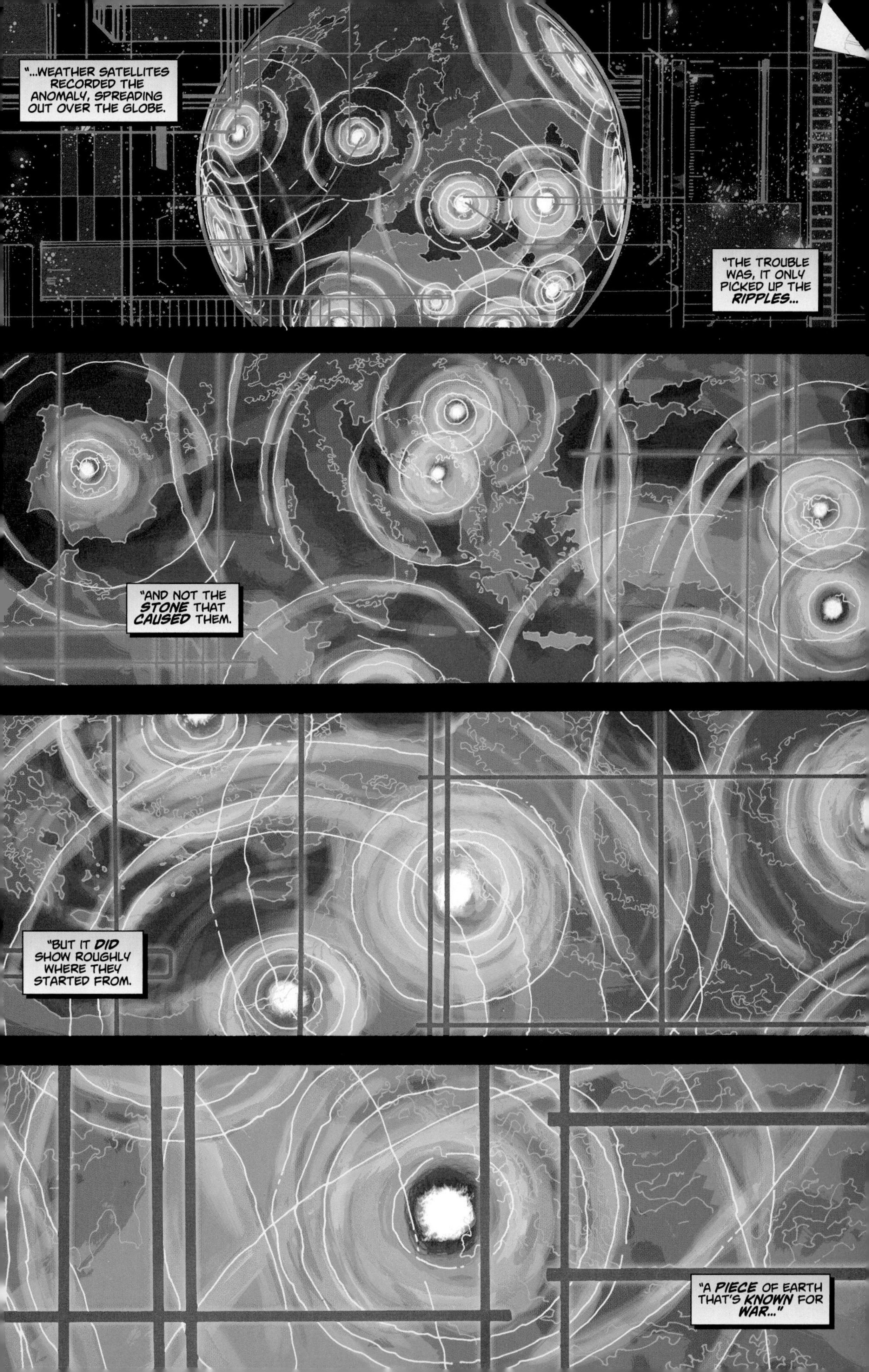
"...WEATHER SATELLITES RECORDED THE ANOMALY, SPREADING OUT OVER THE GLOBE.
"THE TROUBLE WAS, IT ONLY PICKED UP THE *RIPPLES*...
"AND NOT THE *STONE* THAT *CAUSED* THEM.
"BUT IT *DID* SHOW ROUGHLY WHERE THEY STARTED FROM.
"A *PIECE* OF EARTH THAT'S *KNOWN* FOR *WAR*..."

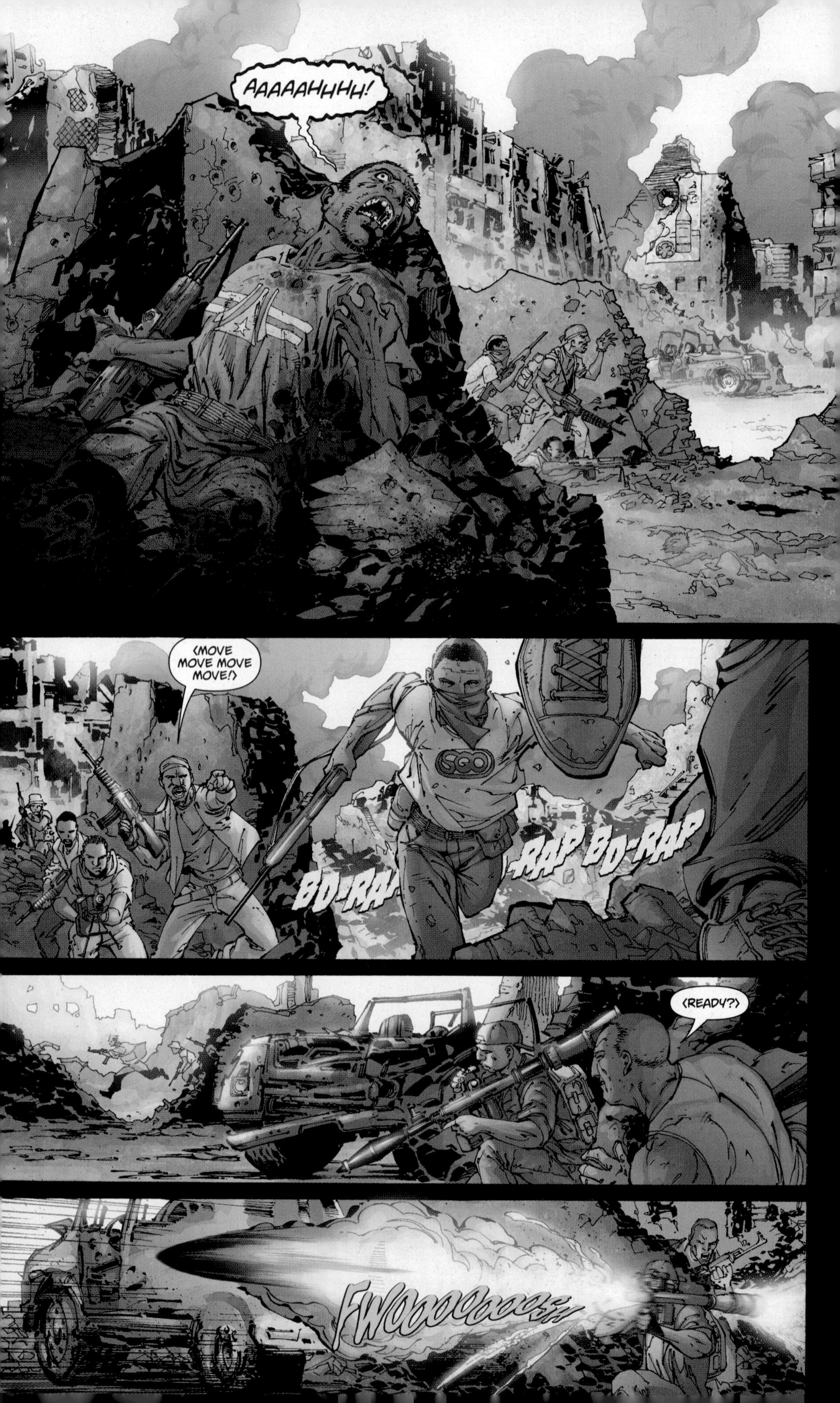
AAAAAHHHH!
(MOVE MOVE MOVE MOVE!)
BD-RA
-RAP BD-RAP
(READY?)
FWOOOOOOSH

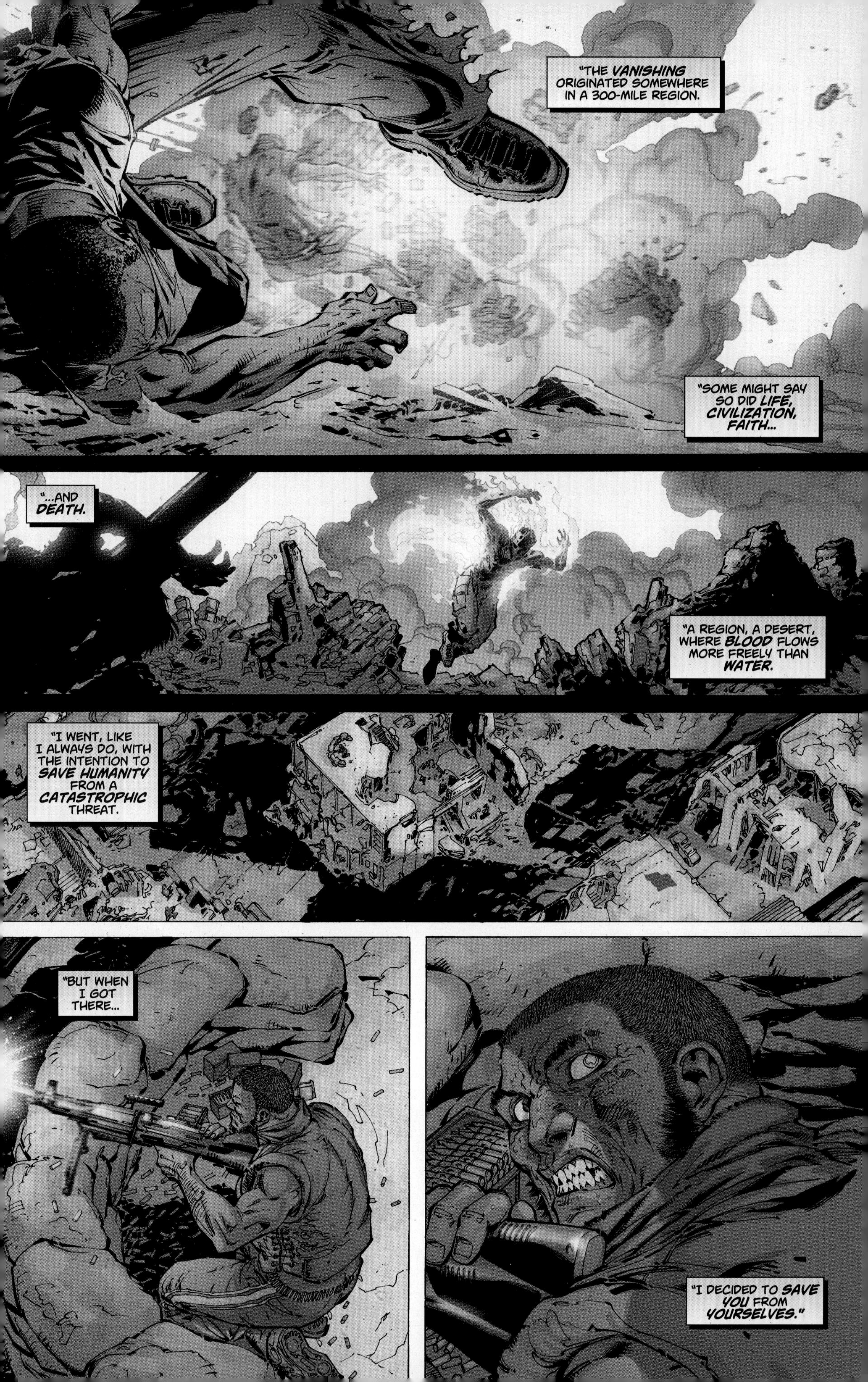
"THE VANISHING ORIGINATED SOMEWHERE IN A 300-MILE REGION.
"SOME MIGHT SAY SO DID LIFE, CIVILIZATION, FAITH...
"...AND DEATH.
"A REGION, A DESERT, WHERE BLOOD FLOWS MORE FREELY THAN WATER.
"I WENT, LIKE I ALWAYS DO, WITH THE INTENTION TO SAVE HUMANITY FROM A CATASTROPHIC THREAT.
"BUT WHEN I GOT THERE...
"I DECIDED TO SAVE YOU FROM YOURSELVES."

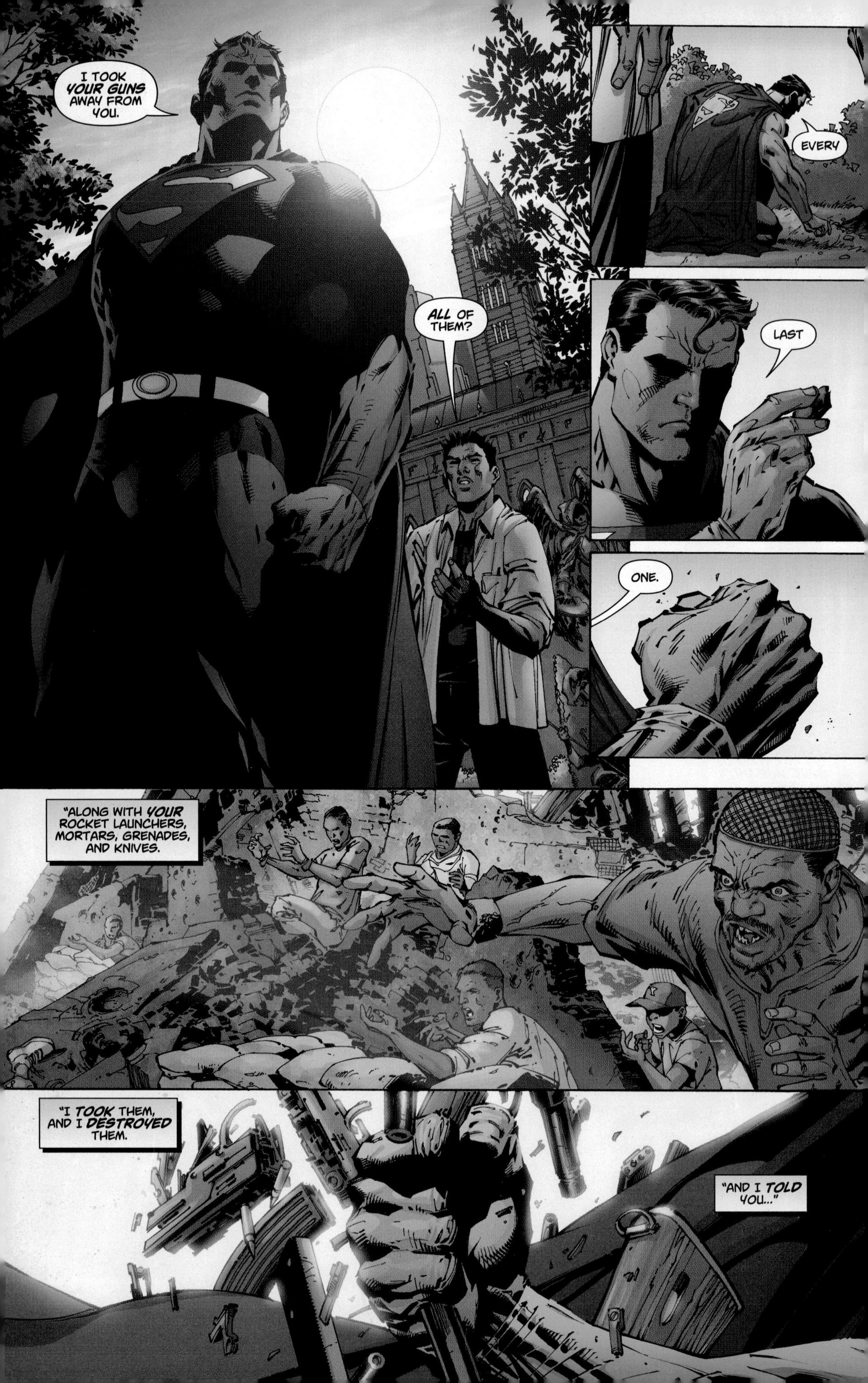
I TOOK YOUR GUNS AWAY FROM YOU.
ALL OF THEM?
EVERY
LAST
ONE.
"ALONG WITH YOUR ROCKET LAUNCHERS, MORTARS, GRENADES, AND KNIVES.
"I TOOK THEM, AND I DESTROYED THEM.
"AND I TOLD YOU..."

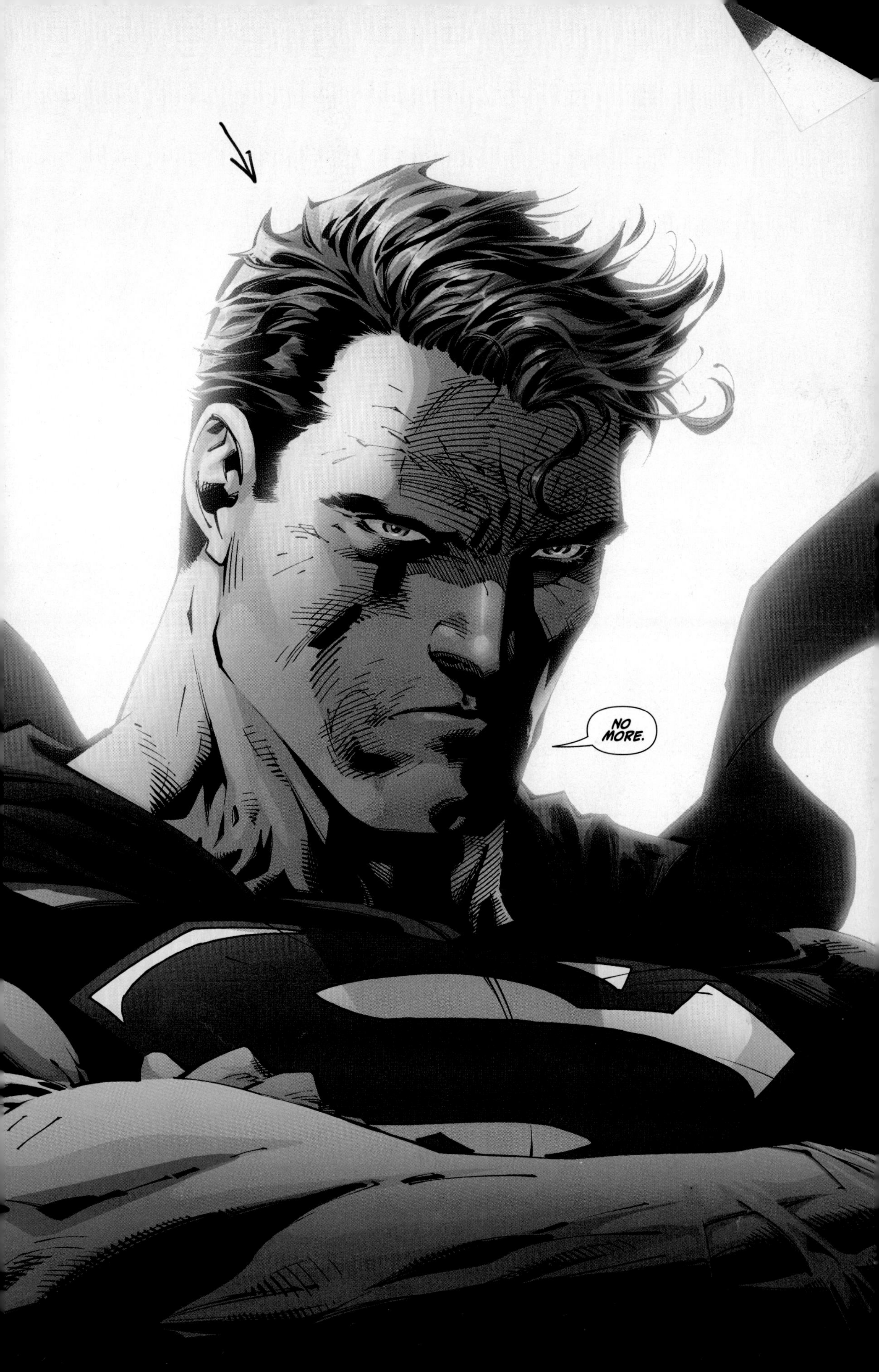
NO MORE.

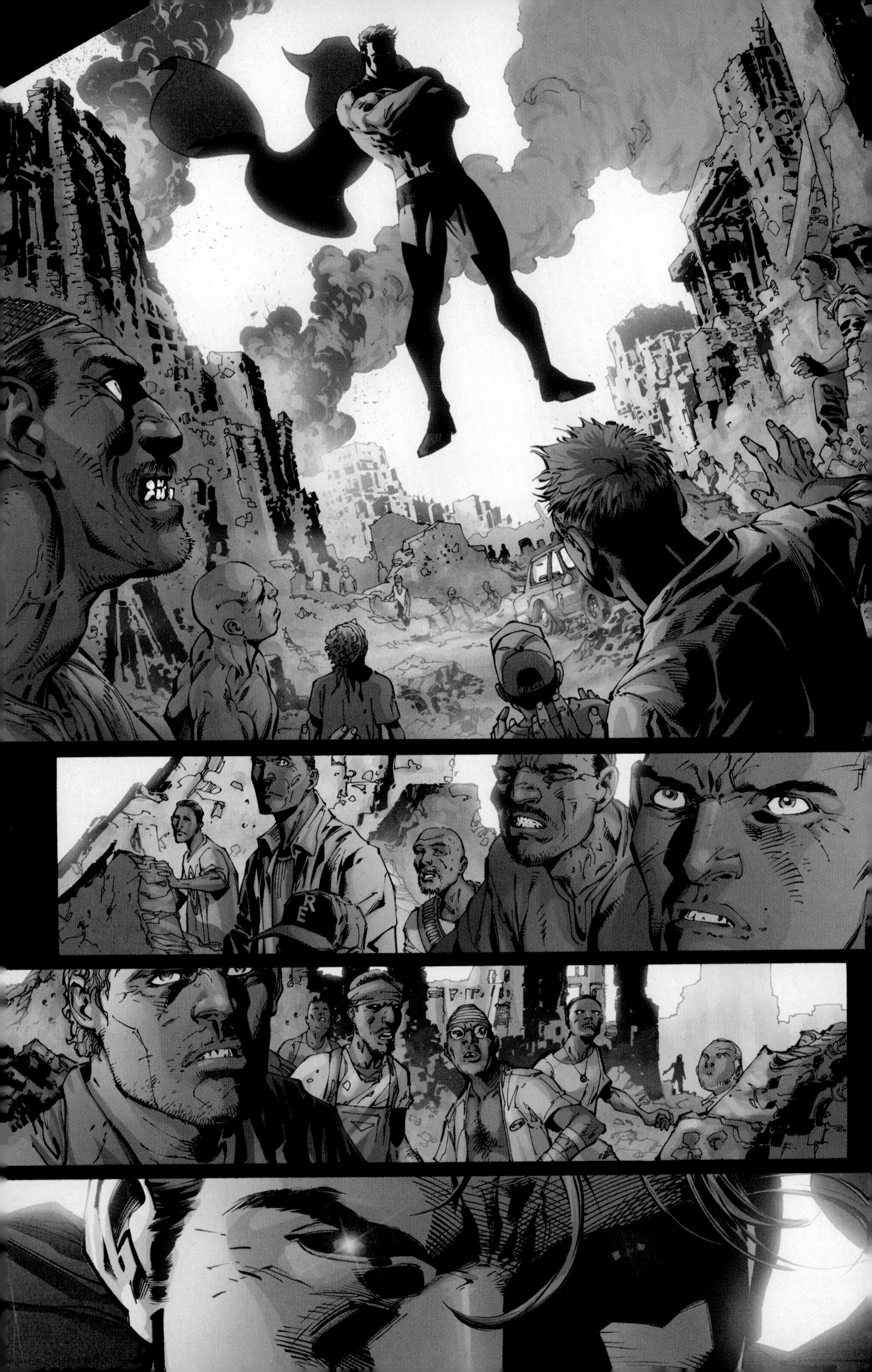

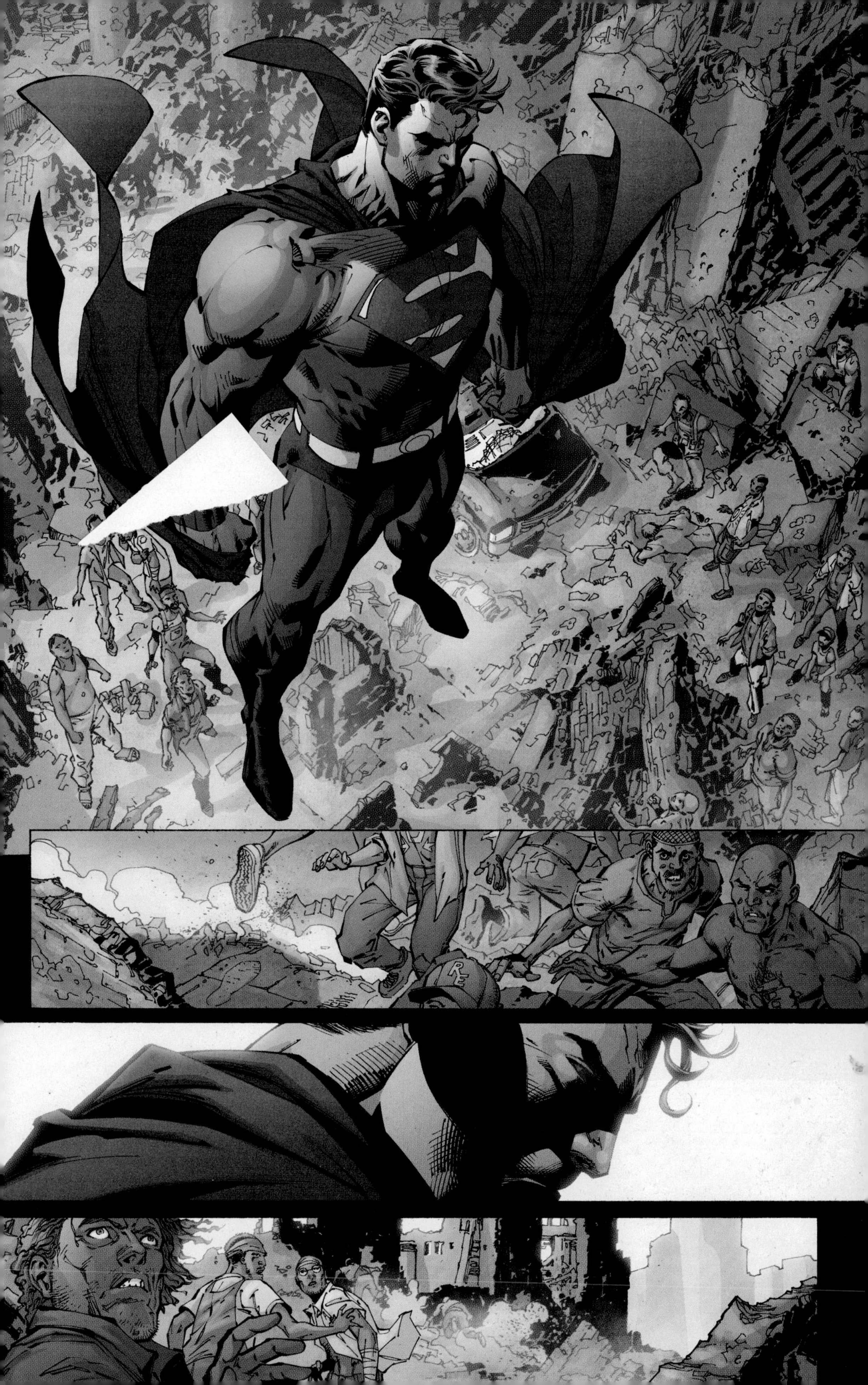

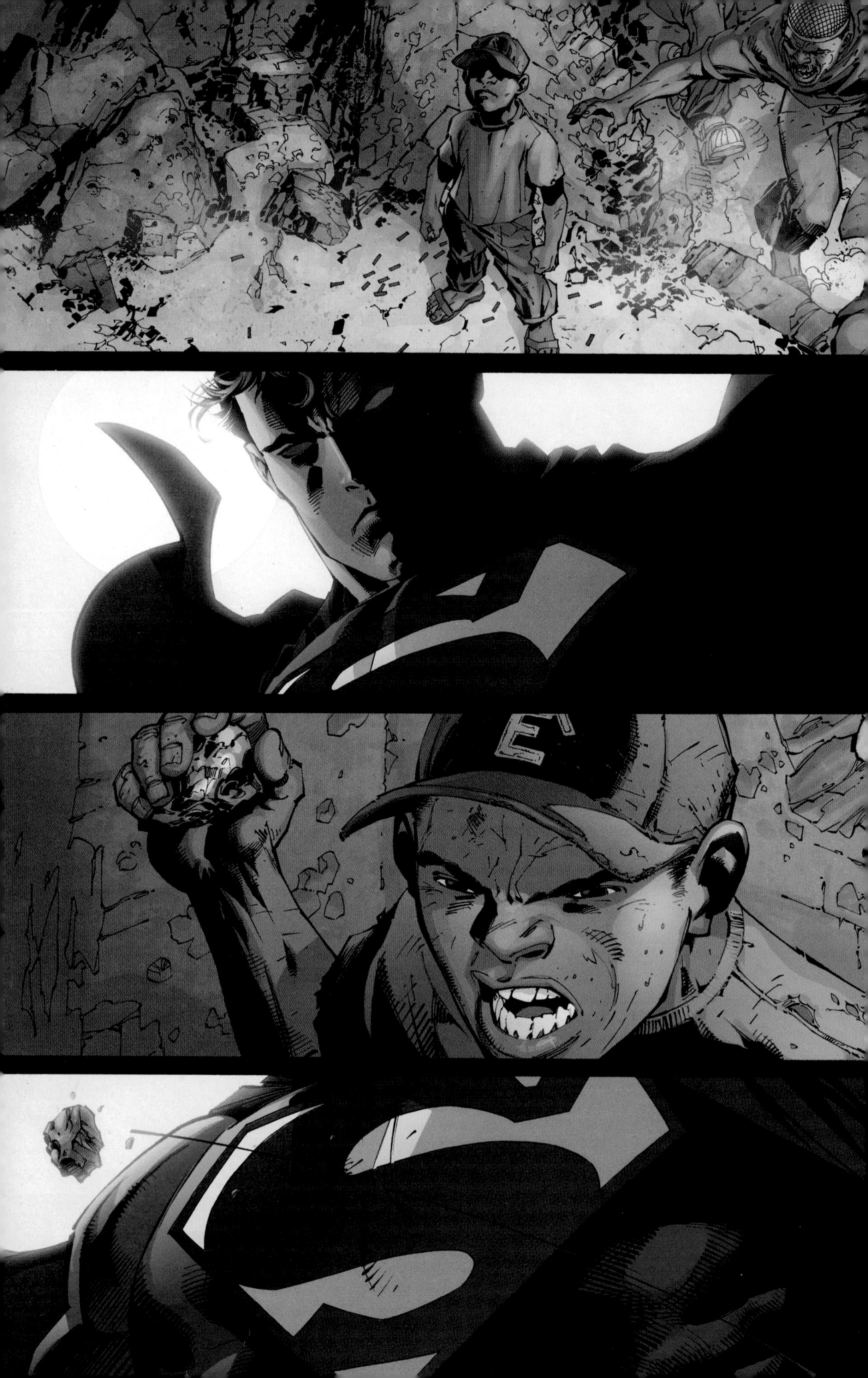

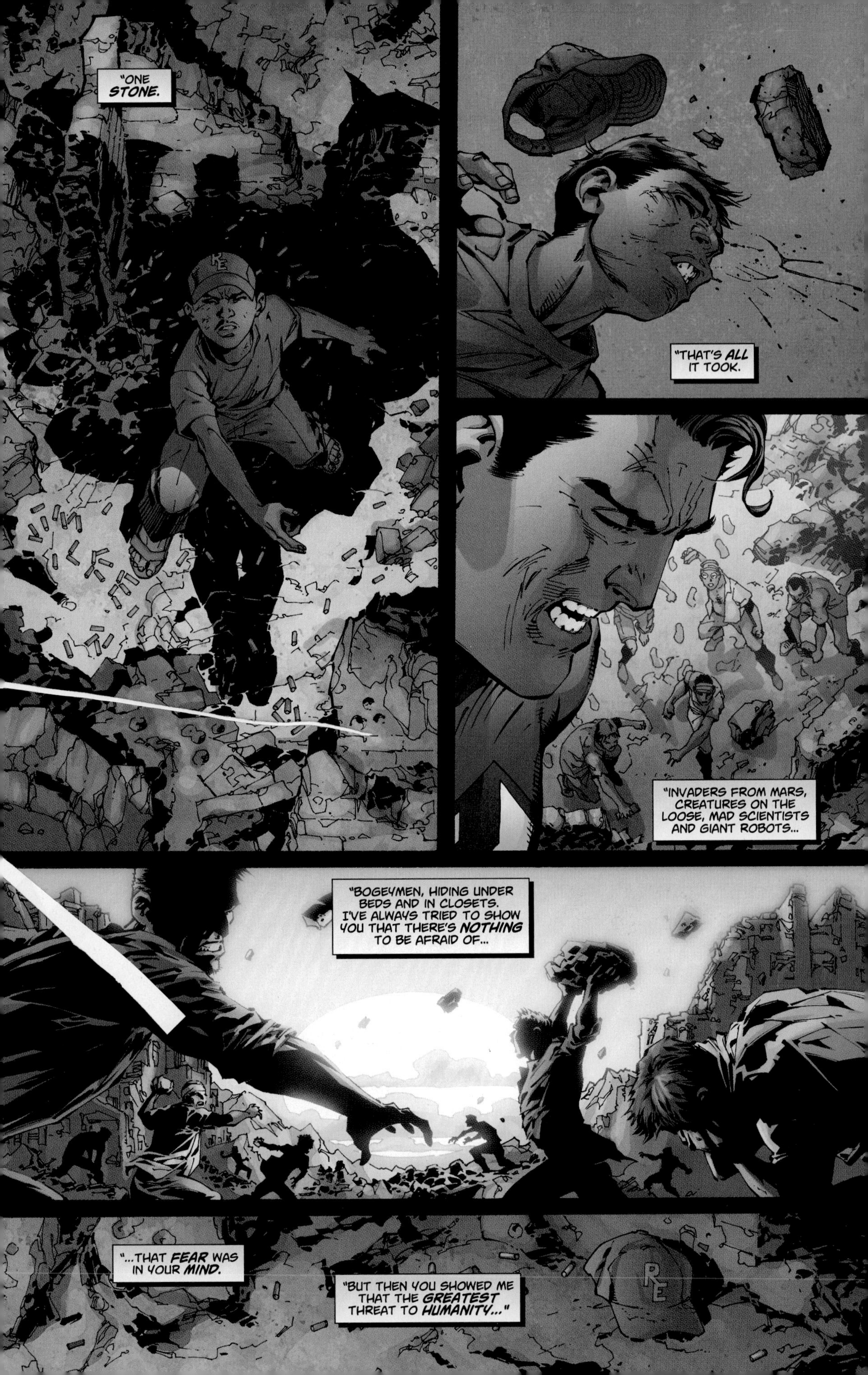
"ONE STONE.
"THAT'S ALL IT TOOK.
"INVADERS FROM MARS, CREATURES ON THE LOOSE, MAD SCIENTISTS AND GIANT ROBOTS...
"BOGEYMEN, HIDING UNDER BEDS AND IN CLOSETS. I'VE ALWAYS TRIED TO SHOW YOU THAT THERE'S NOTHING TO BE AFRAID OF...
"...THAT FEAR WAS IN YOUR MIND.
"BUT THEN YOU SHOWED ME THAT THE GREATEST THREAT TO HUMANITY..."

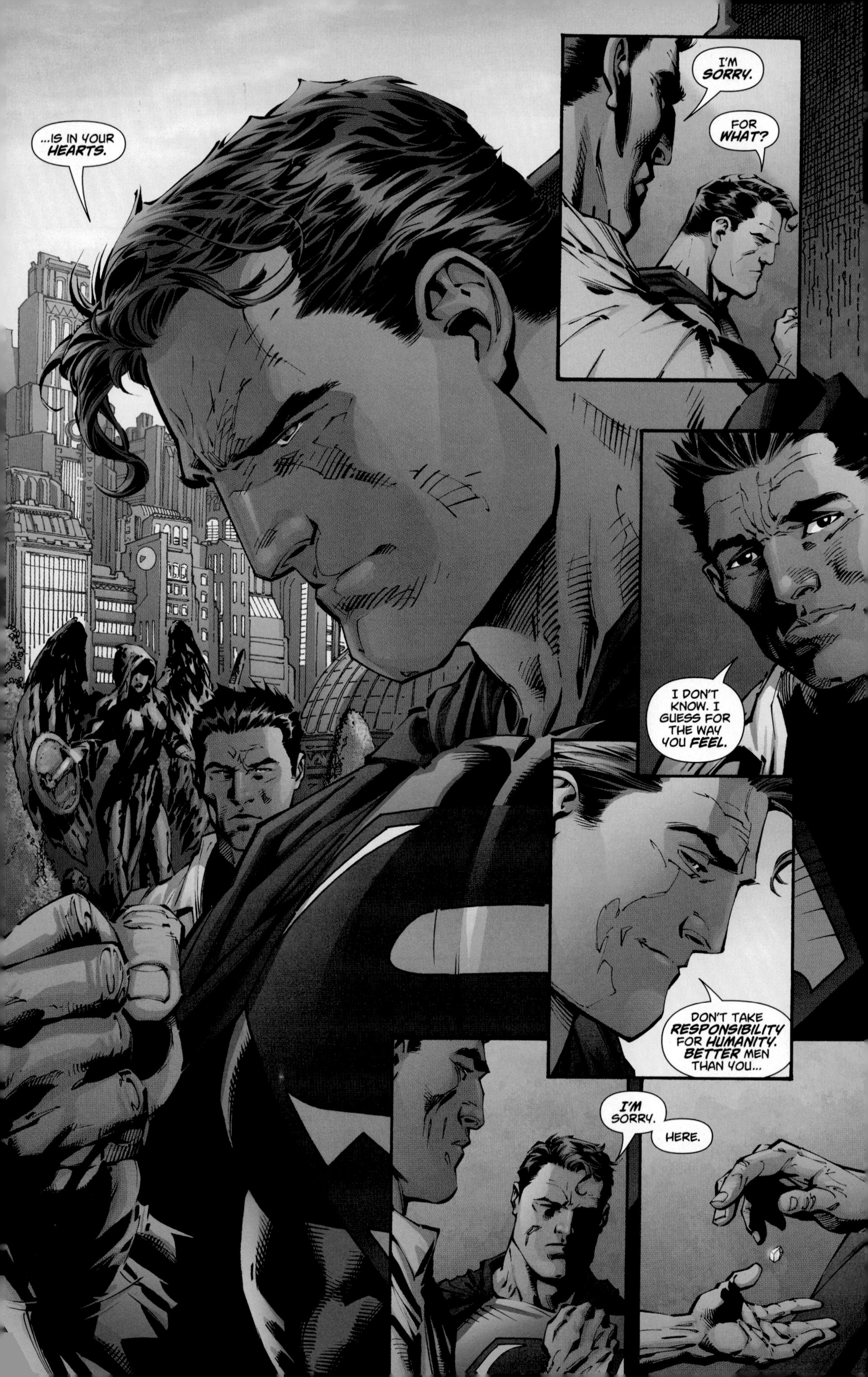
...IS IN YOUR HEARTS.
I'M SORRY.
FOR WHAT?
I DON'T KNOW. I GUESS FOR THE WAY YOU FEEL.
DON'T TAKE RESPONSIBILITY FOR HUMANITY. BETTER MEN THAN YOU...
I'M SORRY.
HERE.

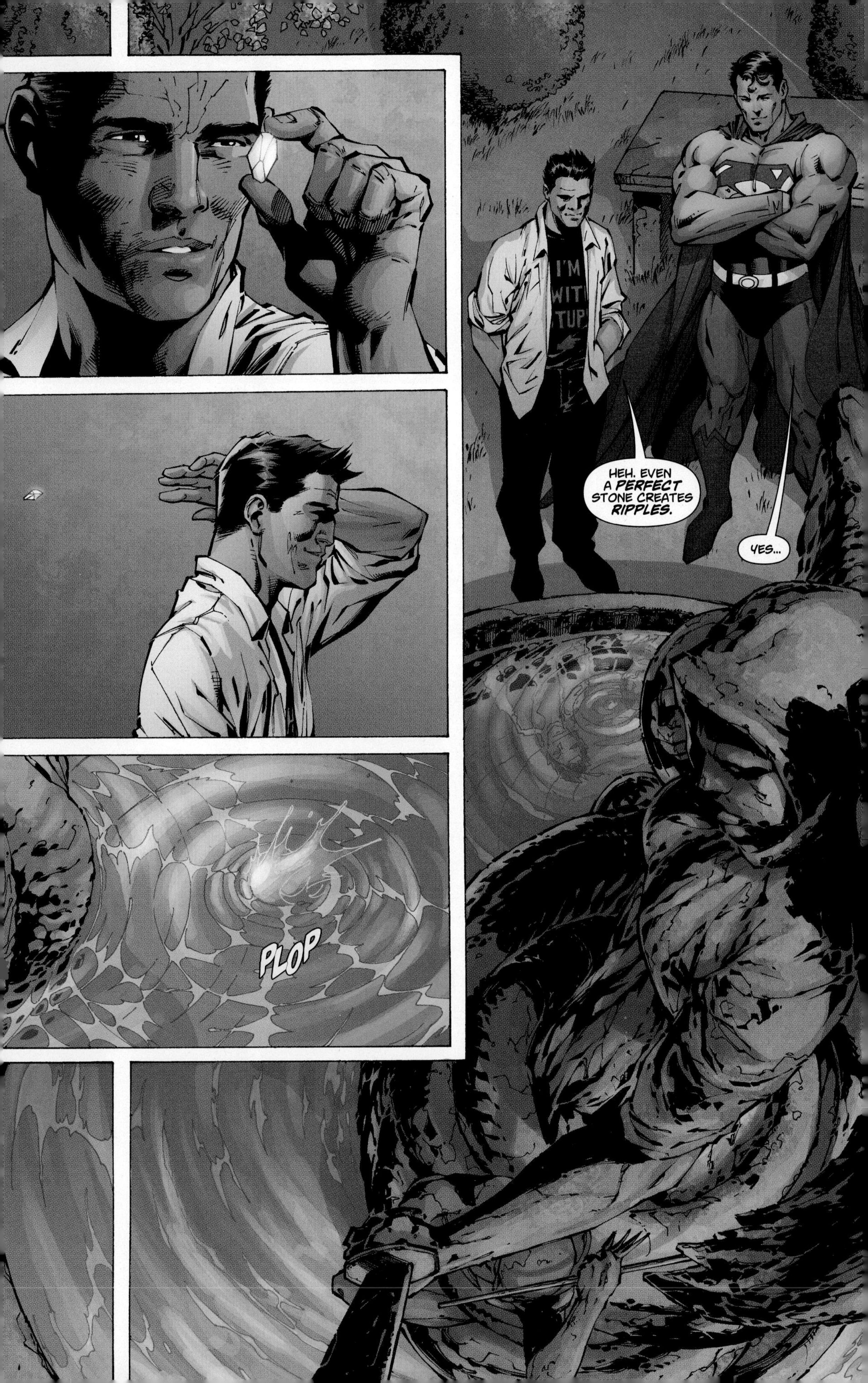
PLOP
HEH. EVEN A PERFECT STONE CREATES RIPPLES.
YES...

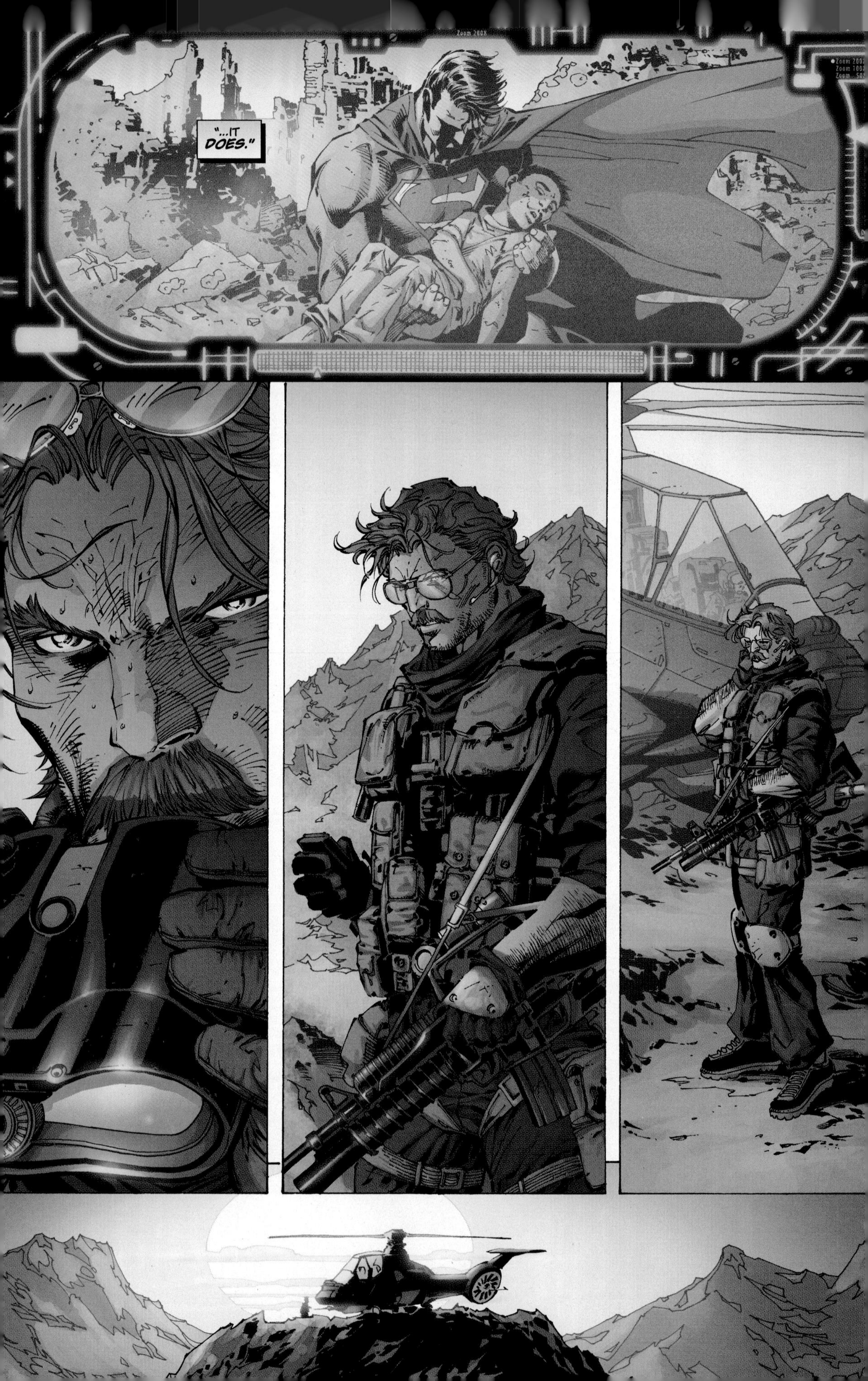
"...IT DOES."

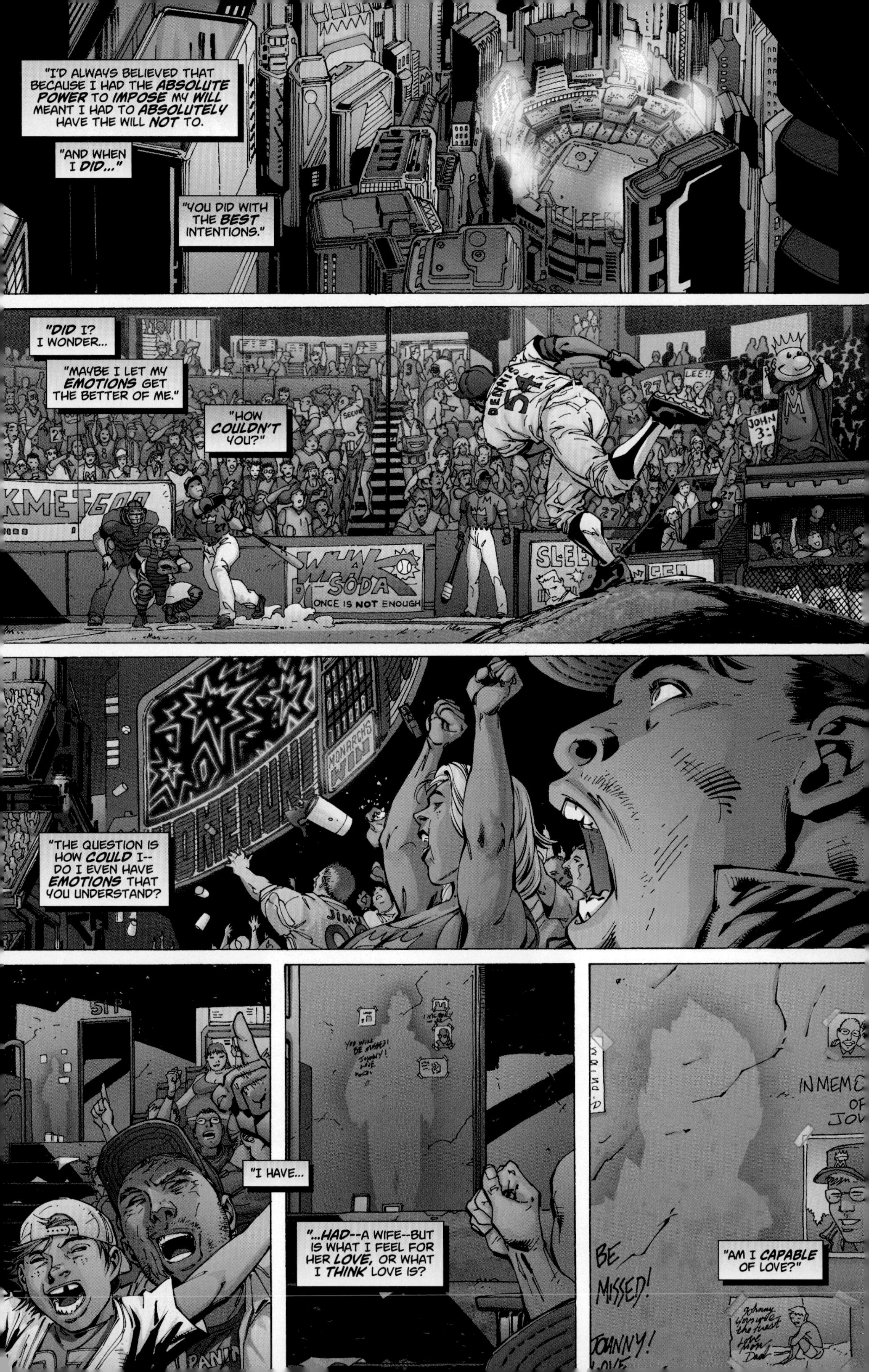
"I'D ALWAYS BELIEVED THAT BECAUSE I HAD THE ABSOLUTE POWER TO IMPOSE MY WILL MEANT I HAD TO ABSOLUTELY HAVE THE WILL NOT TO.
"AND WHEN I DID..."
"YOU DID WITH THE BEST INTENTIONS."
"DID I? I WONDER...
"MAYBE I LET MY EMOTIONS GET THE BETTER OF ME."
"HOW COULDN'T YOU?"
WHAK SODA
ONCE IS NOT ENOUGH
MONARCHS WIN
"THE QUESTION IS HOW COULD I-- DO I EVEN HAVE EMOTIONS THAT YOU UNDERSTAND?
"I HAVE...
"...HAD--A WIFE--BUT IS WHAT I FEEL FOR HER LOVE, OR WHAT I THINK LOVE IS?
"AM I CAPABLE OF LOVE?"
BE MISSED!
JOHNNY!

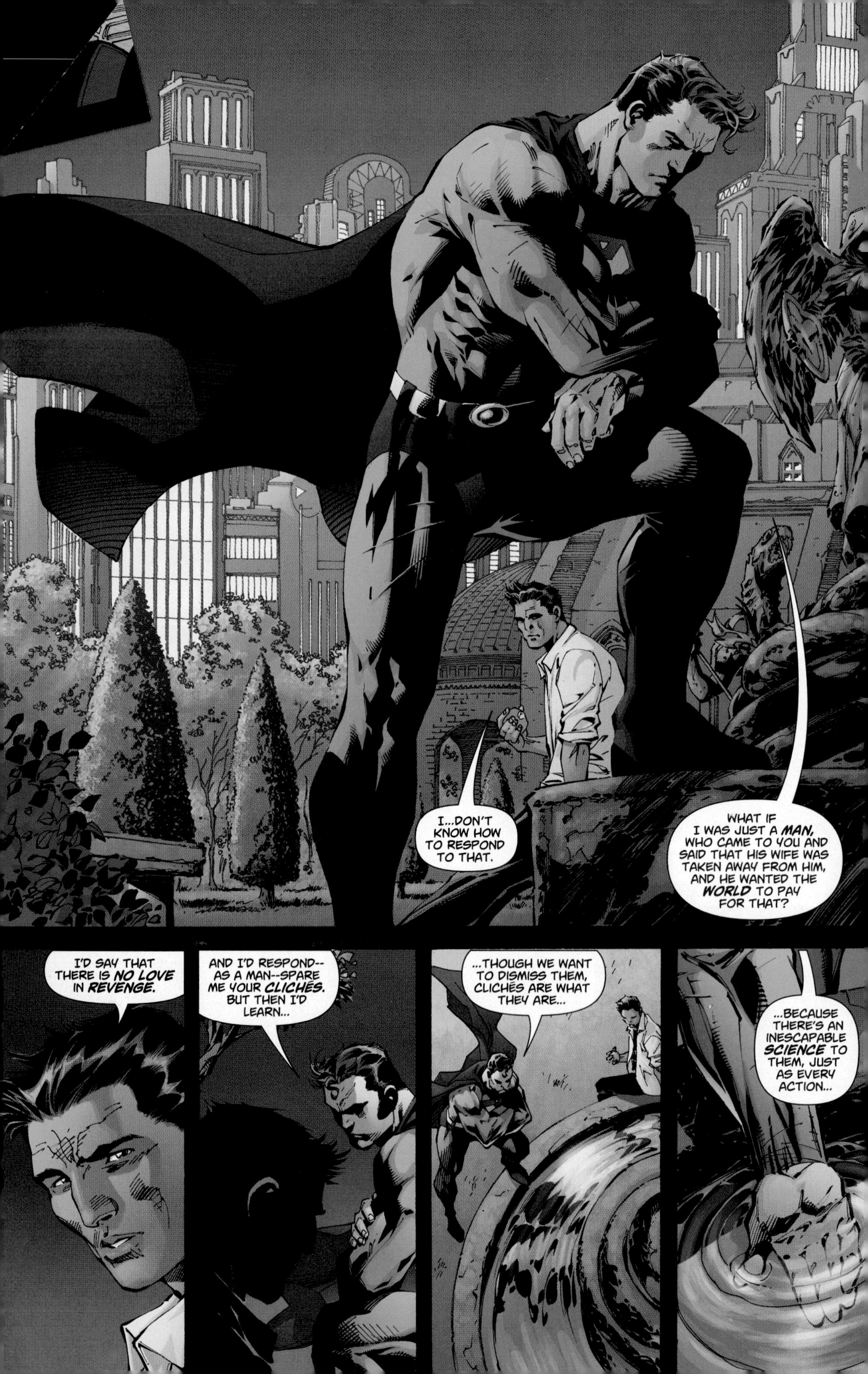
WHAT IF I WAS JUST A MAN, WHO CAME TO YOU AND SAID THAT HIS WIFE WAS TAKEN AWAY FROM HIM, AND HE WANTED THE WORLD TO PAY FOR THAT?
I...DON'T KNOW HOW TO RESPOND TO THAT.
I'D SAY THAT THERE IS NO LOVE IN REVENGE.
AND I'D RESPOND--AS A MAN--SPARE ME YOUR CLICHÉS. BUT THEN I'D LEARN...
...THOUGH WE WANT TO DISMISS THEM, CLICHÉS ARE WHAT THEY ARE...
...BECAUSE THERE'S AN INESCAPABLE SCIENCE TO THEM, JUST AS EVERY ACTION...

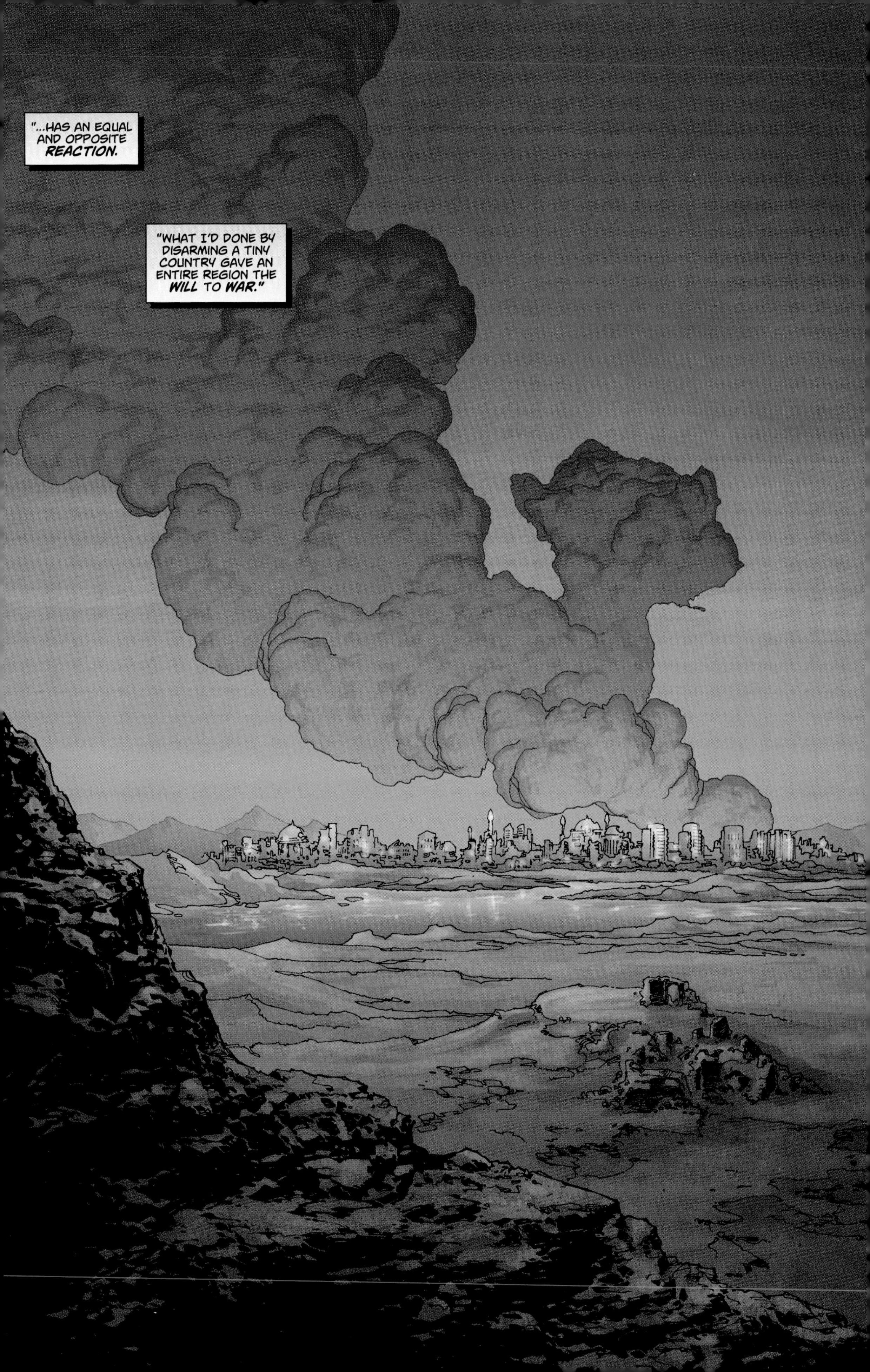
"...HAS AN EQUAL AND OPPOSITE **REACTION**.
"WHAT I'D DONE BY DISARMING A TINY COUNTRY GAVE AN ENTIRE REGION THE **WILL** TO **WAR**."

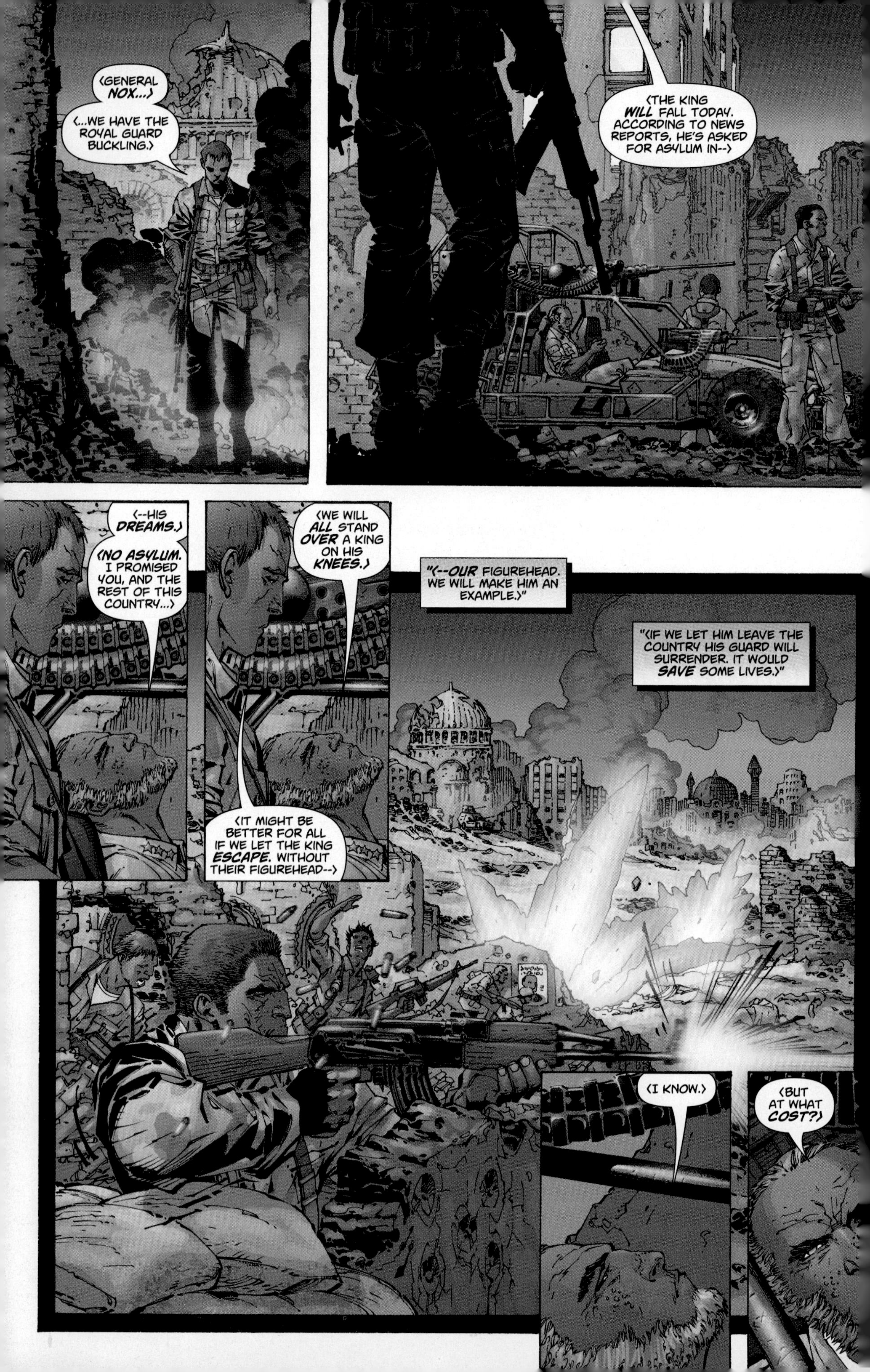

‹GENERAL NOX...›
‹...WE HAVE THE ROYAL GUARD BUCKLING.›
‹THE KING WILL FALL TODAY. ACCORDING TO NEWS REPORTS, HE'S ASKED FOR ASYLUM IN--›
‹--HIS DREAMS.›
‹NO ASYLUM. I PROMISED YOU, AND THE REST OF THIS COUNTRY...›
‹WE WILL ALL STAND OVER A KING ON HIS KNEES.›
‹IT MIGHT BE BETTER FOR ALL IF WE LET THE KING ESCAPE. WITHOUT THEIR FIGUREHEAD--›
"‹--OUR FIGUREHEAD. WE WILL MAKE HIM AN EXAMPLE.›"
"‹IF WE LET HIM LEAVE THE COUNTRY HIS GUARD WILL SURRENDER. IT WOULD SAVE SOME LIVES.›"
‹I KNOW.›
‹BUT AT WHAT COST?›

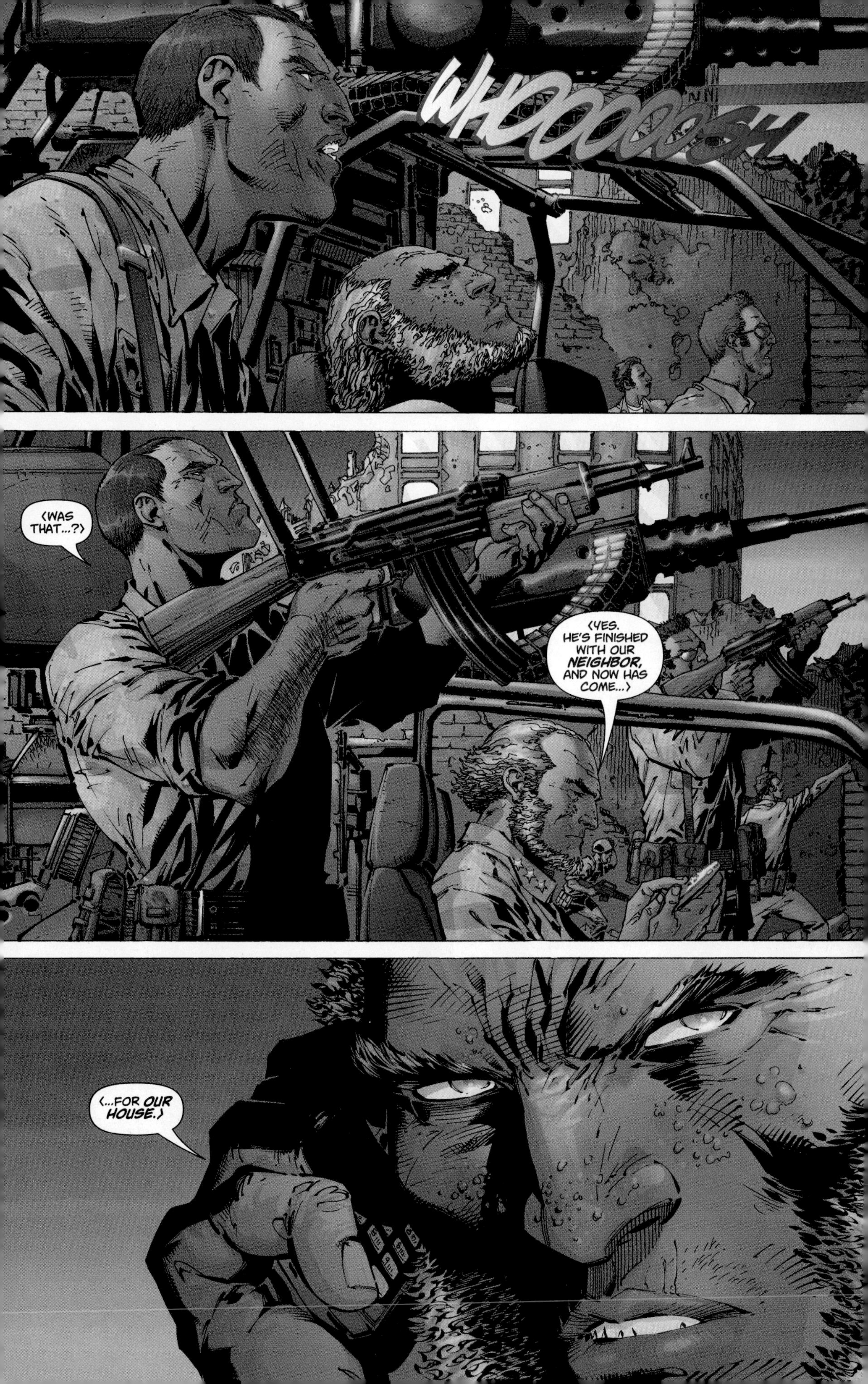
WHOOOOOSH
‹WAS THAT...?›
‹YES. HE'S FINISHED WITH OUR NEIGHBOR, AND NOW HAS COME...›
‹...FOR OUR HOUSE.›

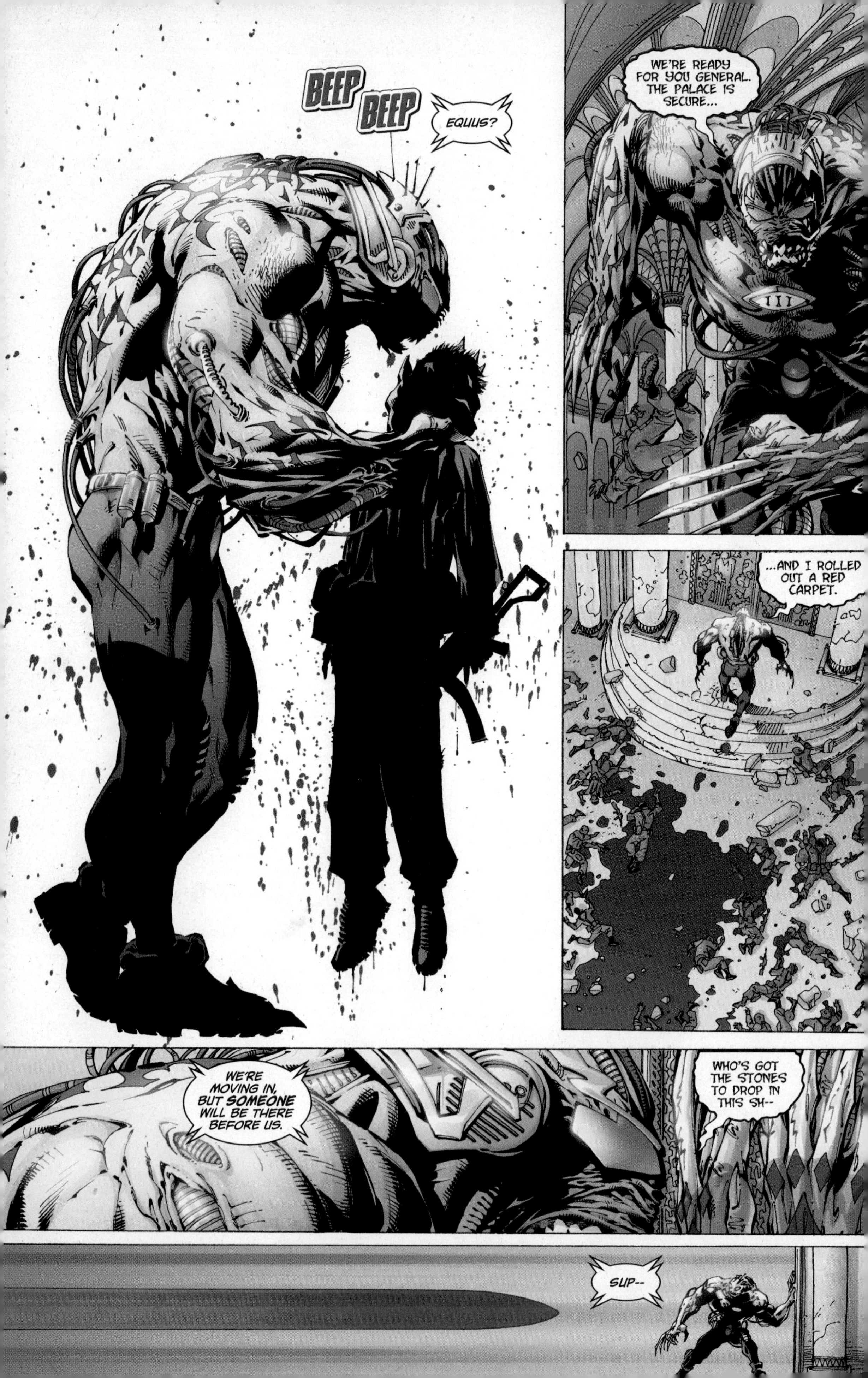
BEEP BEEP
EQUUS?
WE'RE READY FOR YOU GENERAL. THE PALACE IS SECURE...
...AND I ROLLED OUT A RED CARPET.
WE'RE MOVING IN, BUT SOMEONE WILL BE THERE BEFORE US.
WHO'S GOT THE STONES TO DROP IN THIS SH--
SLIP--

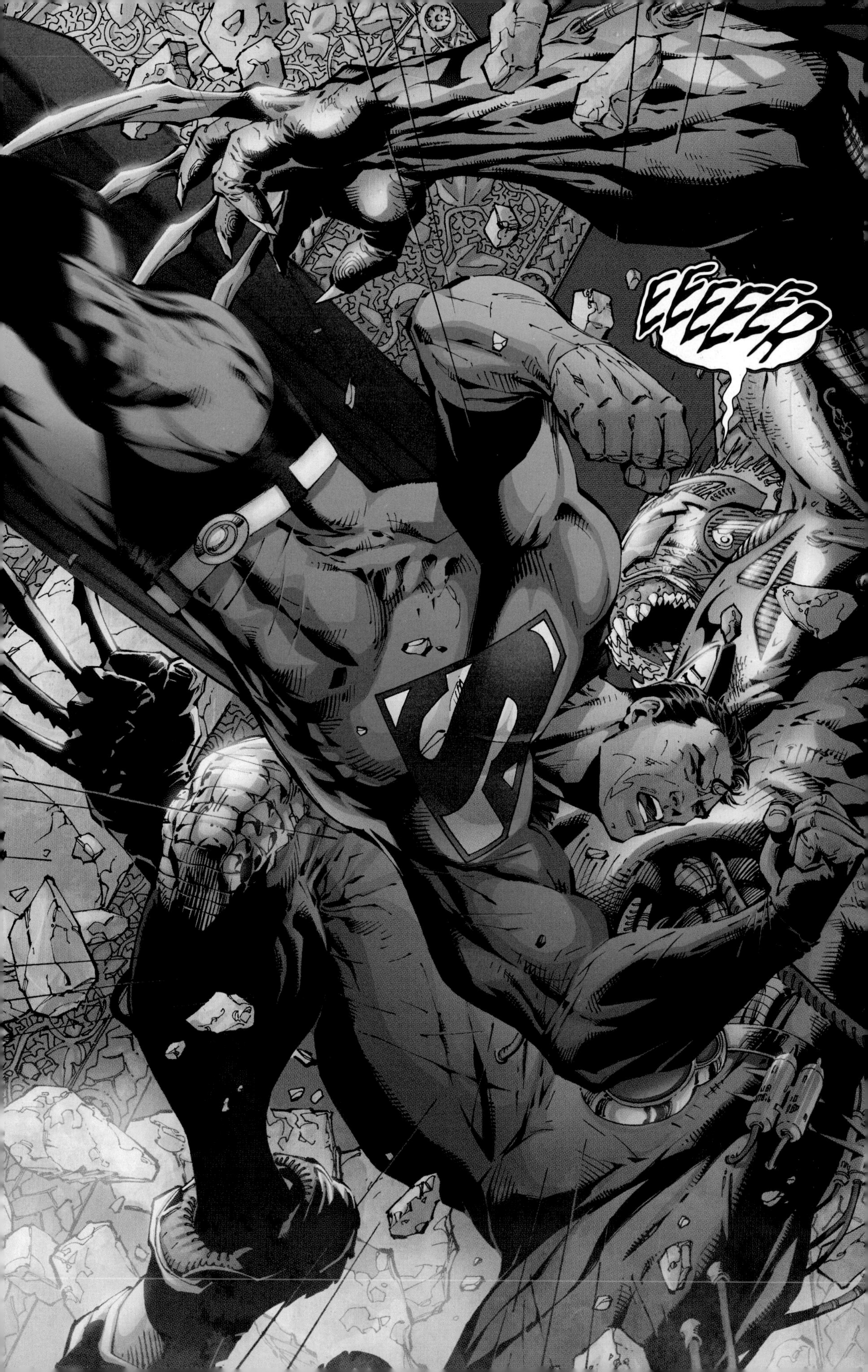
EEEEER

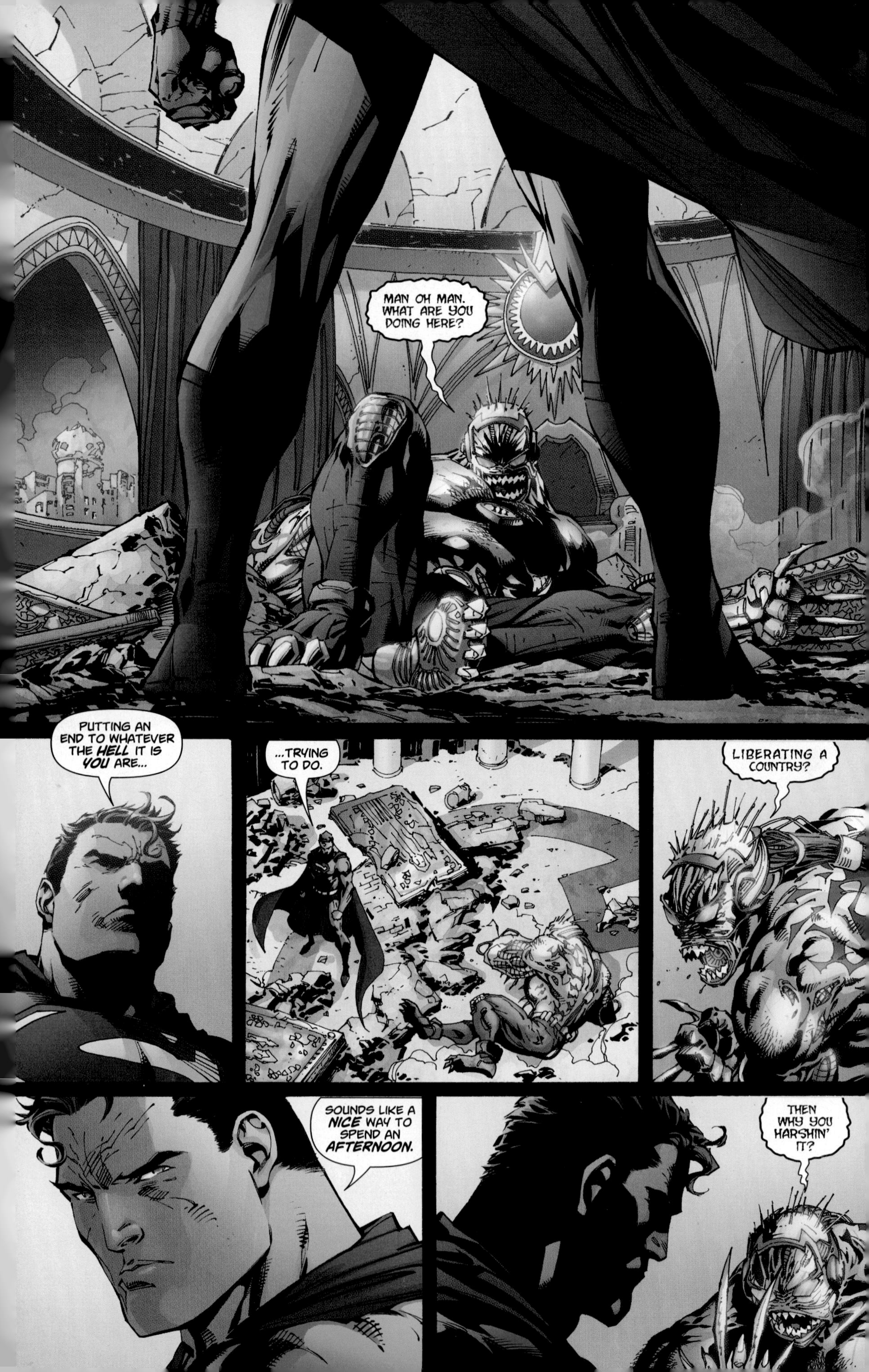
MAN OH MAN. WHAT ARE YOU DOING HERE?
PUTTING AN END TO WHATEVER THE HELL IT IS YOU ARE...
...TRYING TO DO.
LIBERATING A COUNTRY?
SOUNDS LIKE A NICE WAY TO SPEND AN AFTERNOON.
THEN WHY YOU HARSHIN' IT?

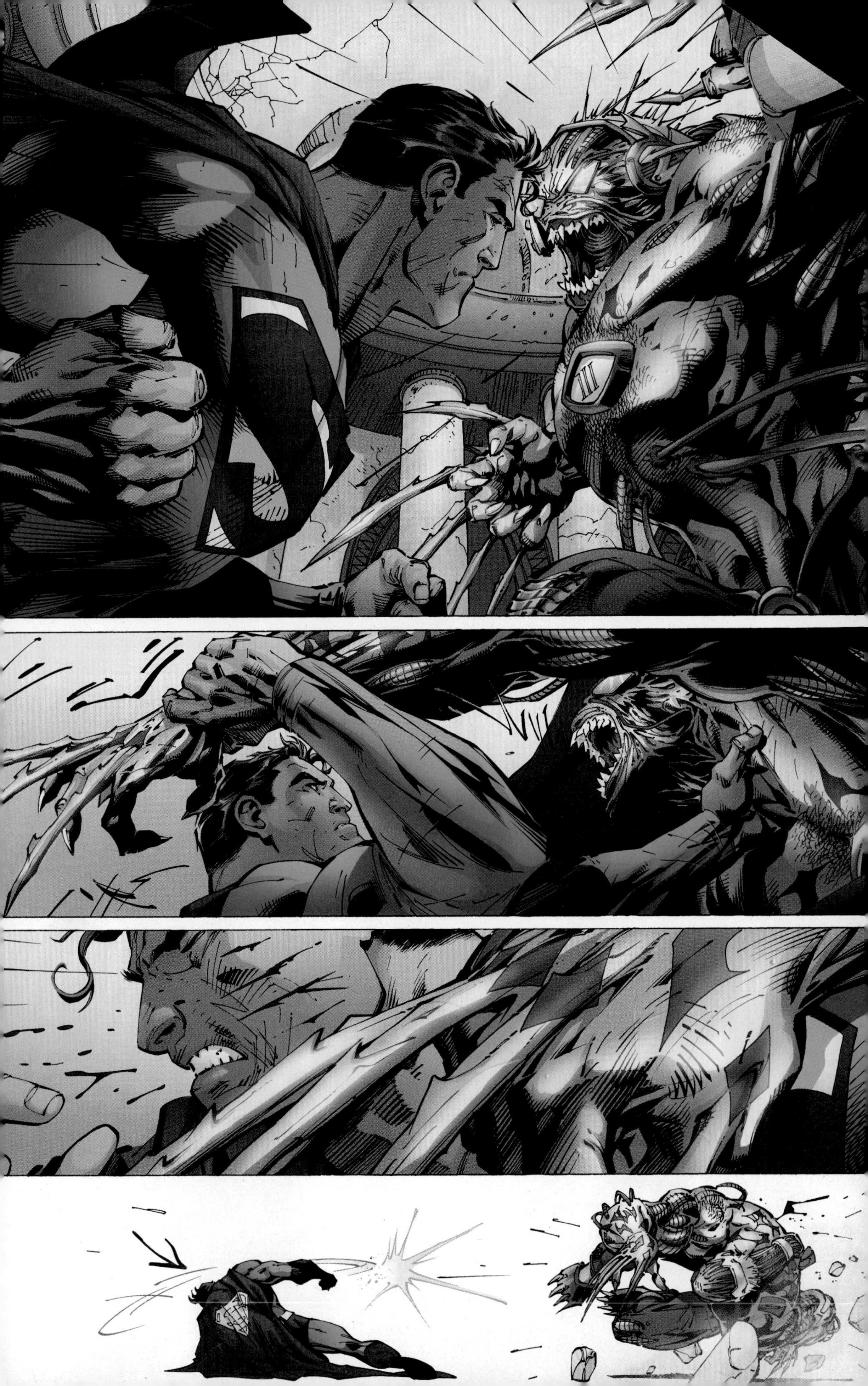

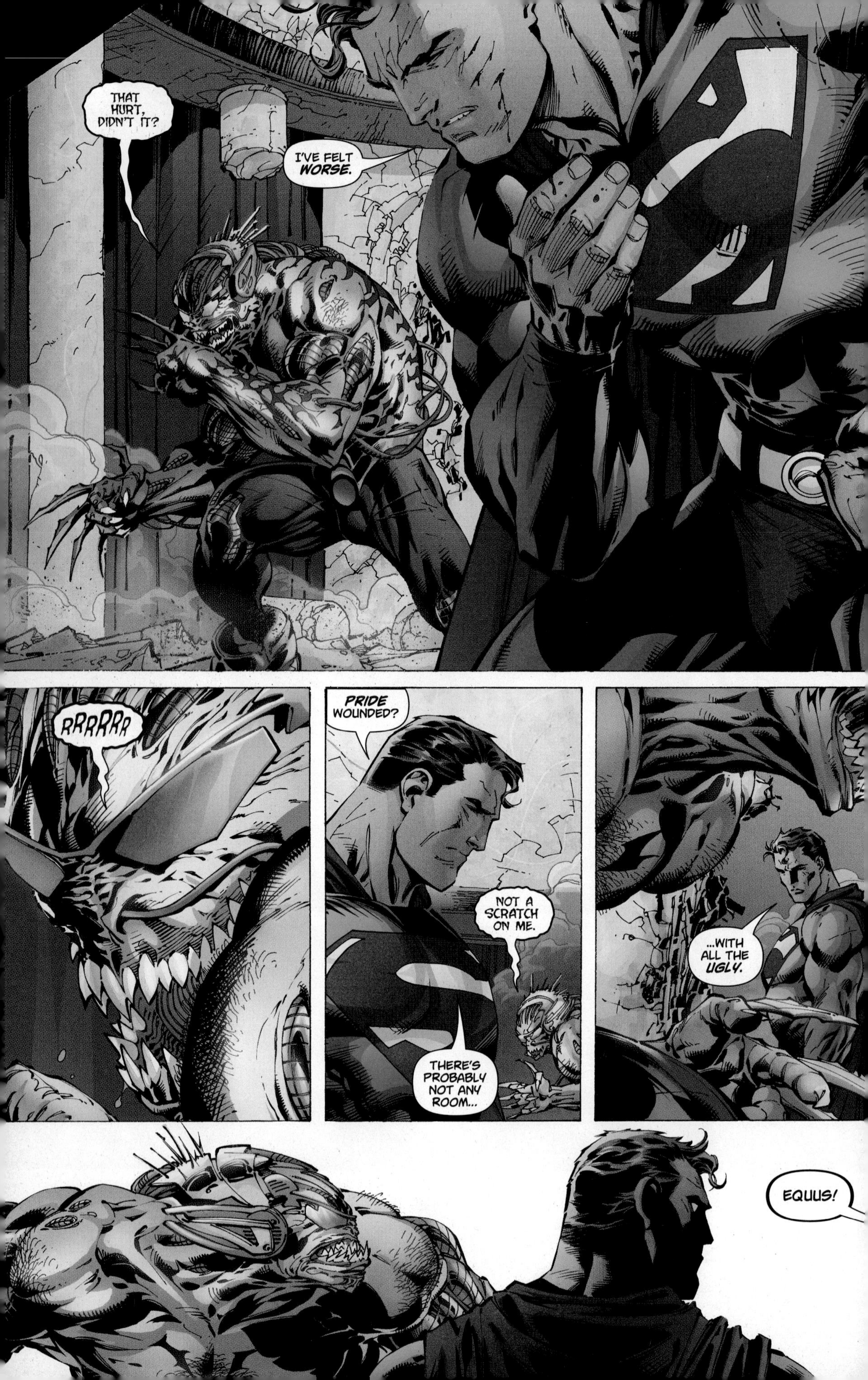
THAT HURT, DIDN'T IT?
I'VE FELT WORSE.
RRRRRR
PRIDE WOUNDED?
NOT A SCRATCH ON ME.
THERE'S PROBABLY NOT ANY ROOM...
...WITH ALL THE UGLY.
EQUUS!

STAND DOWN.

NOX...

WE HAVE NO *QUARREL* WITH SUPERMAN...

...DO WE?

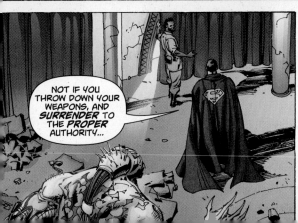

NOT IF YOU THROW DOWN YOUR WEAPONS, AND *SURRENDER* TO THE *PROPER* AUTHORITY...

IF WE DO *THAT*, THEY'LL BE PICKED UP, AND PUT BACK IN *OUR* HANDS...

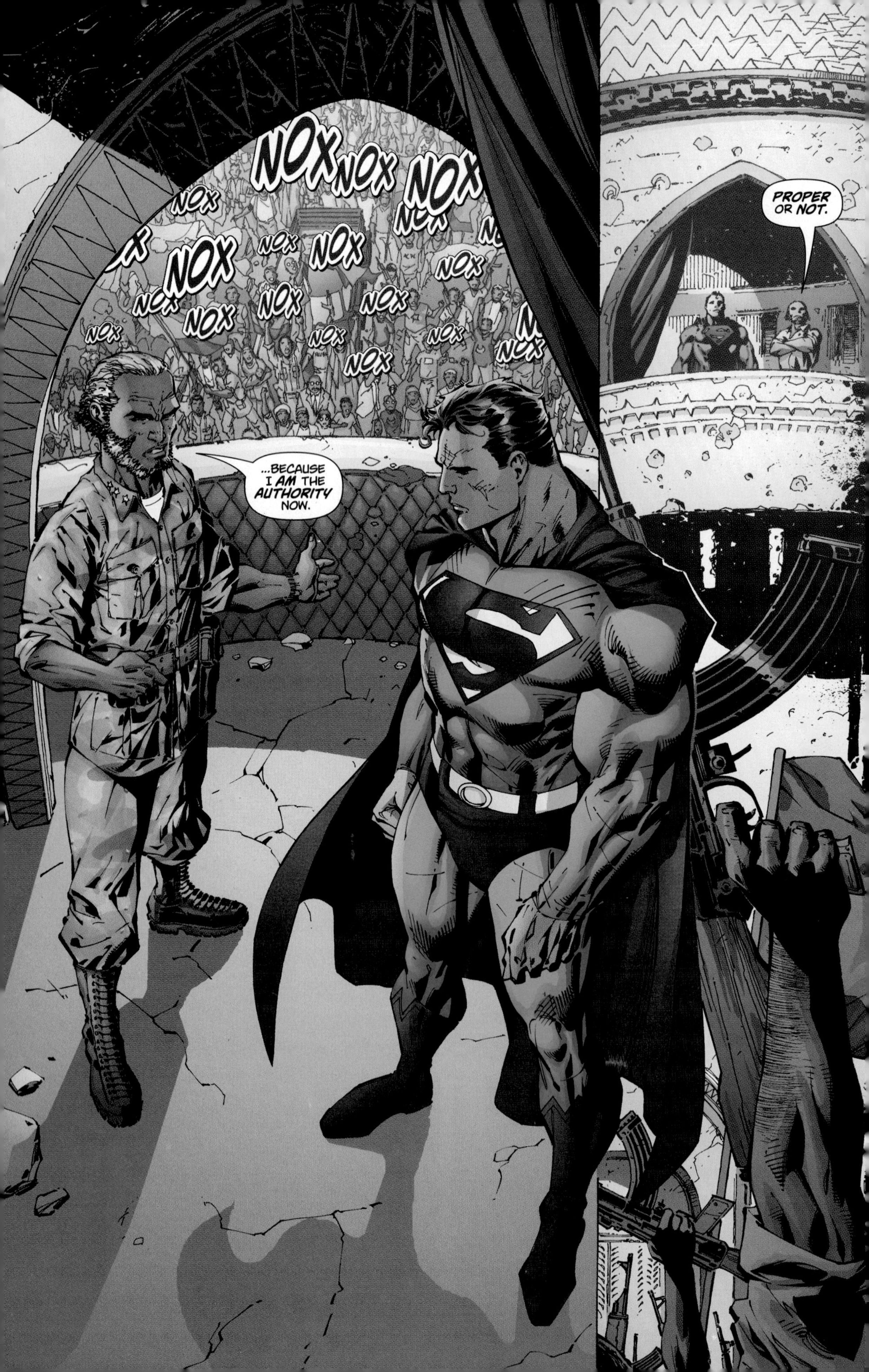
NOX NOX NOX
NOX
NOX
NOX NOX NOX
NOX NOX
NOX NOX NOX NOX
NOX NOX NOX
NOX
...BECAUSE I AM THE AUTHORITY NOW.
PROPER OR NOT.

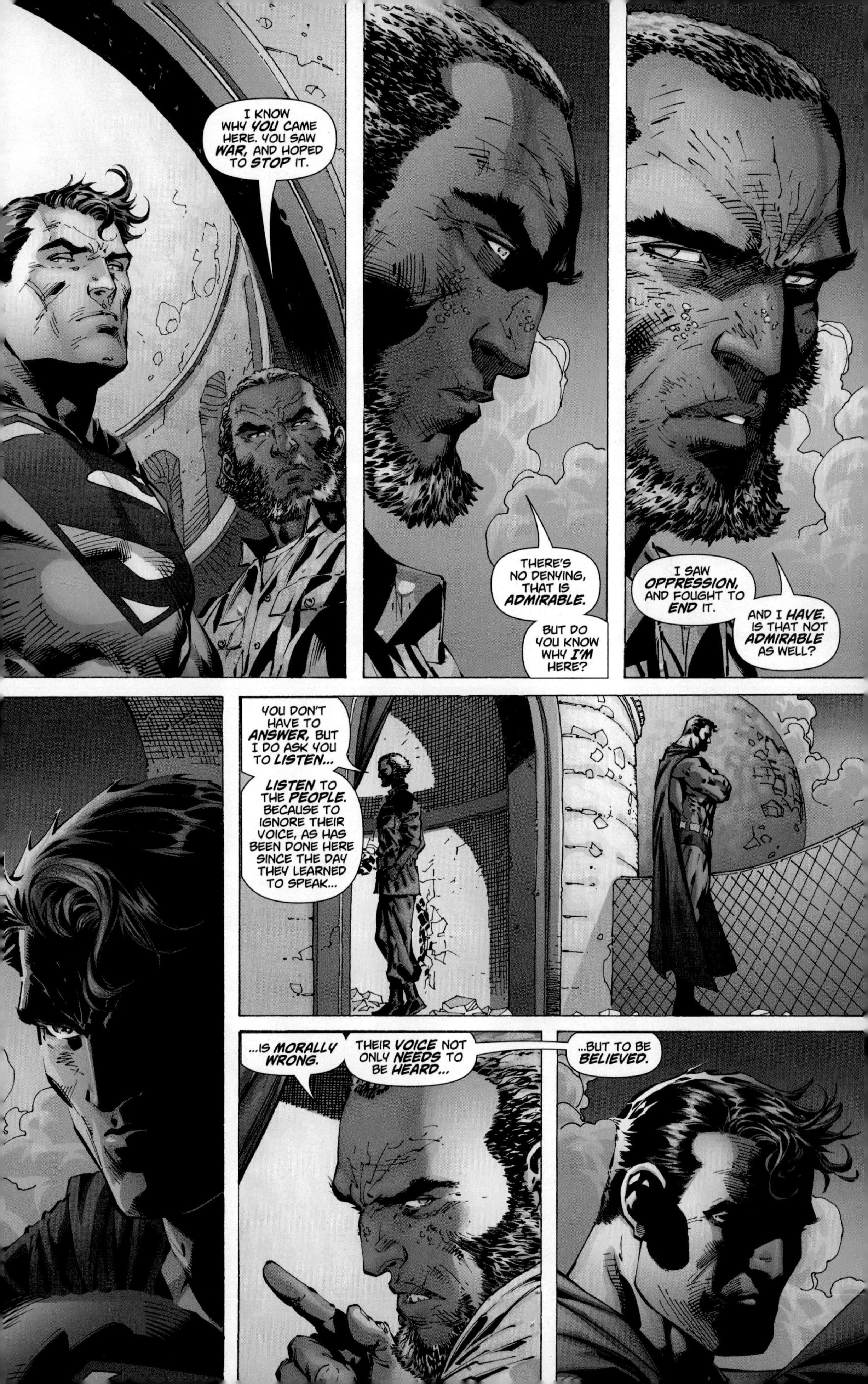
I KNOW WHY *YOU* CAME HERE. YOU SAW *WAR,* AND HOPED TO *STOP* IT.
THERE'S NO DENYING, THAT IS *ADMIRABLE.*
BUT DO YOU KNOW WHY *I'M* HERE?
I SAW *OPPRESSION,* AND FOUGHT TO *END* IT.
AND I *HAVE.* IS THAT NOT *ADMIRABLE* AS WELL?
YOU DON'T HAVE TO *ANSWER,* BUT I DO ASK YOU TO *LISTEN...*
*LISTEN* TO THE *PEOPLE.* BECAUSE TO IGNORE THEIR VOICE, AS HAS BEEN DONE HERE SINCE THE DAY THEY LEARNED TO SPEAK...
...IS *MORALLY WRONG.*
THEIR *VOICE* NOT ONLY *NEEDS* TO BE *HEARD...*
...BUT TO BE *BELIEVED.*

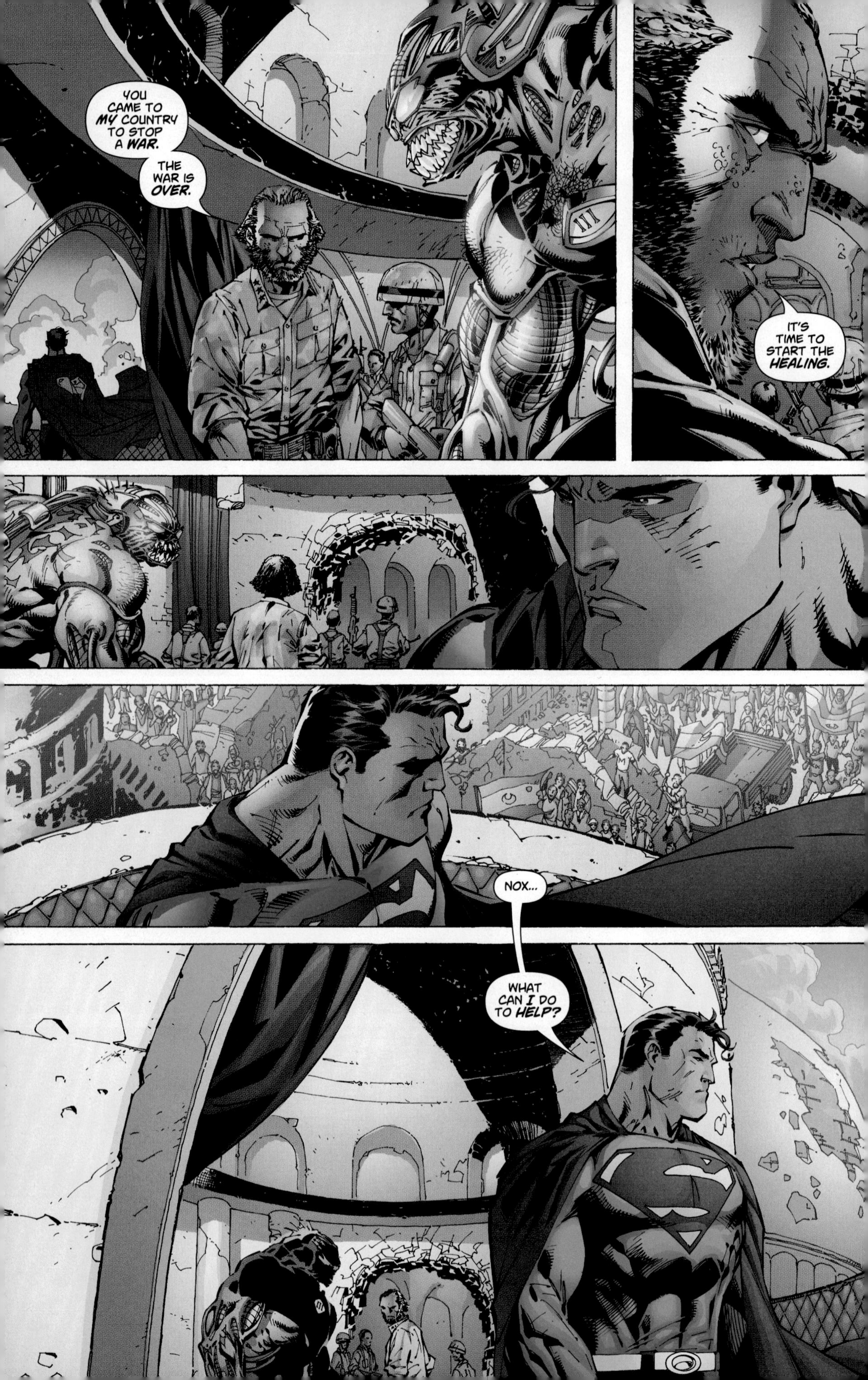
YOU CAME TO **MY** COUNTRY TO STOP A **WAR**.
THE WAR IS **OVER**.
IT'S TIME TO START THE **HEALING**.
NOX...
WHAT CAN **I** DO TO **HELP**?

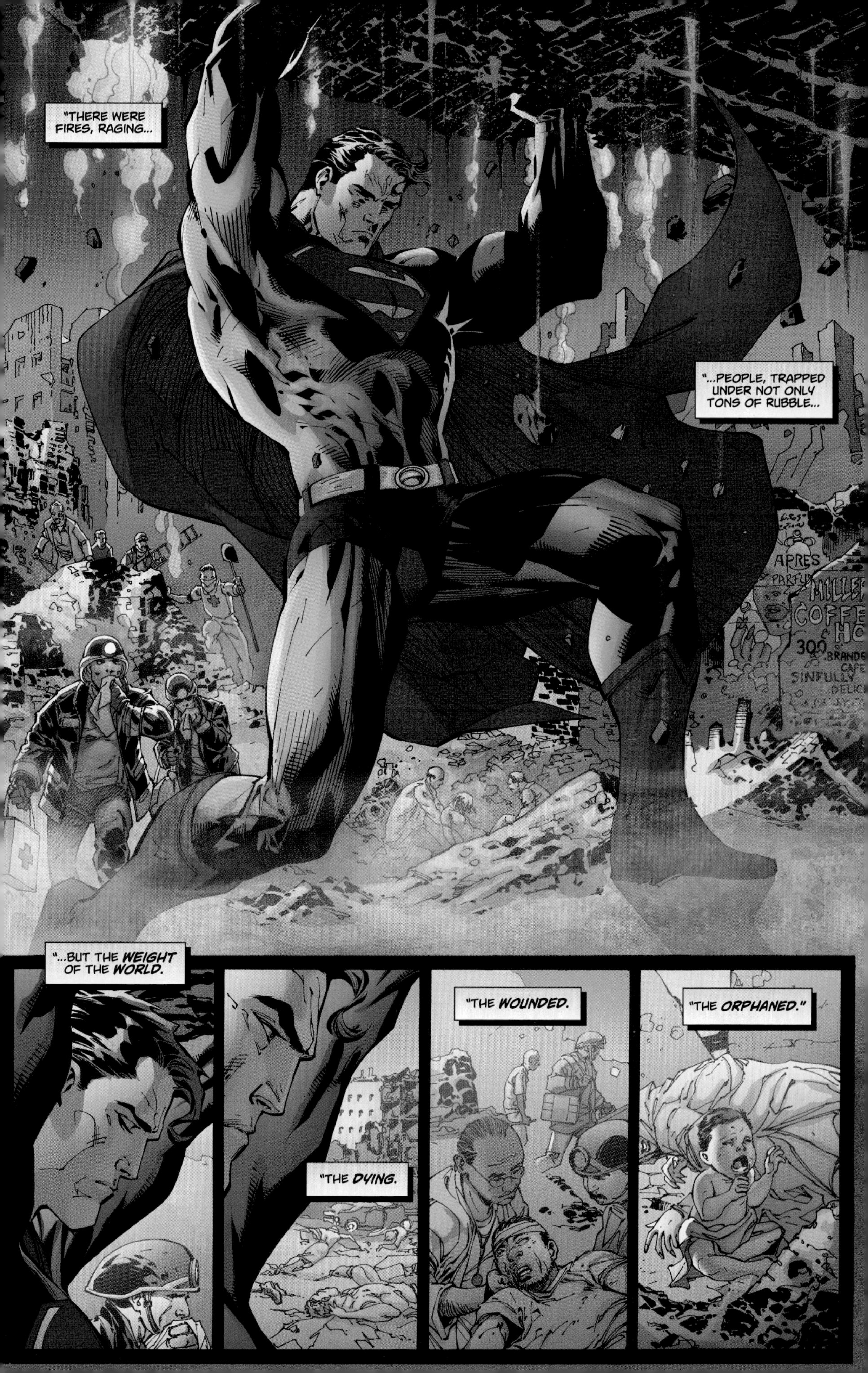
"THERE WERE FIRES, RAGING...
"...PEOPLE, TRAPPED UNDER NOT ONLY TONS OF RUBBLE...
"...BUT THE WEIGHT OF THE WORLD.
"THE DYING.
"THE WOUNDED.
"THE ORPHANED."

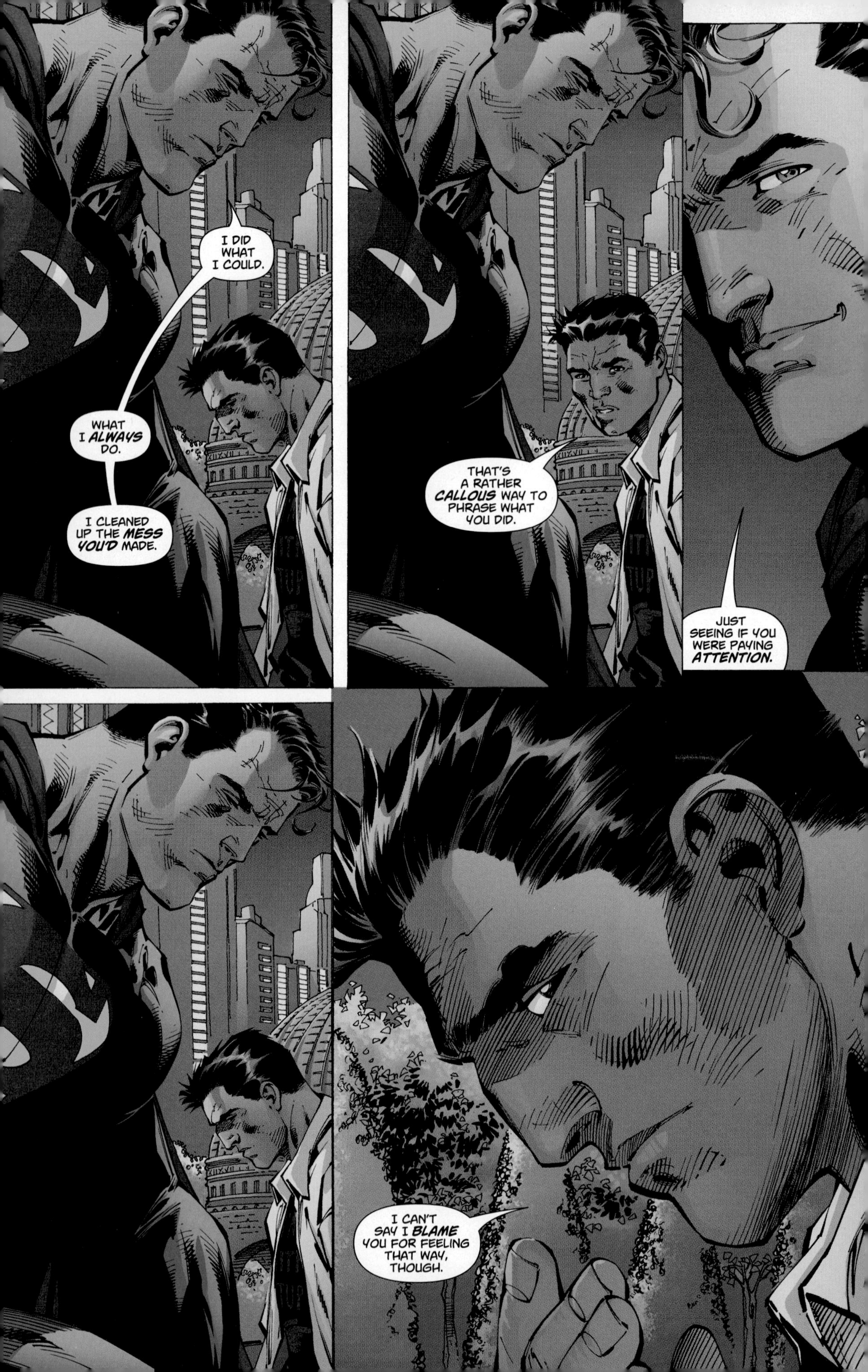
I DID WHAT I COULD.
WHAT I ALWAYS DO.
I CLEANED UP THE MESS YOU'D MADE.
THAT'S A RATHER CALLOUS WAY TO PHRASE WHAT YOU DID.
JUST SEEING IF YOU WERE PAYING ATTENTION.
I CAN'T SAY I BLAME YOU FOR FEELING THAT WAY, THOUGH.

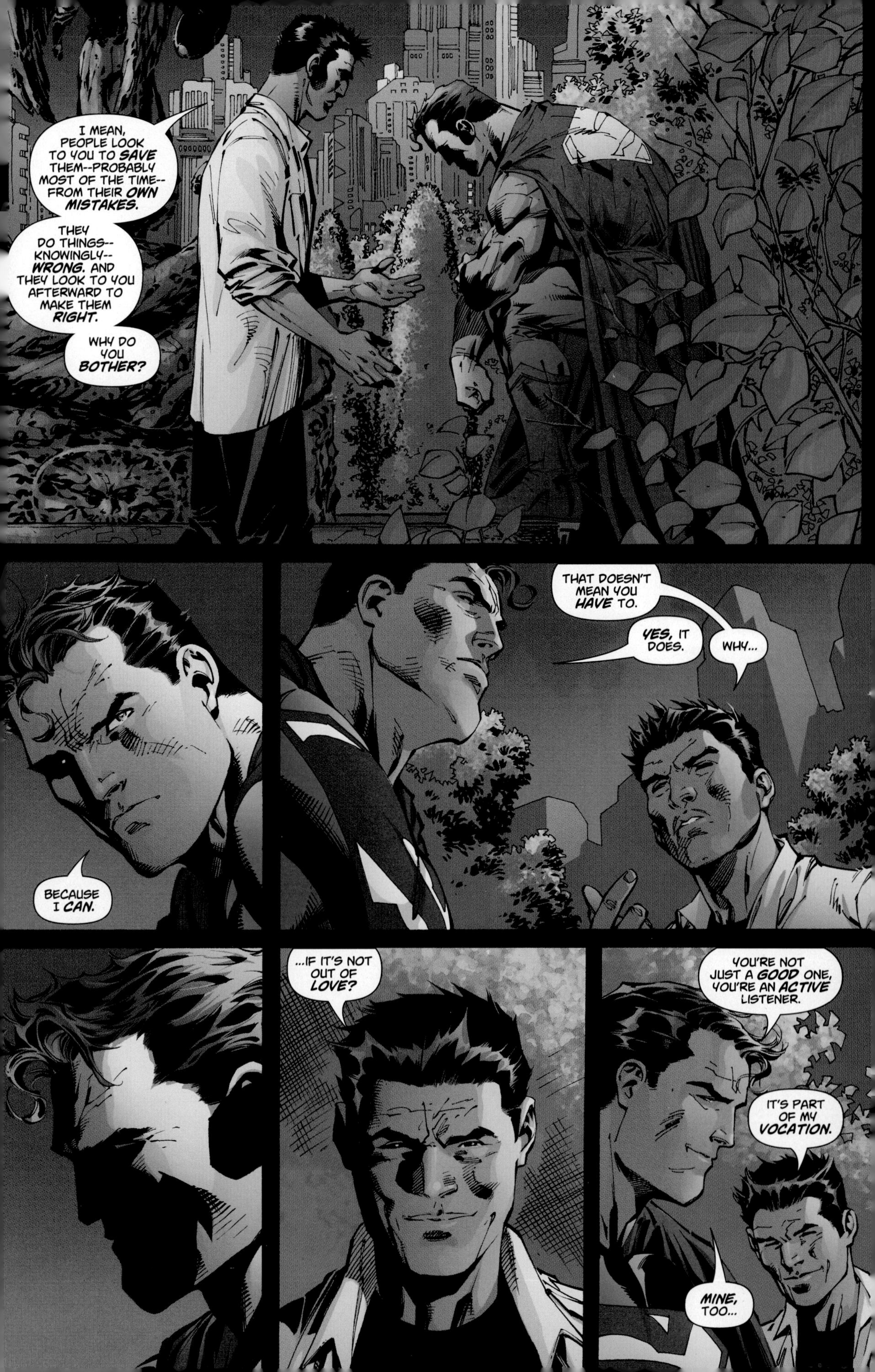
I MEAN, PEOPLE LOOK TO YOU TO SAVE THEM--PROBABLY MOST OF THE TIME--FROM THEIR OWN MISTAKES.
THEY DO THINGS--KNOWINGLY--WRONG. AND THEY LOOK TO YOU AFTERWARD TO MAKE THEM RIGHT.
WHY DO YOU BOTHER?
BECAUSE I CAN.
THAT DOESN'T MEAN YOU HAVE TO.
YES, IT DOES.
WHY...
...IF IT'S NOT OUT OF LOVE?
YOU'RE NOT JUST A GOOD ONE, YOU'RE AN ACTIVE LISTENER.
IT'S PART OF MY VOCATION.
MINE, TOO...

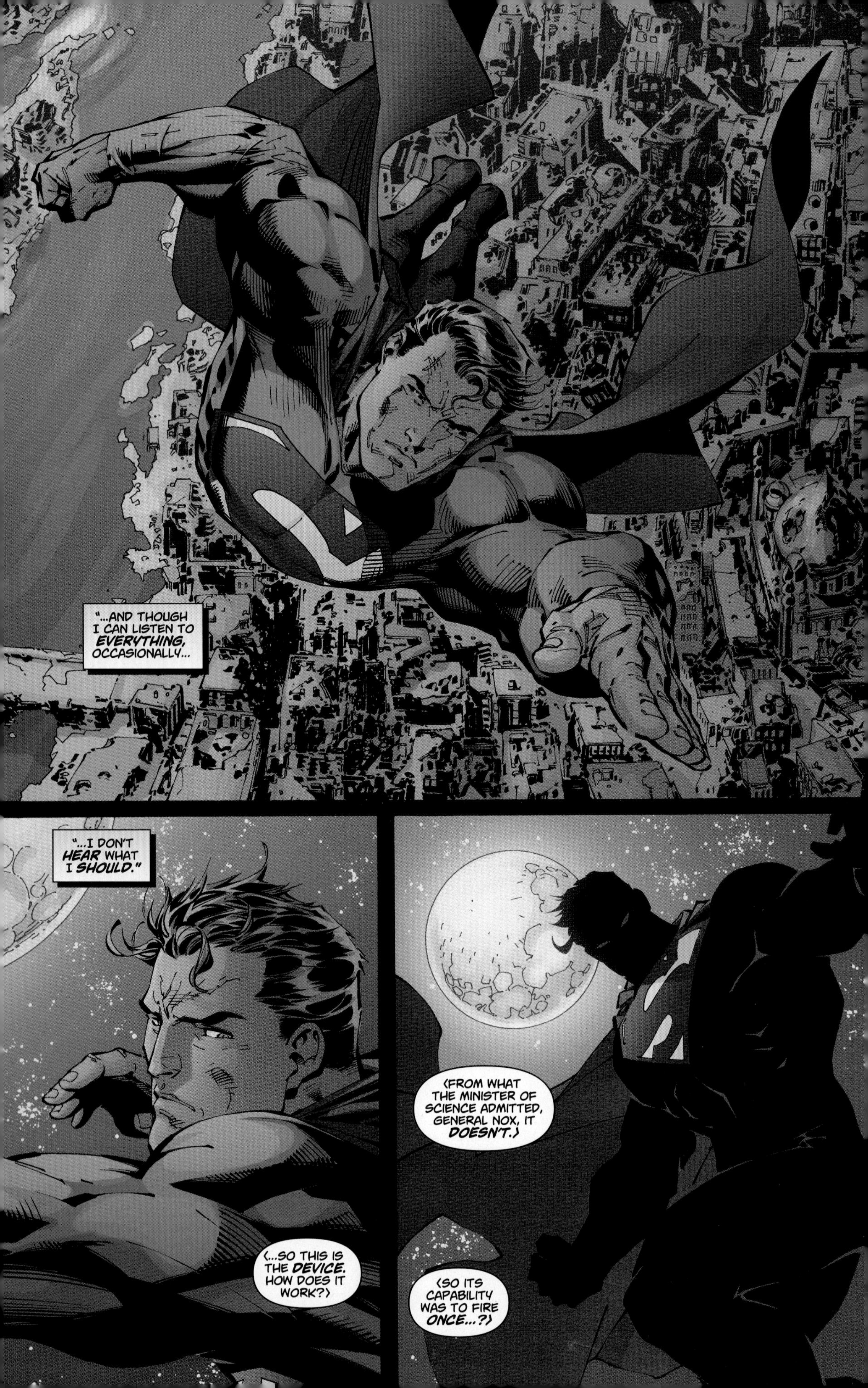
"...AND THOUGH I CAN LISTEN TO EVERYTHING, OCCASIONALLY...
"...I DON'T HEAR WHAT I SHOULD."
‹...SO THIS IS THE DEVICE. HOW DOES IT WORK?›
‹FROM WHAT THE MINISTER OF SCIENCE ADMITTED, GENERAL NOX, IT DOESN'T.›
‹SO ITS CAPABILITY WAS TO FIRE ONCE...?›

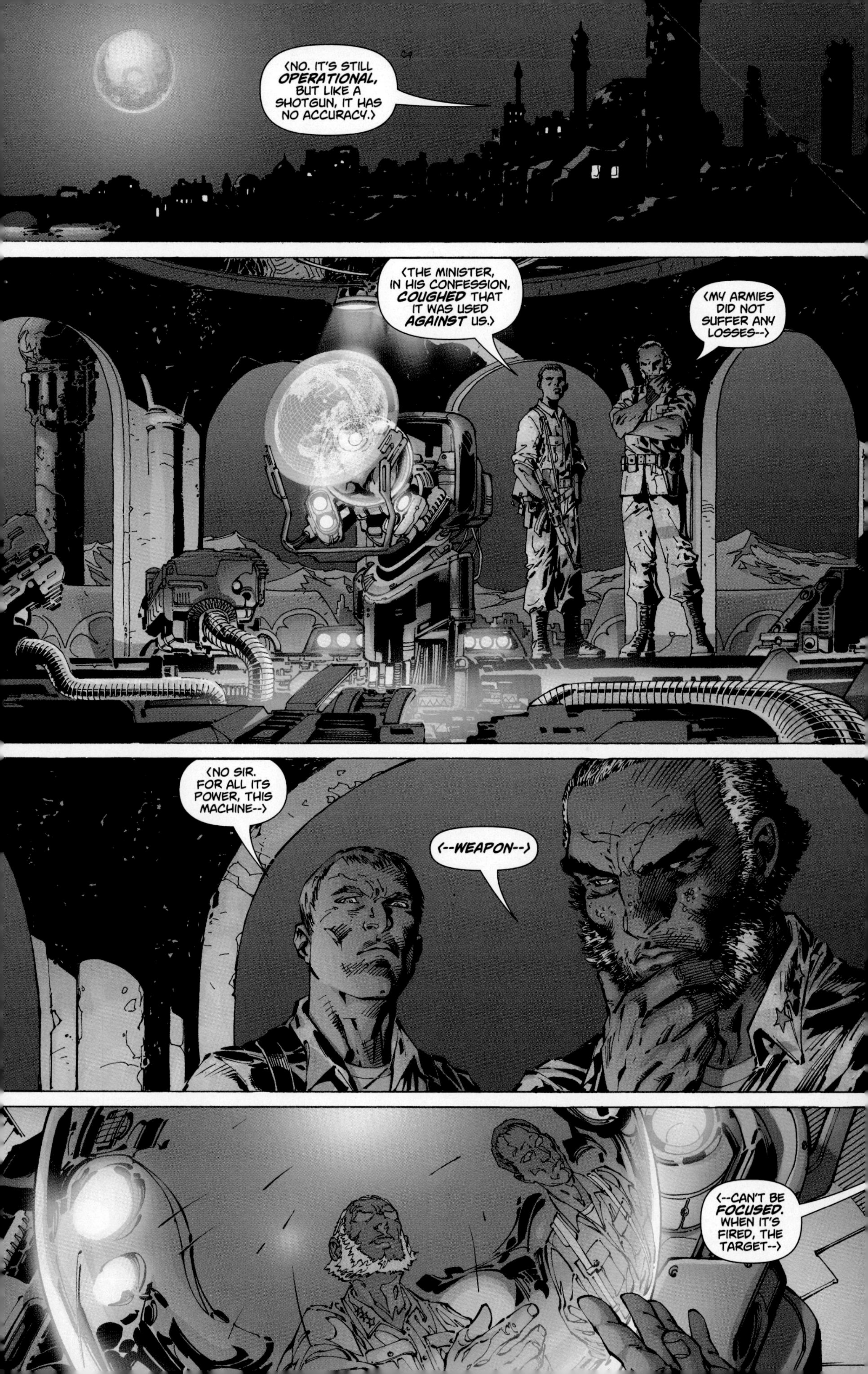
‹NO. IT'S STILL OPERATIONAL, BUT LIKE A SHOTGUN, IT HAS NO ACCURACY.›
‹THE MINISTER, IN HIS CONFESSION, COUGHED THAT IT WAS USED AGAINST US.›
‹MY ARMIES DID NOT SUFFER ANY LOSSES--›
‹NO SIR. FOR ALL ITS POWER, THIS MACHINE--›
‹--WEAPON--›
‹--CAN'T BE FOCUSED. WHEN IT'S FIRED, THE TARGET--›

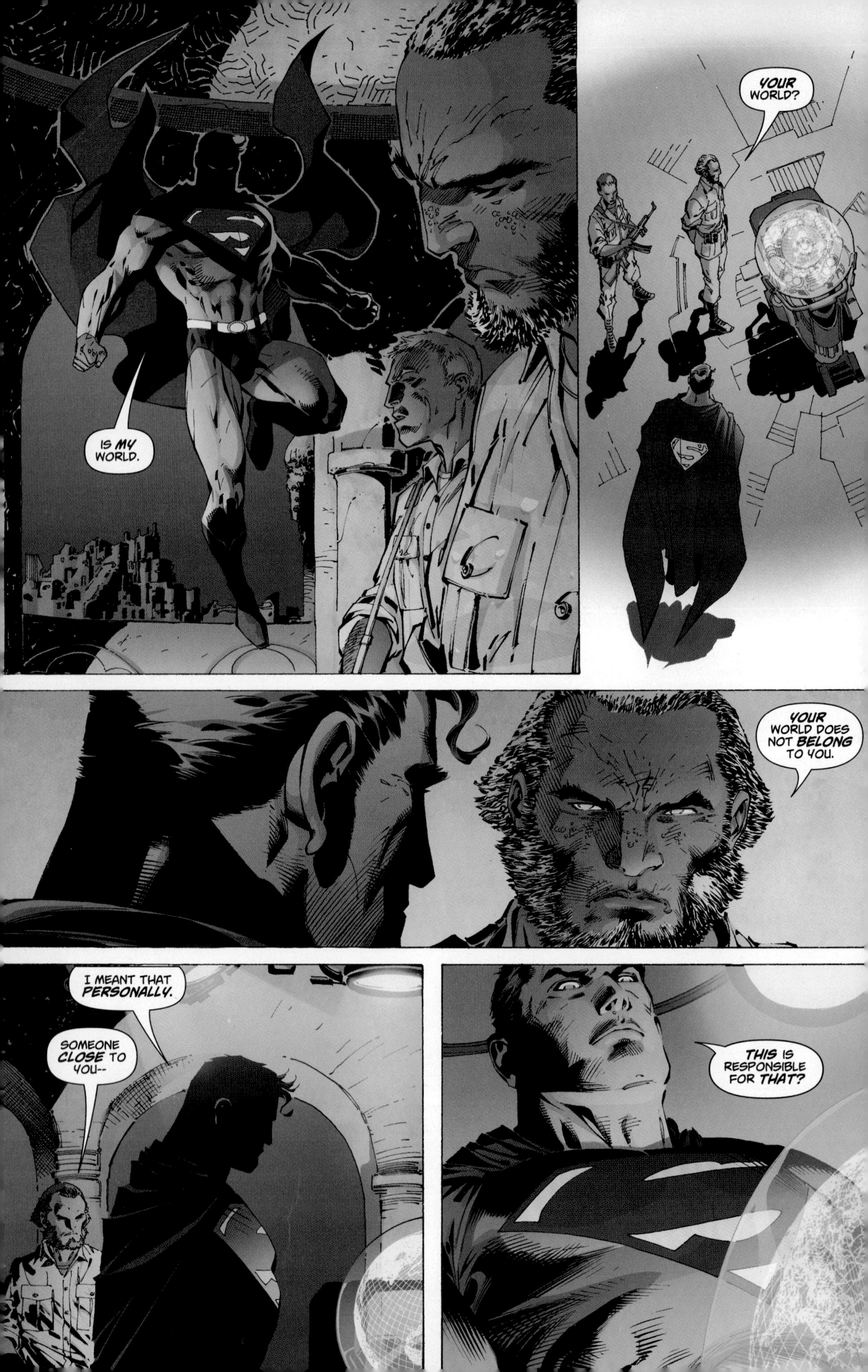
IS MY WORLD.
YOUR WORLD?
YOUR WORLD DOES NOT BELONG TO YOU.
I MEANT THAT PERSONALLY.
SOMEONE CLOSE TO YOU--
THIS IS RESPONSIBLE FOR THAT?

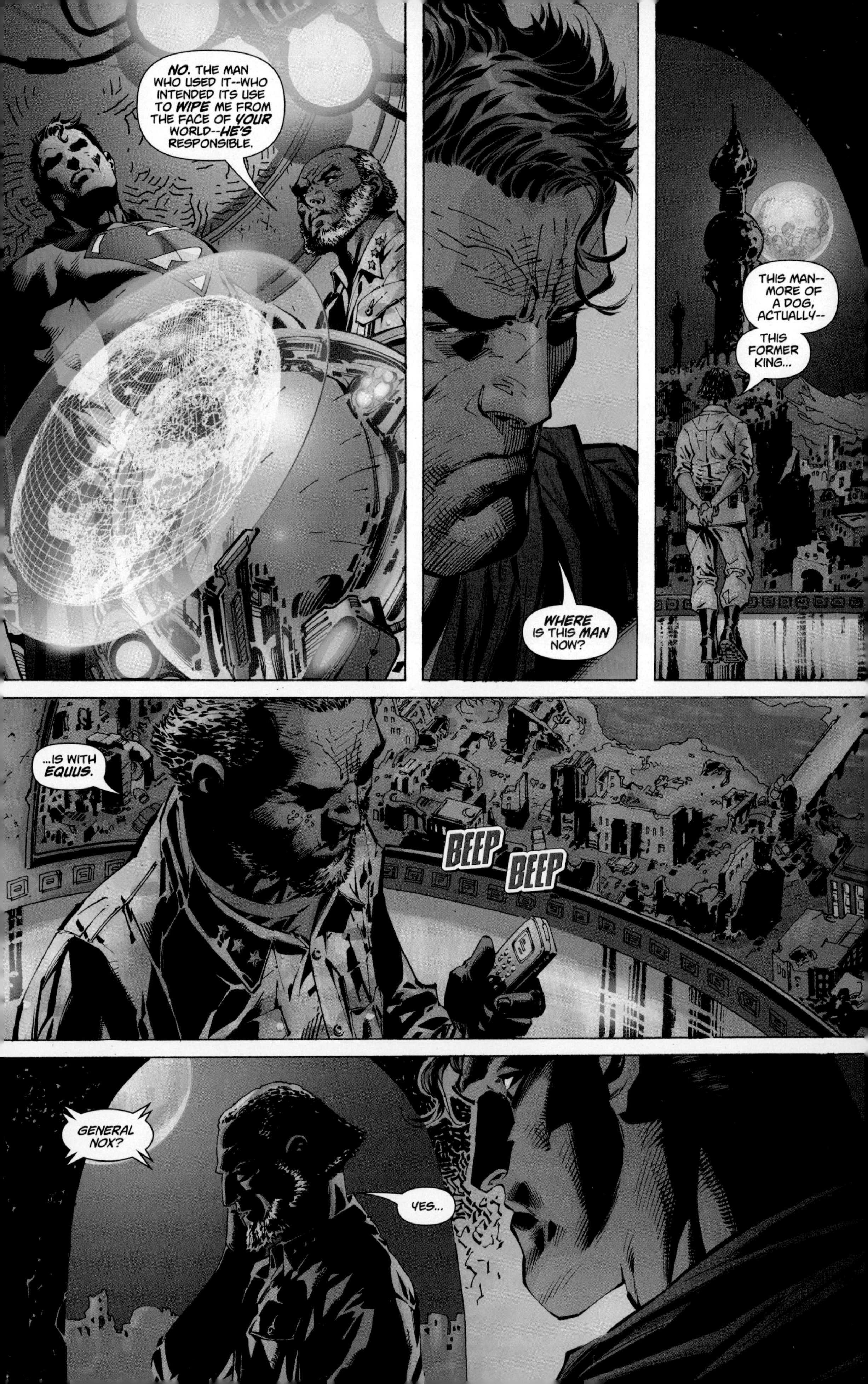
NO. THE MAN WHO USED IT--WHO INTENDED ITS USE TO WIPE ME FROM THE FACE OF YOUR WORLD--HE'S RESPONSIBLE.
WHERE IS THIS MAN NOW?
THIS MAN-- MORE OF A DOG, ACTUALLY--
THIS FORMER KING...
...IS WITH EQUUS.
BEEP
BEEP
GENERAL NOX?
YES...

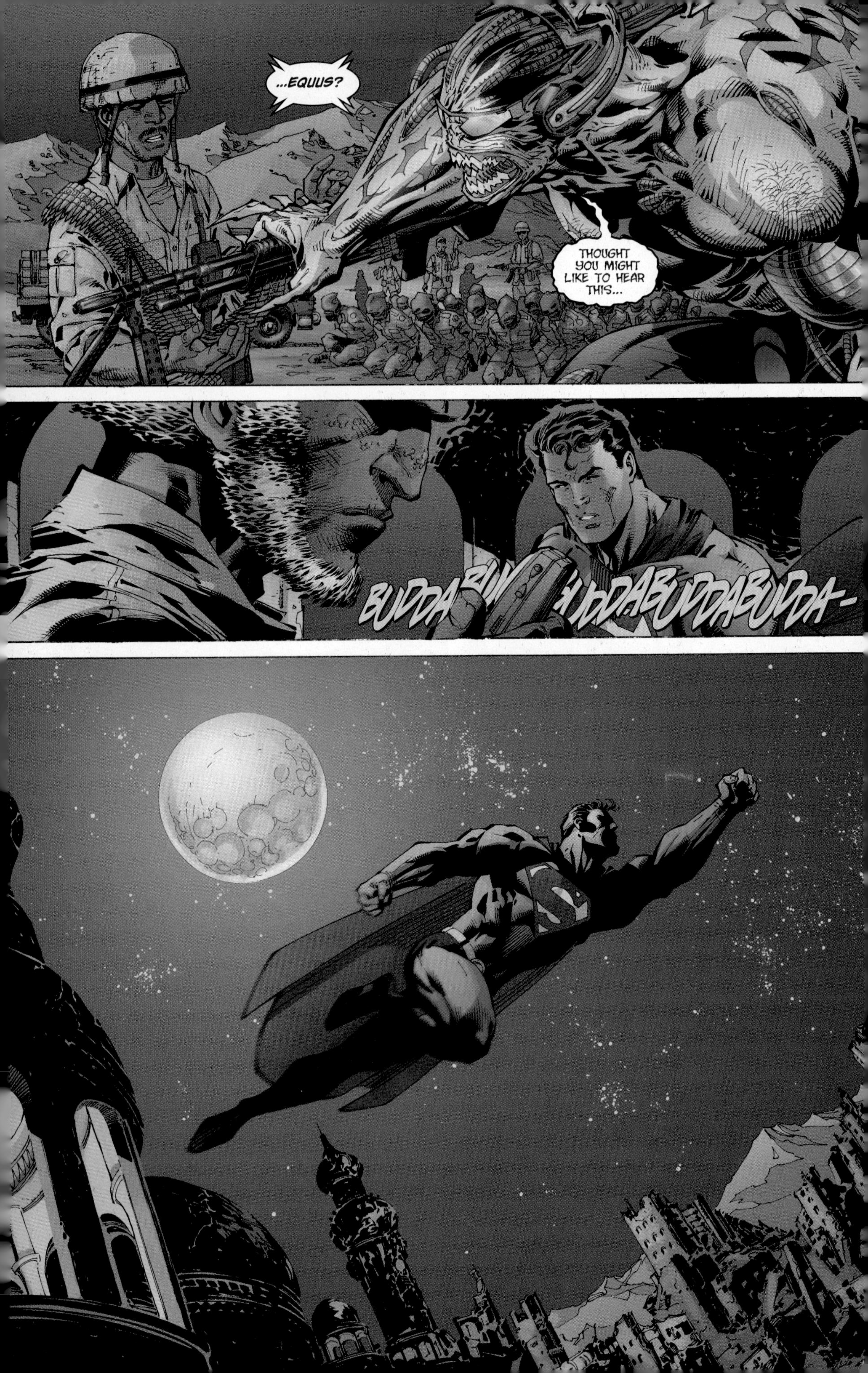
...EQUUS?
THOUGHT YOU MIGHT LIKE TO HEAR THIS...
BUDDABUDDABUDDABUDDA-

"SIX HUNDRED SEVENTY-TWO MILES PER HOUR.

"THAT'S THE SPEED OF A BULLET FIRED FROM AN M-60.

"IT'S BEEN SAID THAT I'M FASTER THAN A SPEEDING BULLET.

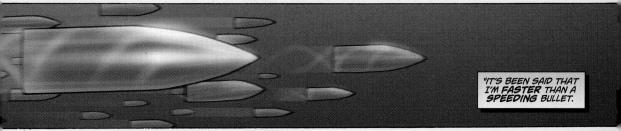

"AND I AM."

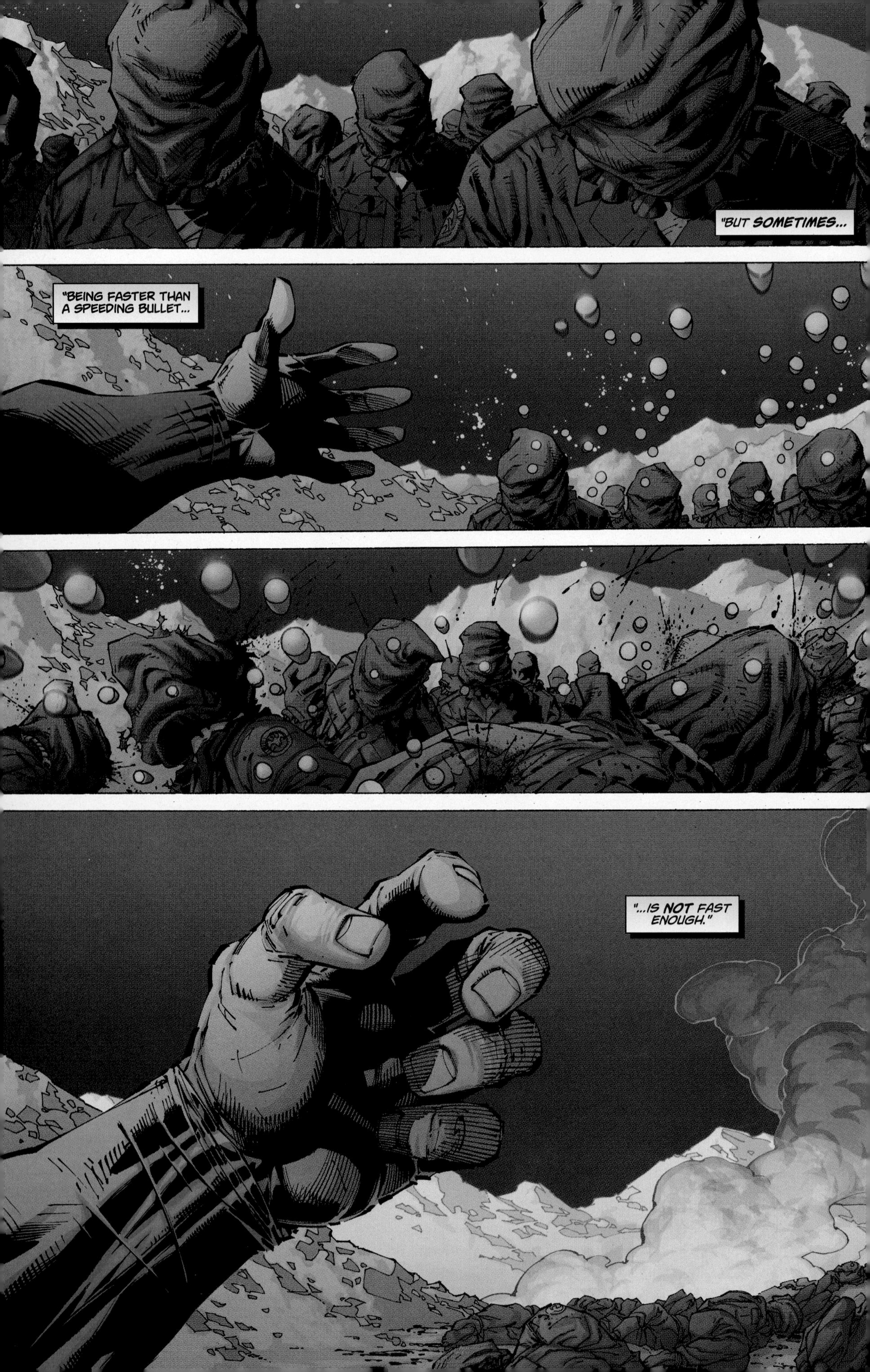
"BUT SOMETIMES...
"BEING FASTER THAN A SPEEDING BULLET...
"...IS NOT FAST ENOUGH."

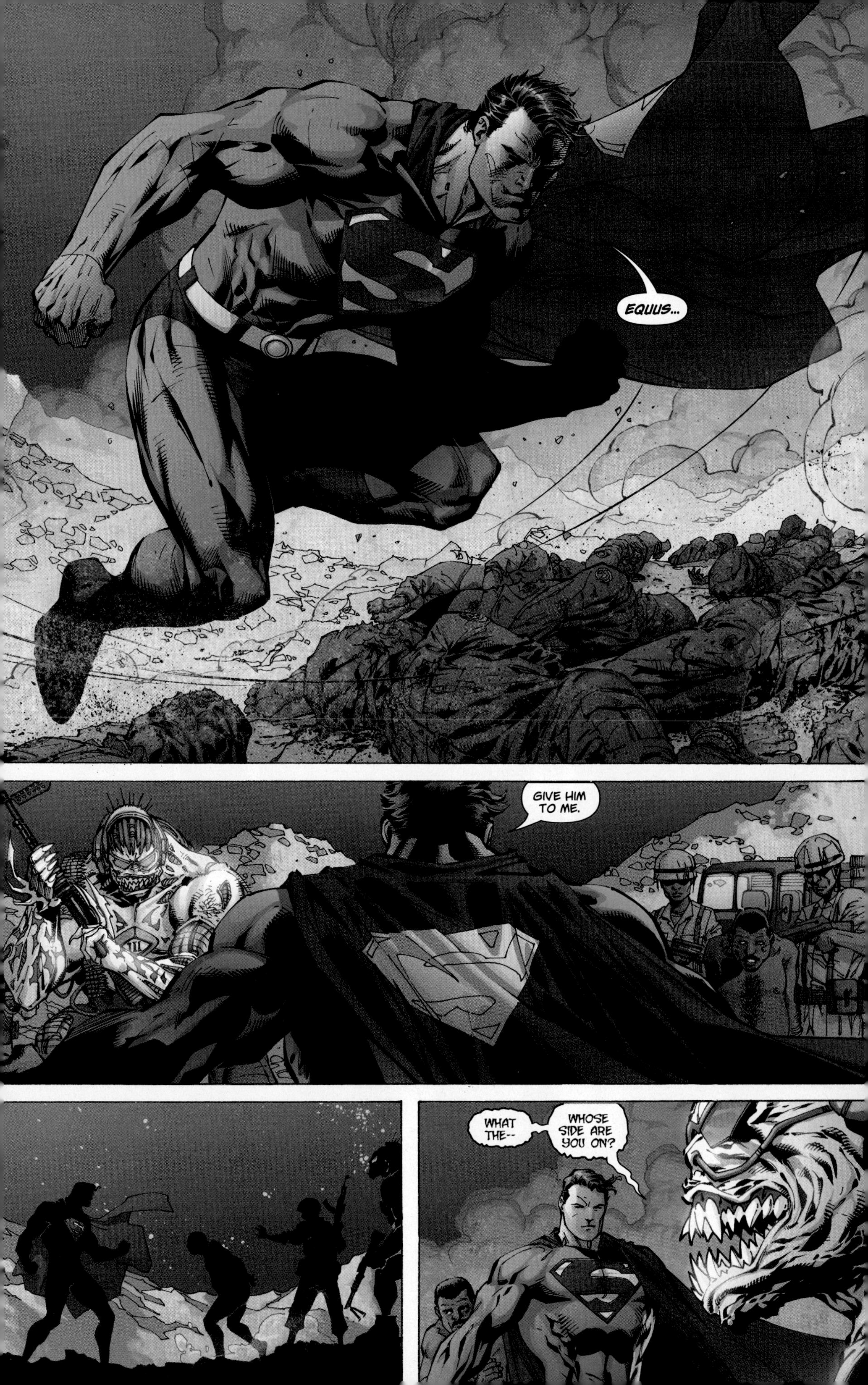
EQUUS...
GIVE HIM TO ME.
WHAT THE--
WHOSE SIDE ARE YOU ON?

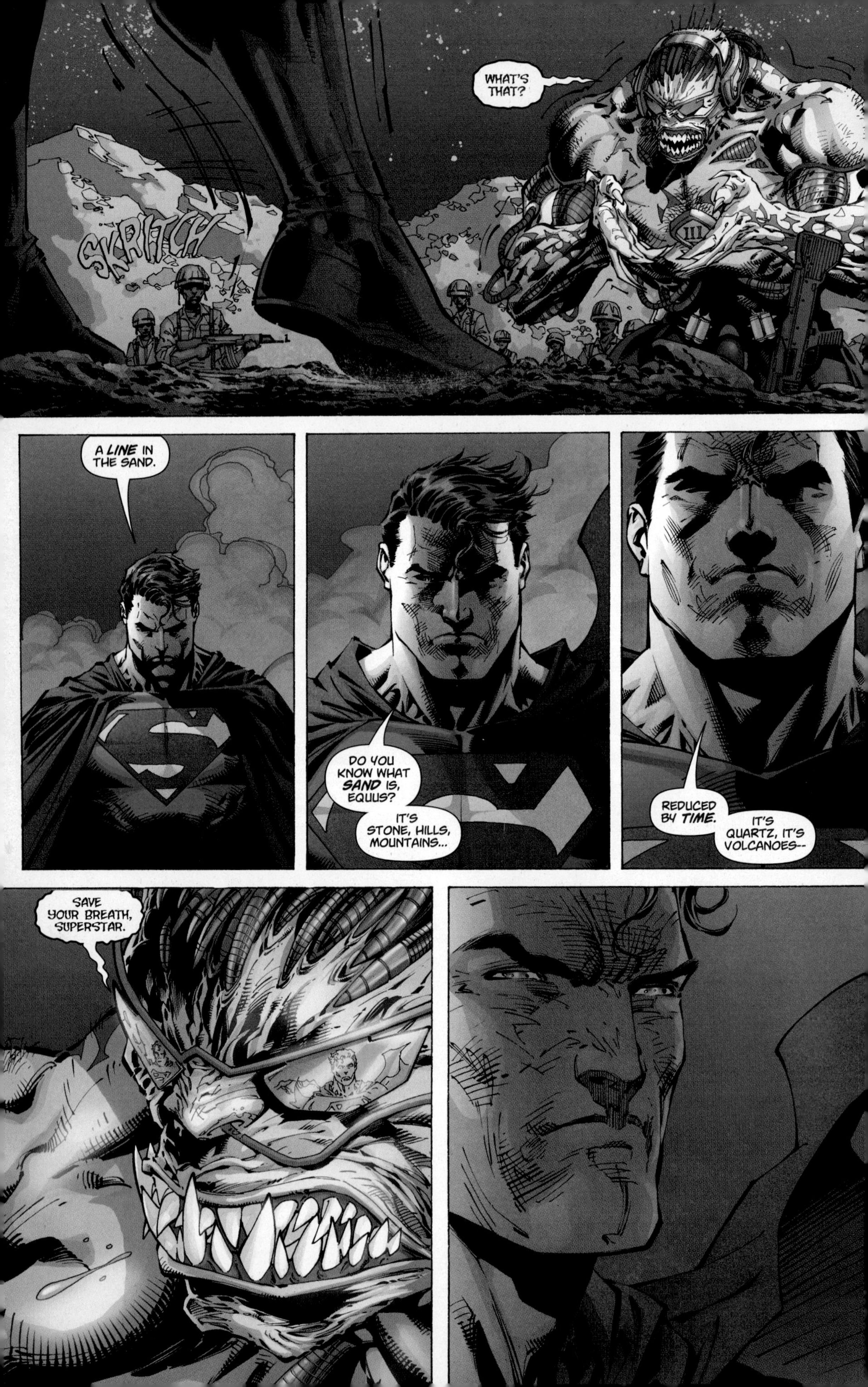
WHAT'S THAT?
SKRITCH
A LINE IN THE SAND.
DO YOU KNOW WHAT SAND IS, EQUUS?
IT'S STONE, HILLS, MOUNTAINS...
REDUCED BY TIME.
IT'S QUARTZ, IT'S VOLCANOES--
SAVE YOUR BREATH, SUPERSTAR.

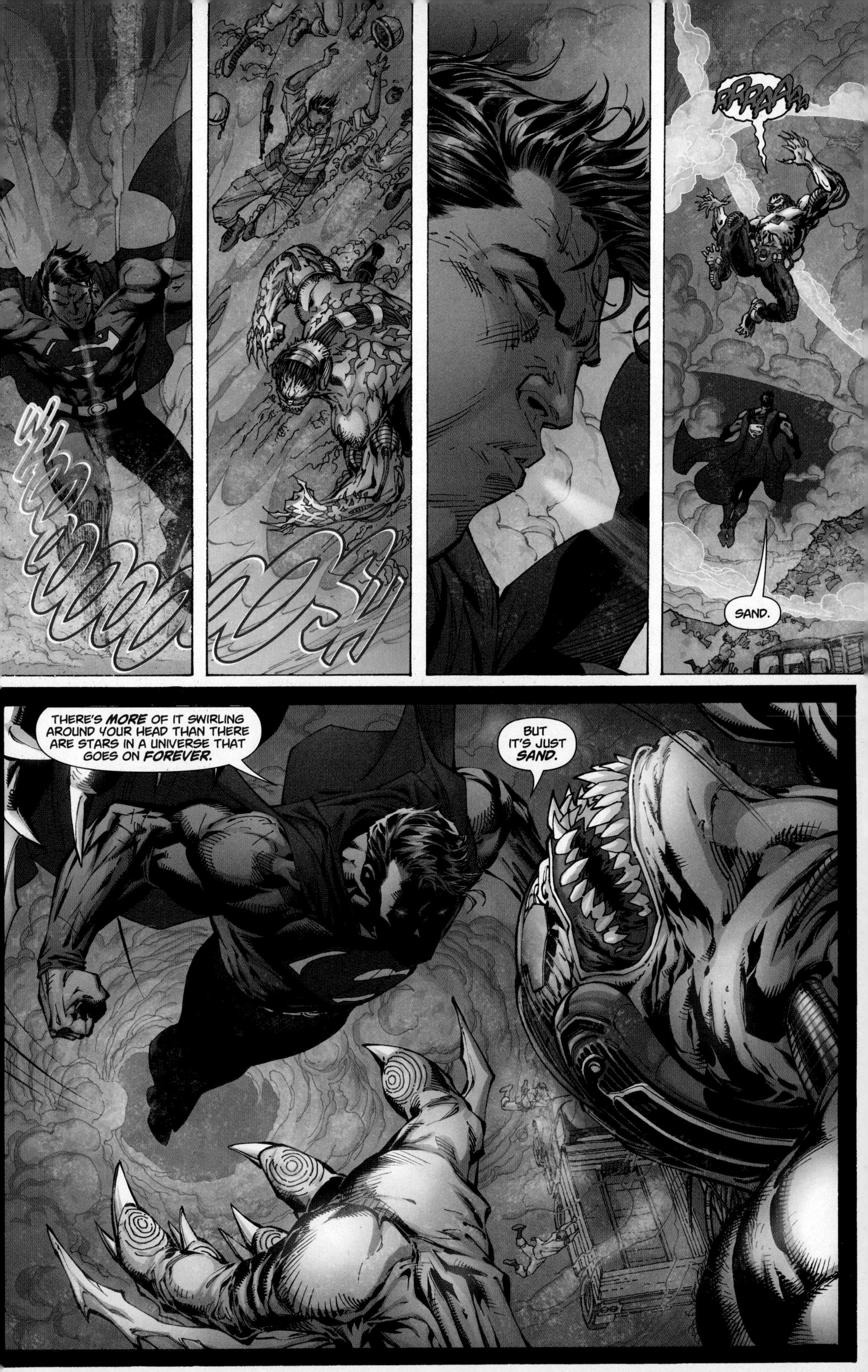
SHWOOOOOOOOSH
RRRAAA...
SAND.
THERE'S MORE OF IT SWIRLING AROUND YOUR HEAD THAN THERE ARE STARS IN A UNIVERSE THAT GOES ON FOREVER.
BUT IT'S JUST SAND.

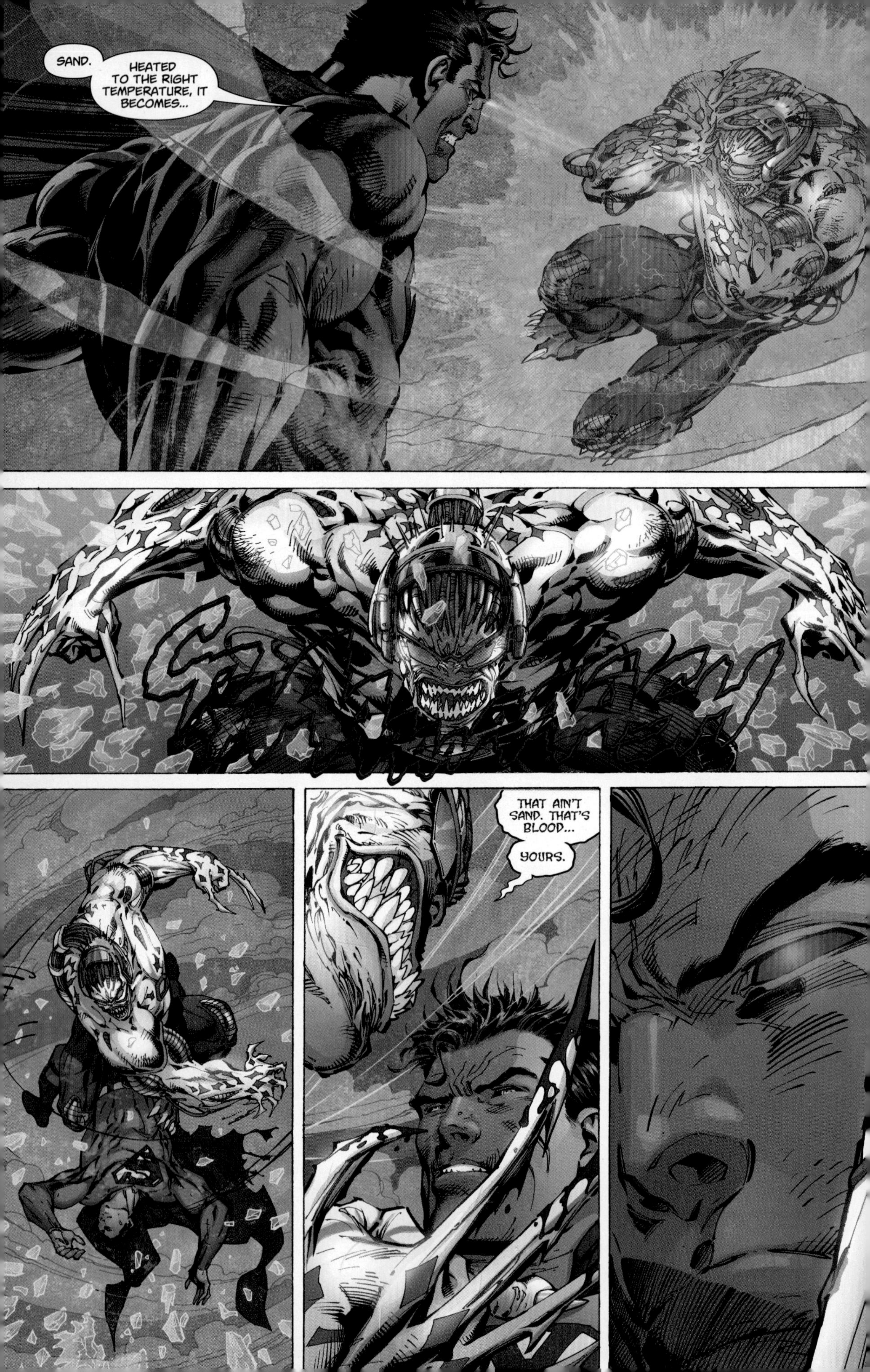
SAND.
HEATED TO THE RIGHT TEMPERATURE, IT BECOMES...
THAT AIN'T SAND. THAT'S BLOOD...
YOURS.

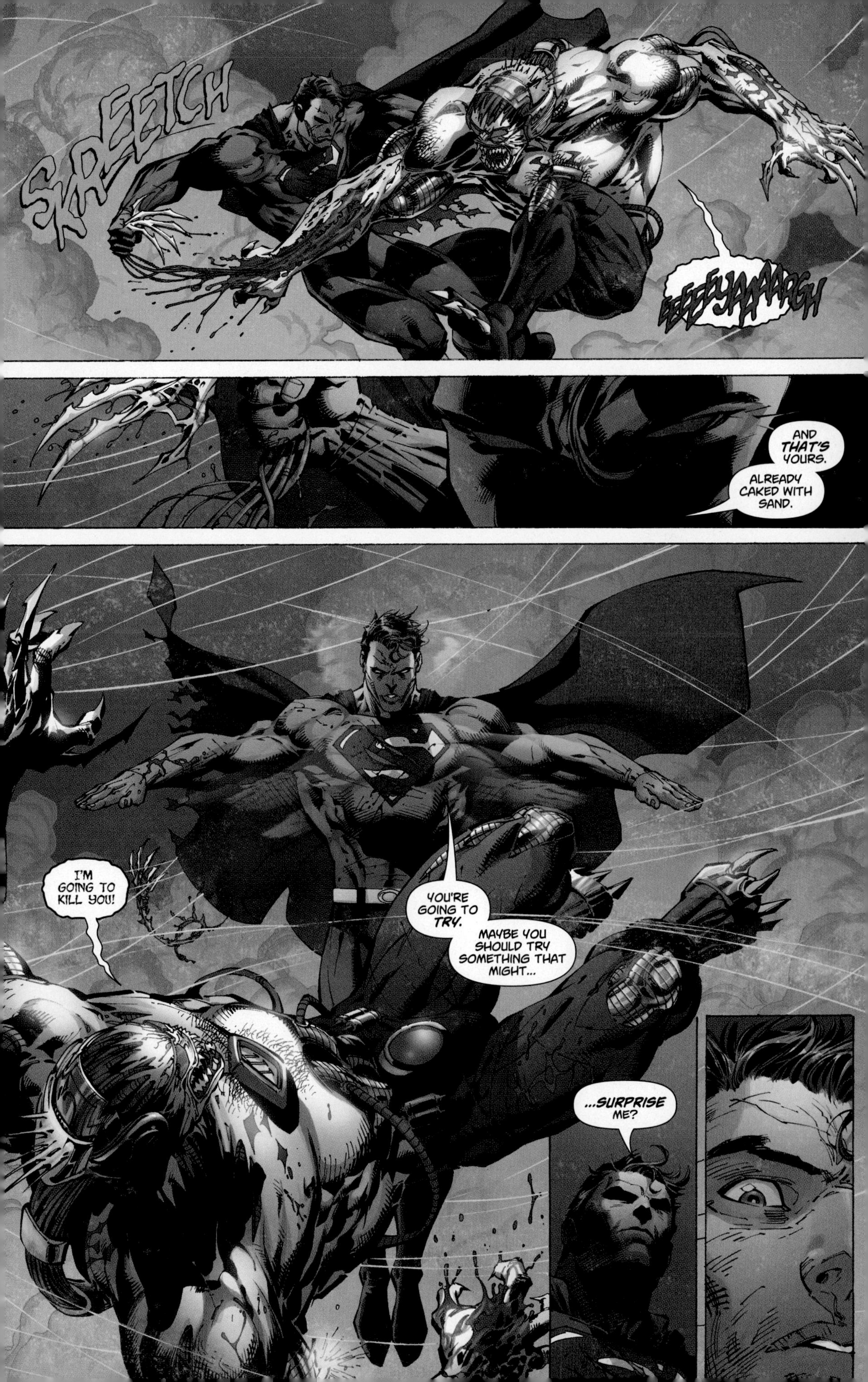
SKREEETCH
EEEEEYAAAAARGH
AND THAT'S YOURS.
ALREADY CAKED WITH SAND.
I'M GOING TO KILL YOU!
YOU'RE GOING TO TRY.
MAYBE YOU SHOULD TRY SOMETHING THAT MIGHT...
...SURPRISE ME?

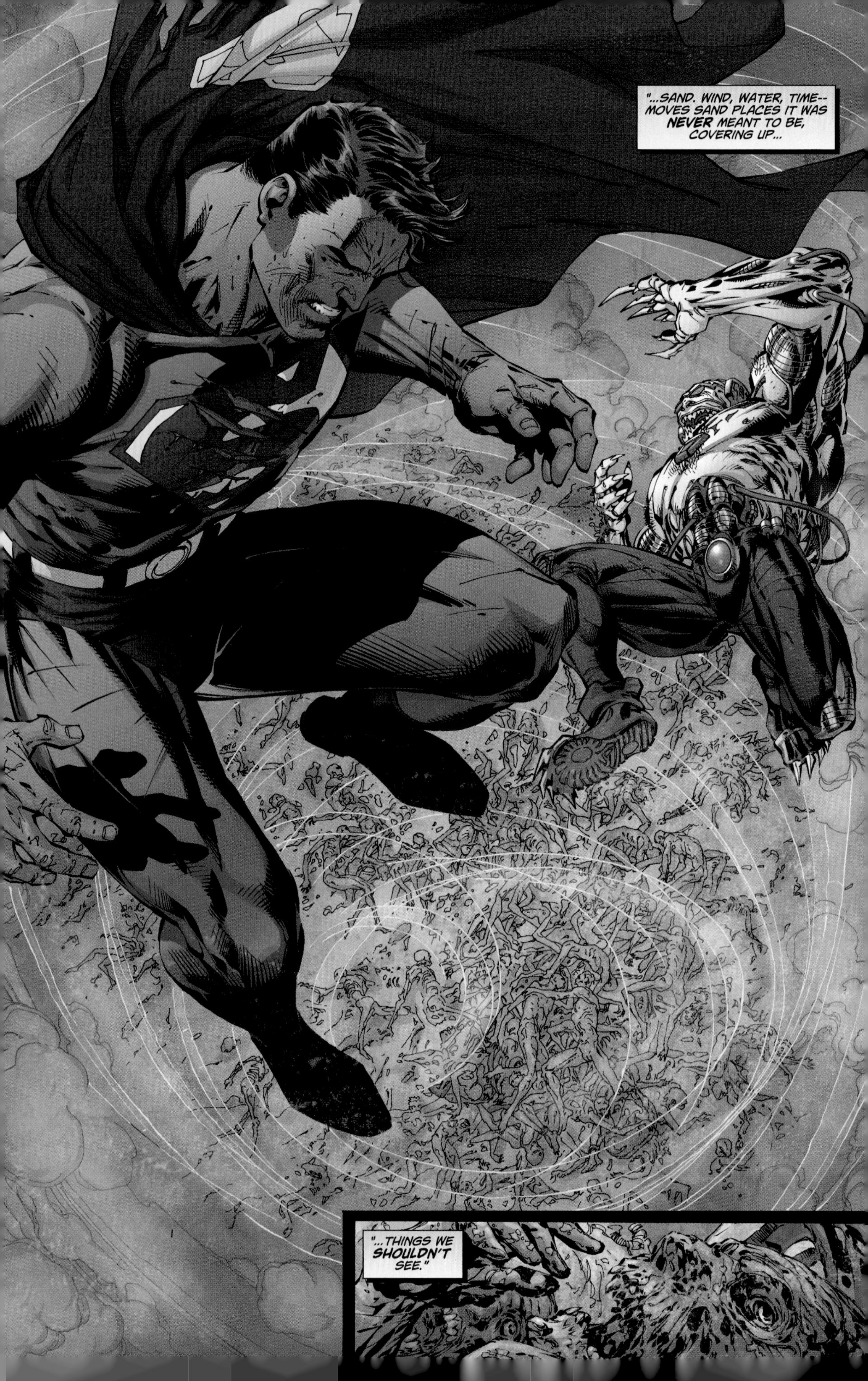
"...SAND. WIND, WATER, TIME--MOVES SAND PLACES IT WAS NEVER MEANT TO BE, COVERING UP...
"...THINGS WE SHOULDN'T SEE."

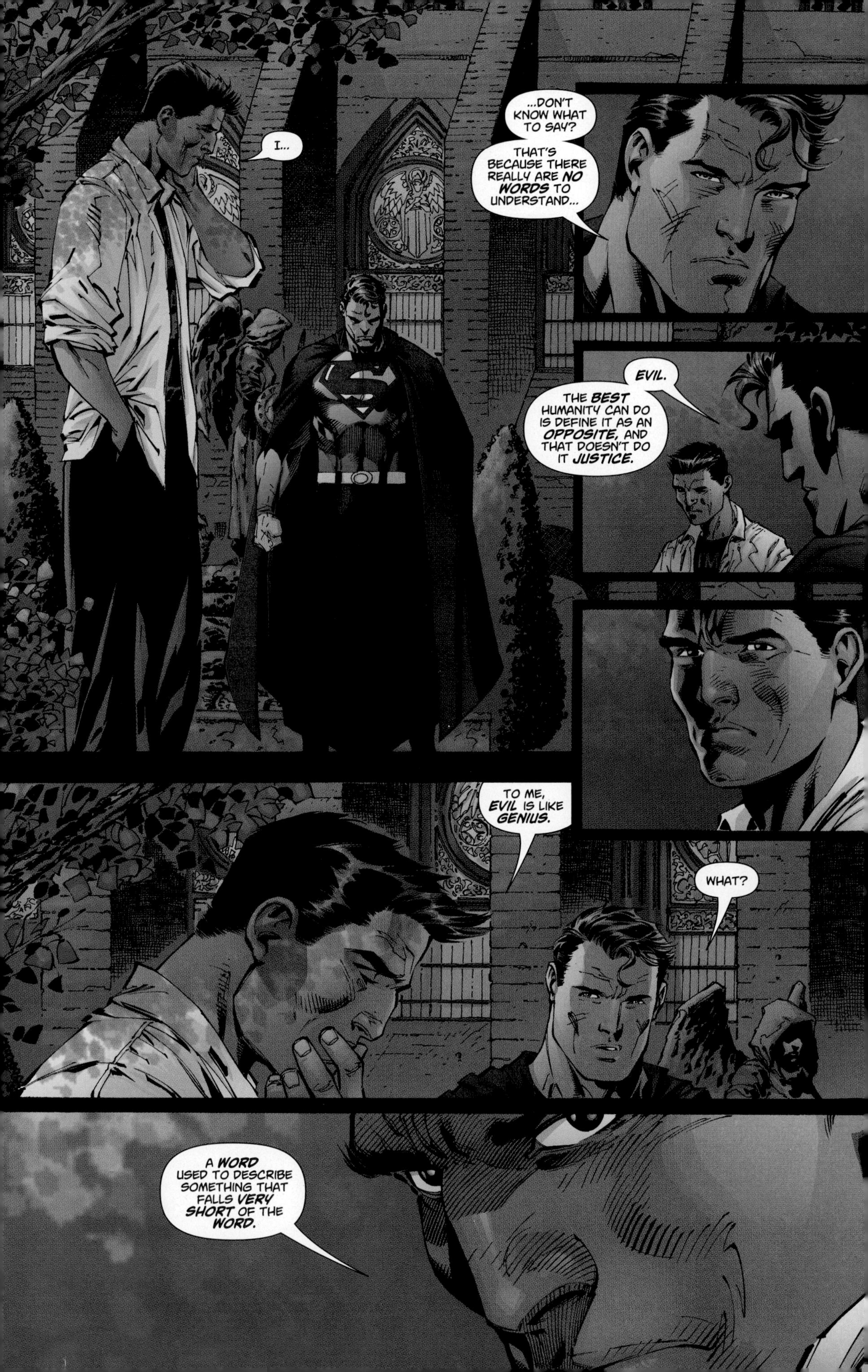
I...
...DON'T KNOW WHAT TO SAY?
THAT'S BECAUSE THERE REALLY ARE NO WORDS TO UNDERSTAND...
EVIL.
THE BEST HUMANITY CAN DO IS DEFINE IT AS AN OPPOSITE, AND THAT DOESN'T DO IT JUSTICE.
TO ME, EVIL IS LIKE GENIUS.
WHAT?
A WORD USED TO DESCRIBE SOMETHING THAT FALLS VERY SHORT OF THE WORD.

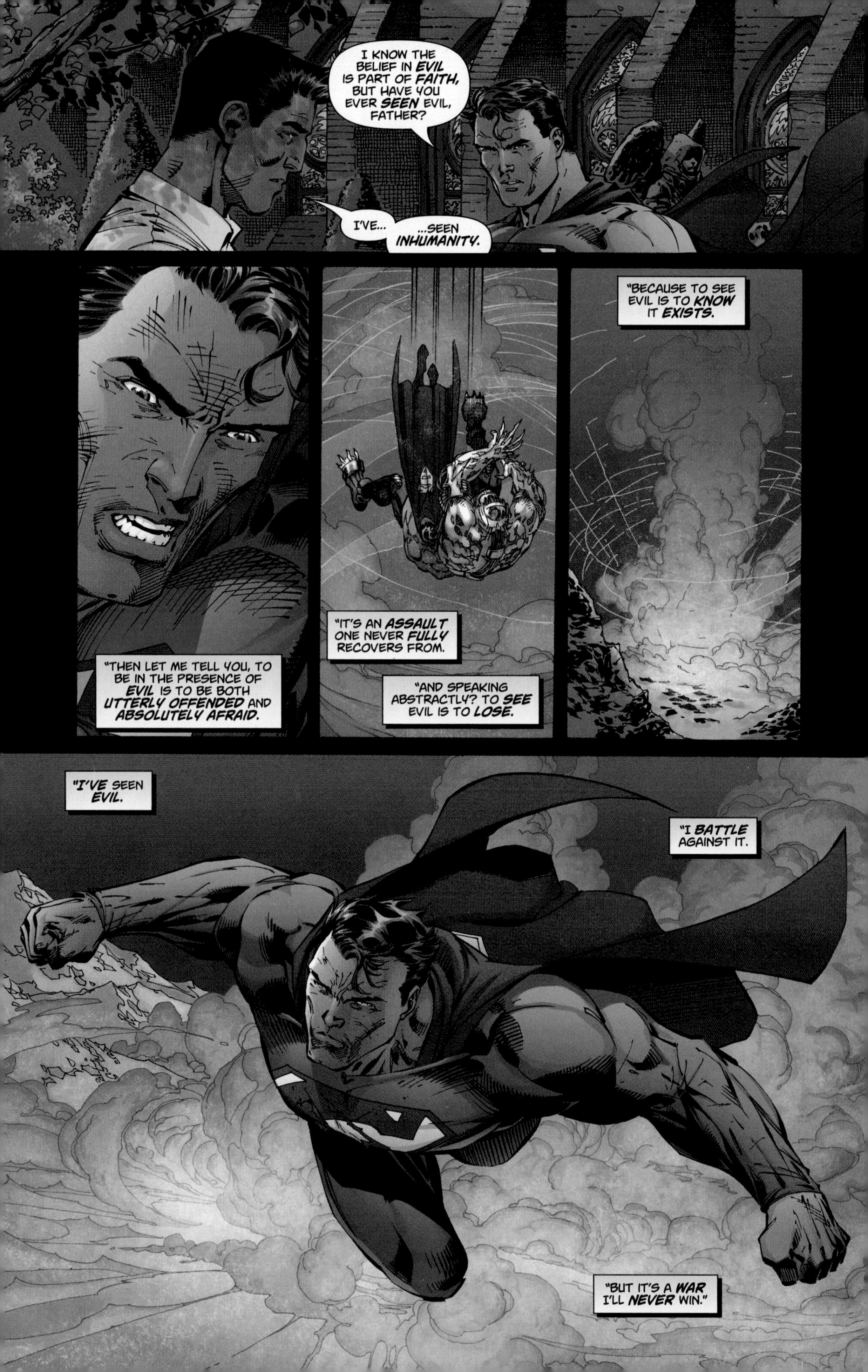
I KNOW THE BELIEF IN EVIL IS PART OF FAITH, BUT HAVE YOU EVER SEEN EVIL, FATHER?
I'VE...
...SEEN INHUMANITY.
"THEN LET ME TELL YOU, TO BE IN THE PRESENCE OF EVIL IS TO BE BOTH UTTERLY OFFENDED AND ABSOLUTELY AFRAID.
"IT'S AN ASSAULT ONE NEVER FULLY RECOVERS FROM.
"AND SPEAKING ABSTRACTLY? TO SEE EVIL IS TO LOSE.
"BECAUSE TO SEE EVIL IS TO KNOW IT EXISTS.
"I'VE SEEN EVIL.
"I BATTLE AGAINST IT.
"BUT IT'S A WAR I'LL NEVER WIN."

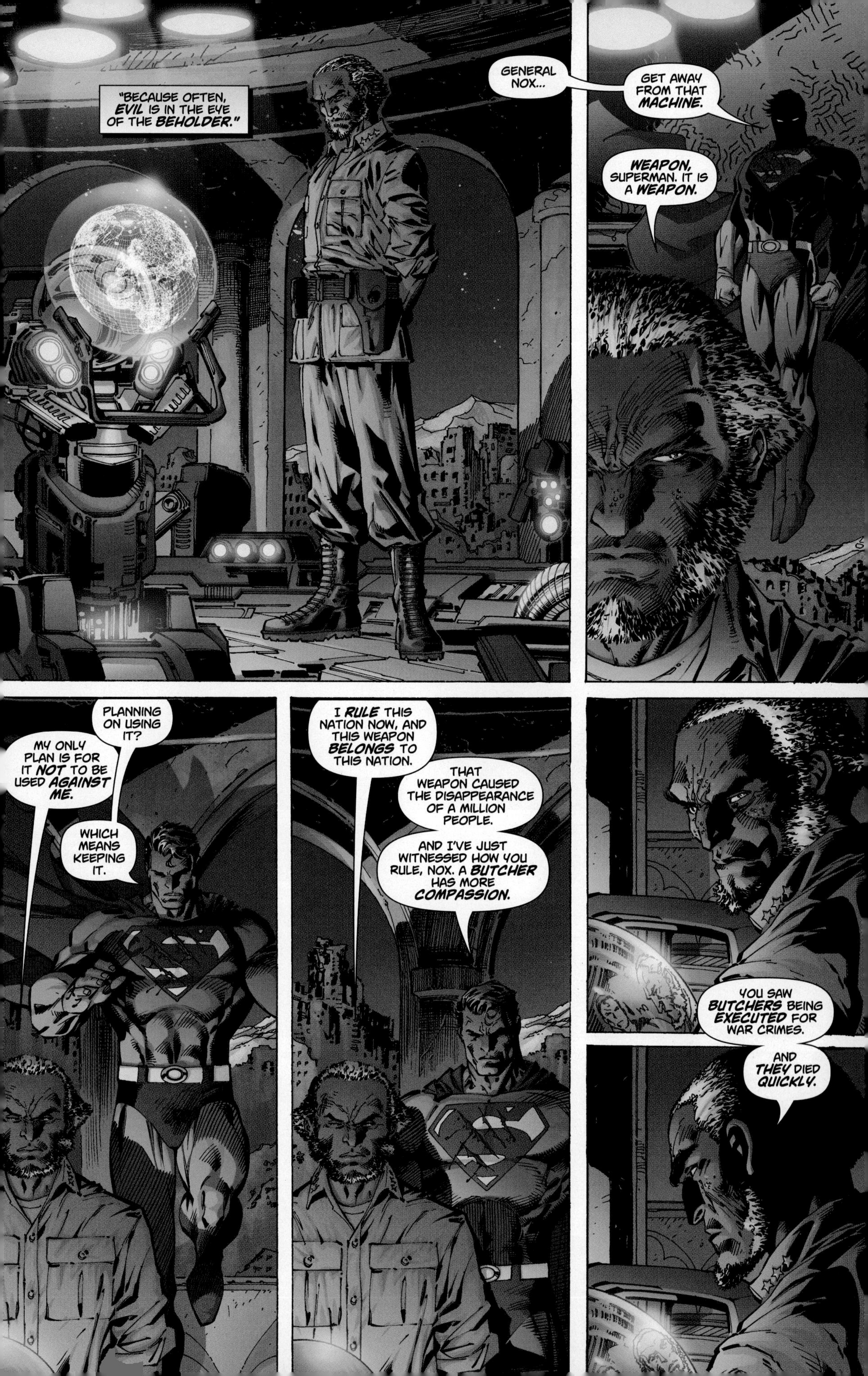
"BECAUSE OFTEN, EVIL IS IN THE EYE OF THE BEHOLDER."
GENERAL NOX...
GET AWAY FROM THAT MACHINE.
WEAPON, SUPERMAN. IT IS A WEAPON.
PLANNING ON USING IT?
MY ONLY PLAN IS FOR IT NOT TO BE USED AGAINST ME.
WHICH MEANS KEEPING IT.
I RULE THIS NATION NOW, AND THIS WEAPON BELONGS TO THIS NATION.
THAT WEAPON CAUSED THE DISAPPEARANCE OF A MILLION PEOPLE.
AND I'VE JUST WITNESSED HOW YOU RULE, NOX. A BUTCHER HAS MORE COMPASSION.
YOU SAW BUTCHERS BEING EXECUTED FOR WAR CRIMES.
AND THEY DIED QUICKLY.

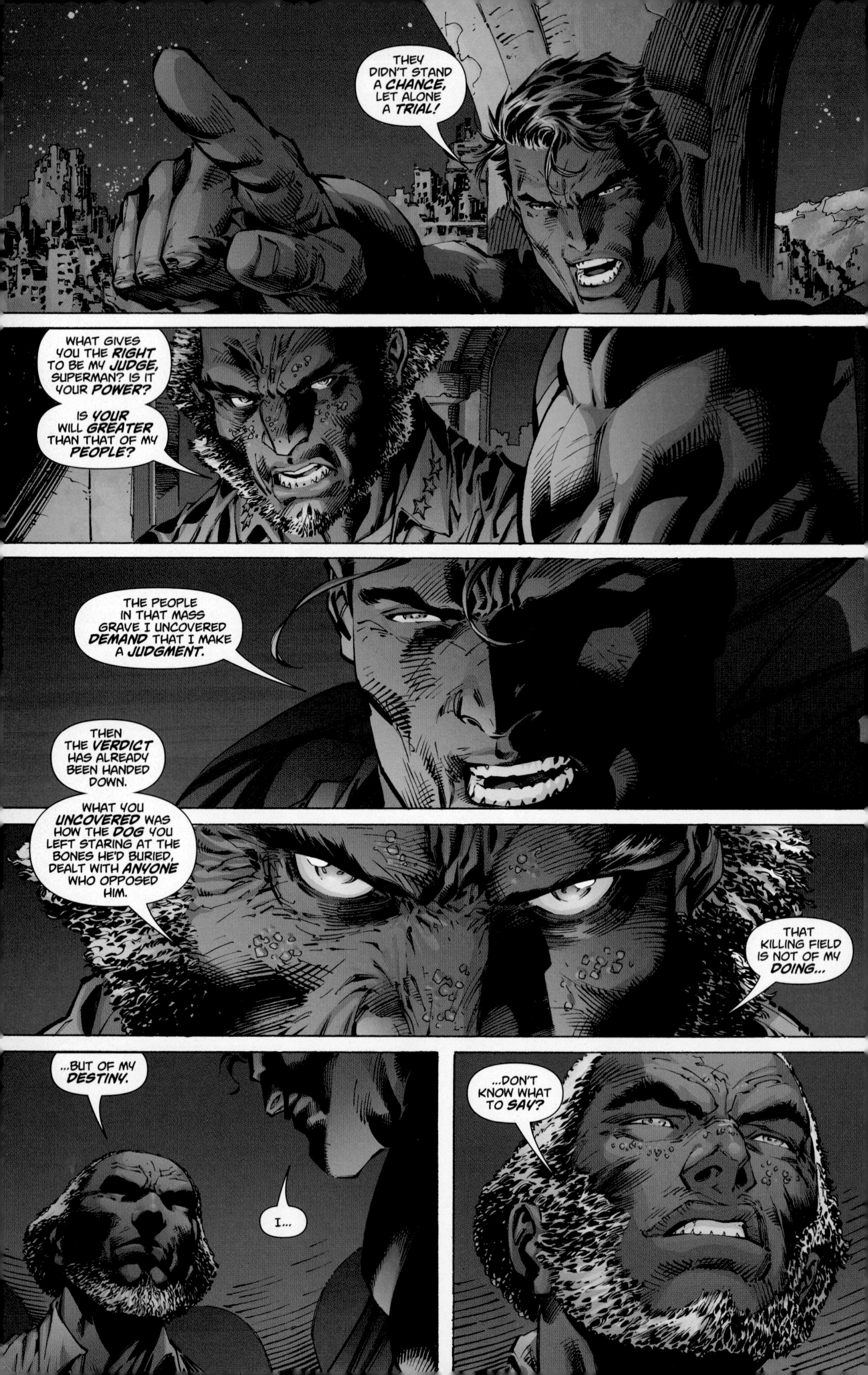
THEY DIDN'T STAND A CHANCE, LET ALONE A TRIAL!
WHAT GIVES YOU THE RIGHT TO BE MY JUDGE, SUPERMAN? IS IT YOUR POWER?
IS YOUR WILL GREATER THAN THAT OF MY PEOPLE?
THE PEOPLE IN THAT MASS GRAVE I UNCOVERED DEMAND THAT I MAKE A JUDGMENT.
THEN THE VERDICT HAS ALREADY BEEN HANDED DOWN.
WHAT YOU UNCOVERED WAS HOW THE DOG YOU LEFT STARING AT THE BONES HE'D BURIED, DEALT WITH ANYONE WHO OPPOSED HIM.
THAT KILLING FIELD IS NOT OF MY DOING...
...BUT OF MY DESTINY.
I...
...DON'T KNOW WHAT TO SAY?

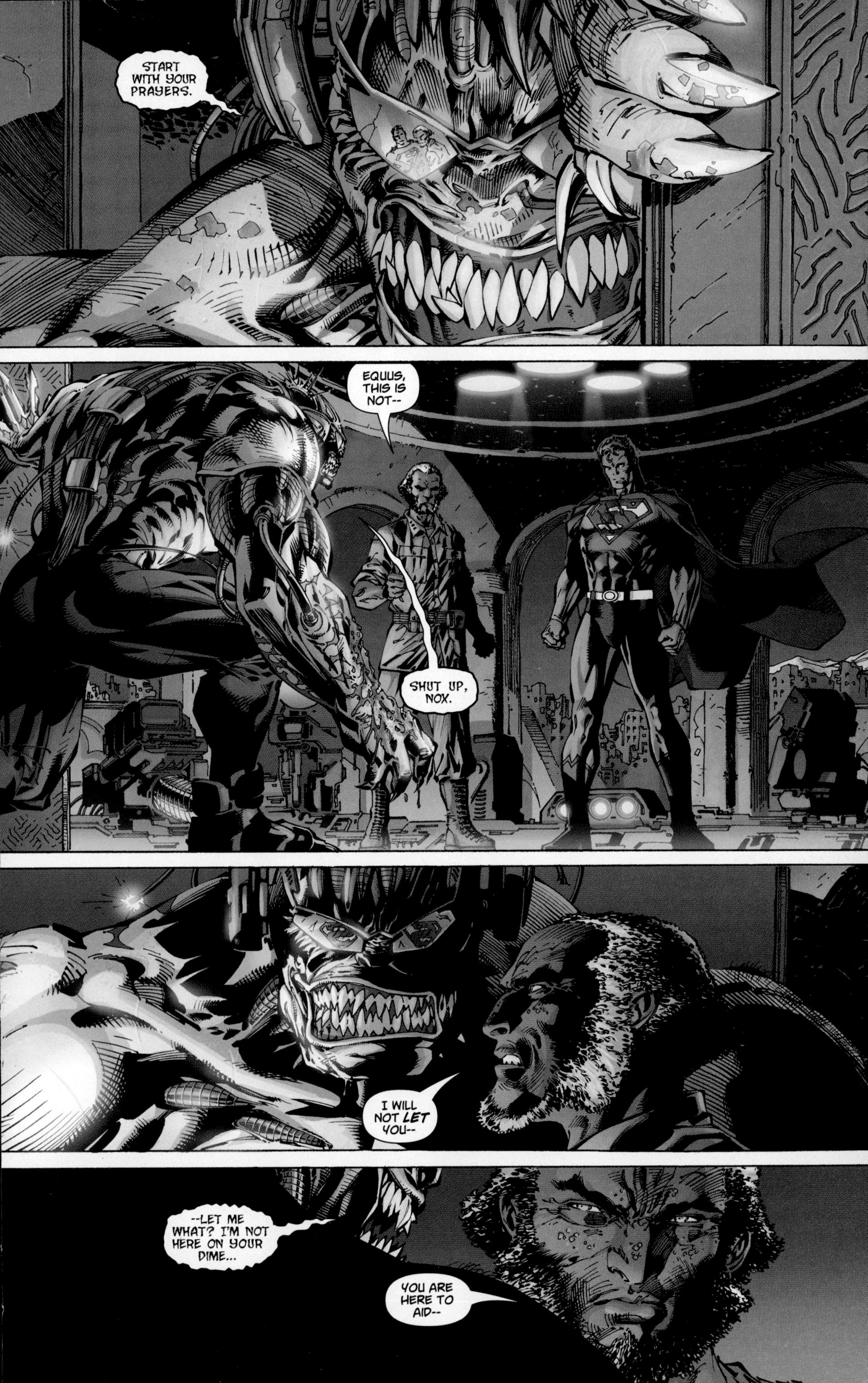
START WITH YOUR PRAYERS.
EQUUS, THIS IS NOT--
SHUT UP, NOX.
I WILL NOT LET YOU--
--LET ME WHAT? I'M NOT HERE ON YOUR DIME...
YOU ARE HERE TO AID--

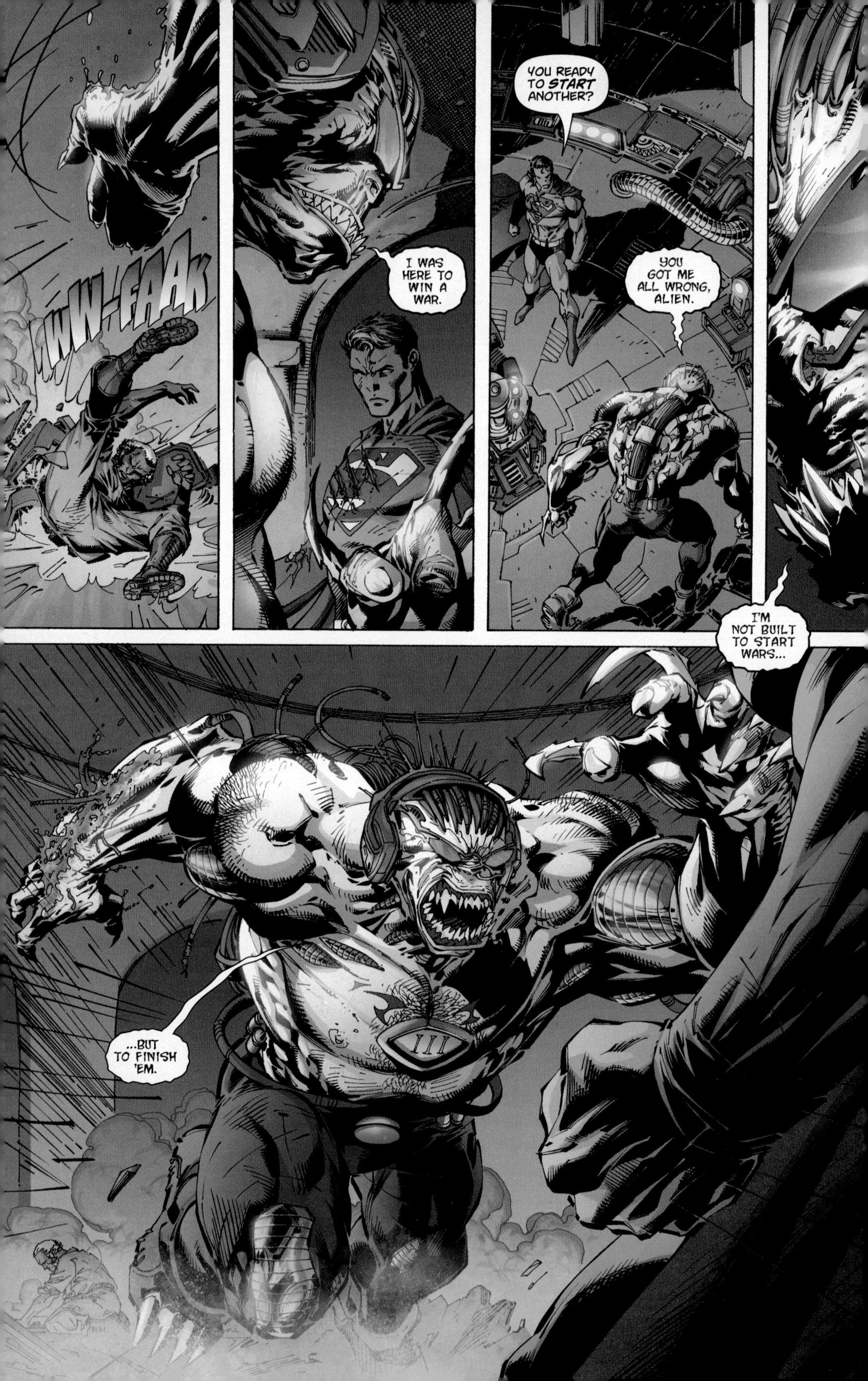
WW-FAAK
I WAS HERE TO WIN A WAR.
YOU READY TO START ANOTHER?
YOU GOT ME ALL WRONG, ALIEN.
I'M NOT BUILT TO START WARS...
...BUT TO FINISH 'EM.

"ALIEN. EQUUS HAD CALLED ME ALIEN. UP TO THAT POINT, I HADN'T EVEN THOUGHT ABOUT WHAT *HE* WAS...

"...BEYOND HIS SURFACE.

"SO OPENING MY EYES...

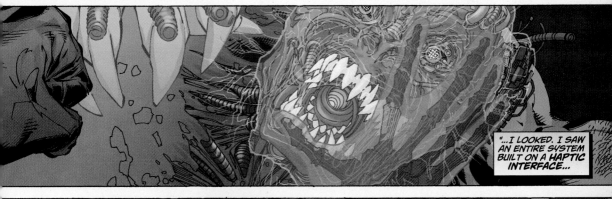

"...I LOOKED. I SAW AN ENTIRE SYSTEM BUILT ON A *HAPTIC* INTERFACE...

"CROCODILIAN SKIN CELLS LACED WITH SELF-HEALING *HINGE* MOLECULES."

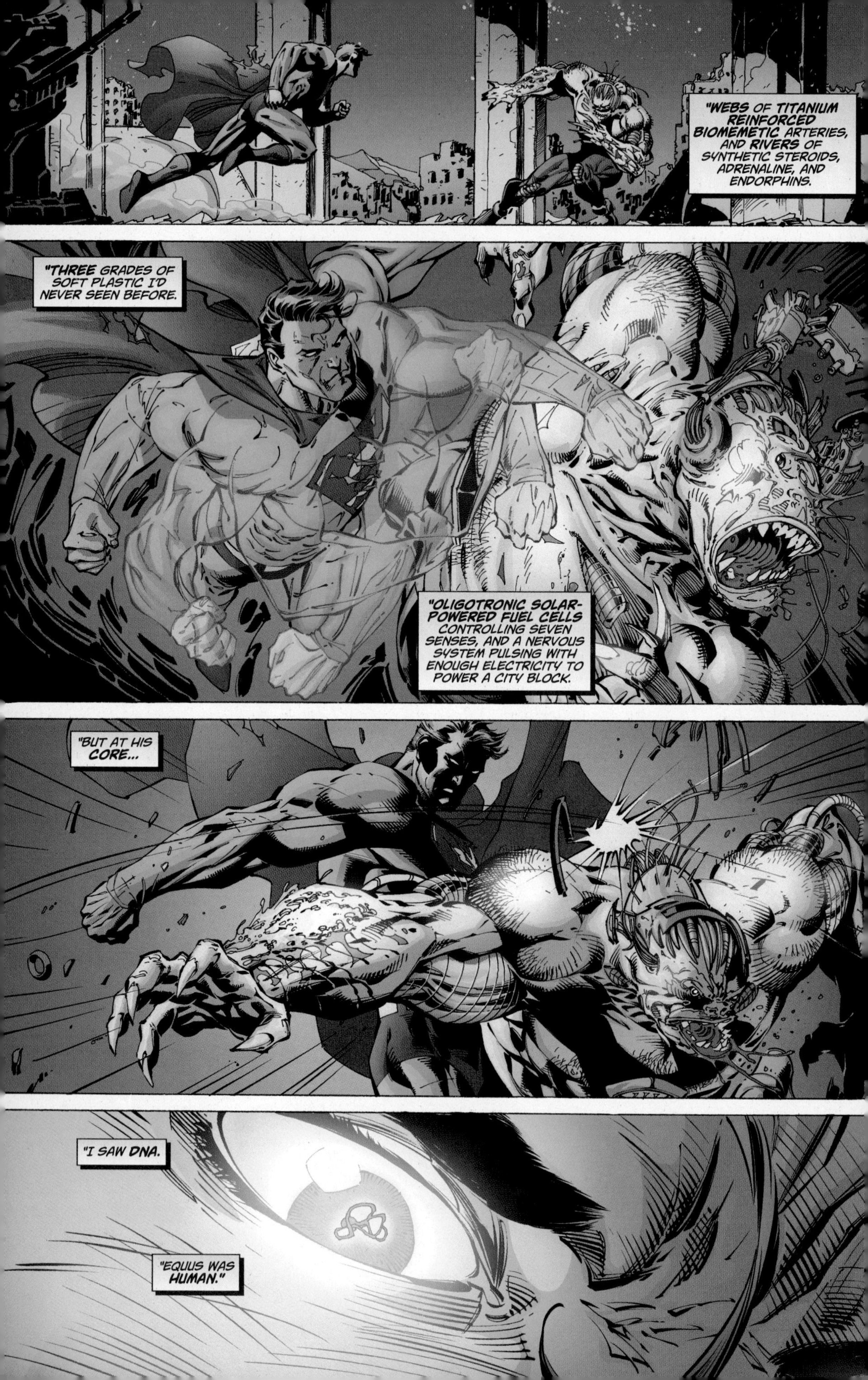
"WEBS OF TITANIUM REINFORCED BIOMEMETIC ARTERIES, AND RIVERS OF SYNTHETIC STEROIDS, ADRENALINE, AND ENDORPHINS.
"THREE GRADES OF SOFT PLASTIC I'D NEVER SEEN BEFORE.
"OLIGOTRONIC SOLAR-POWERED FUEL CELLS CONTROLLING SEVEN SENSES, AND A NERVOUS SYSTEM PULSING WITH ENOUGH ELECTRICITY TO POWER A CITY BLOCK.
"BUT AT HIS CORE...
"I SAW DNA.
"EQUUS WAS HUMAN."

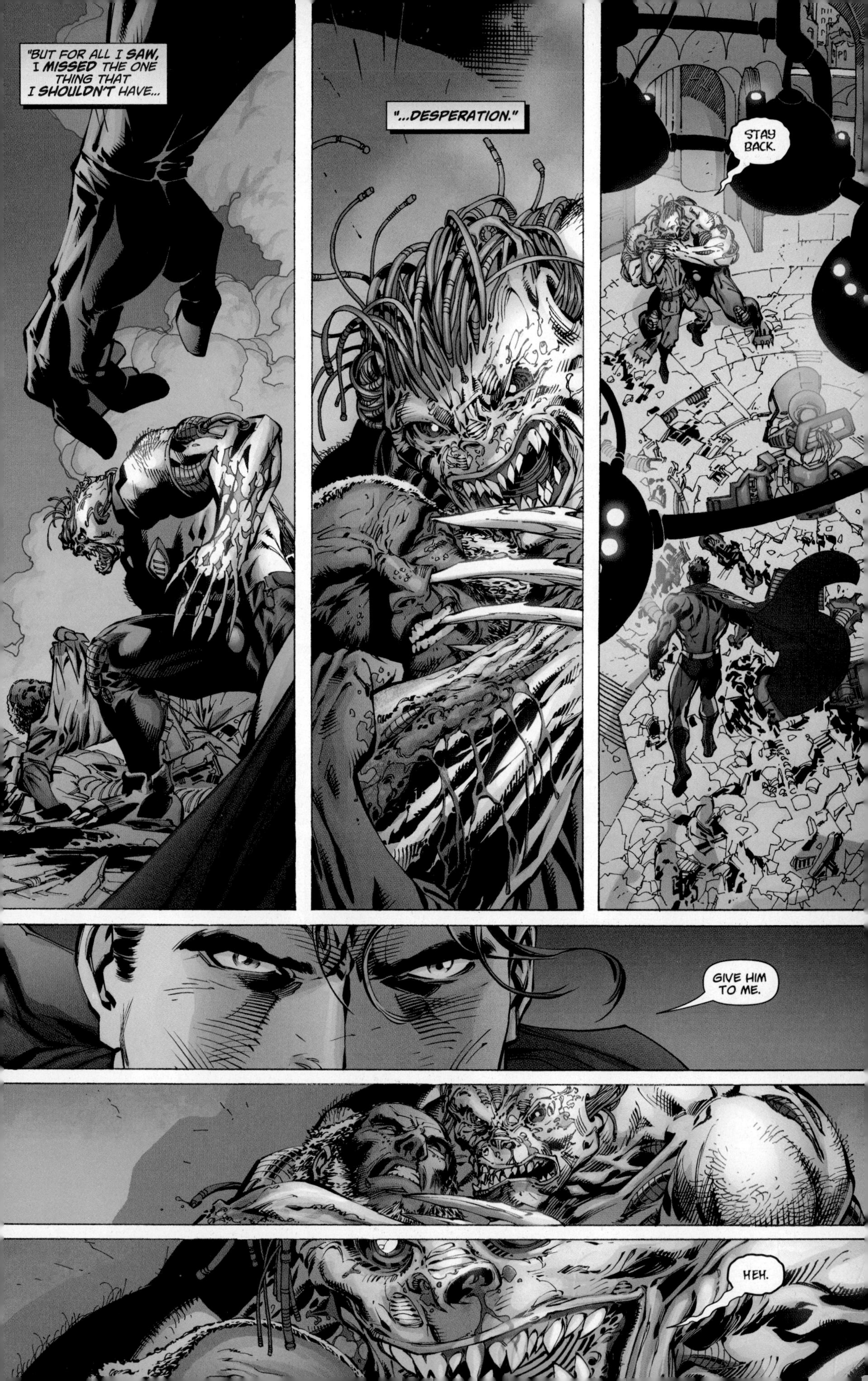
"BUT FOR ALL I SAW, I MISSED THE ONE THING THAT I SHOULDN'T HAVE...
"...DESPERATION."
STAY BACK.
GIVE HIM TO ME.
HEH.

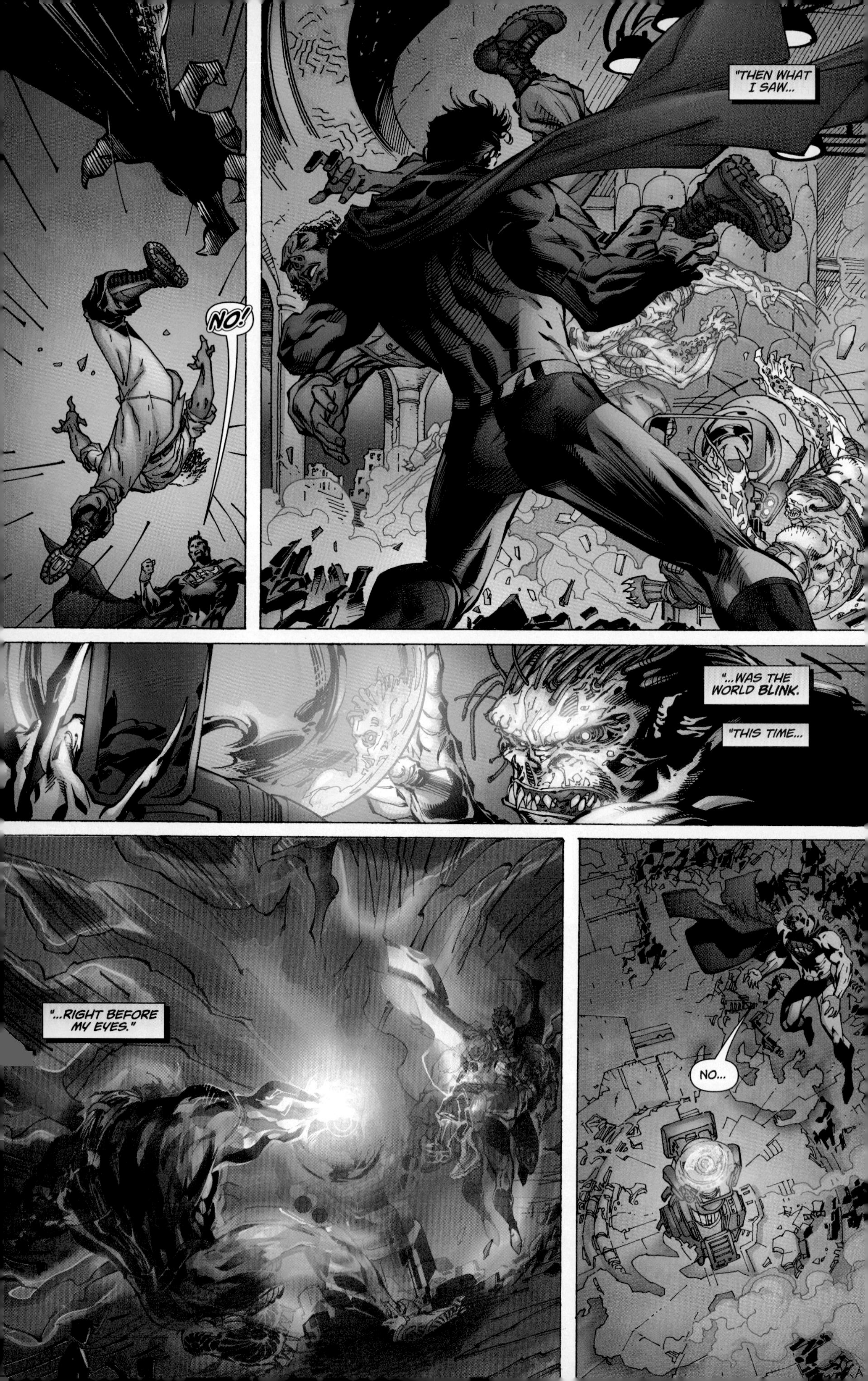
"THEN WHAT I SAW...
NO!
"...WAS THE WORLD BLINK.
"THIS TIME...
"...RIGHT BEFORE MY EYES."
NO...

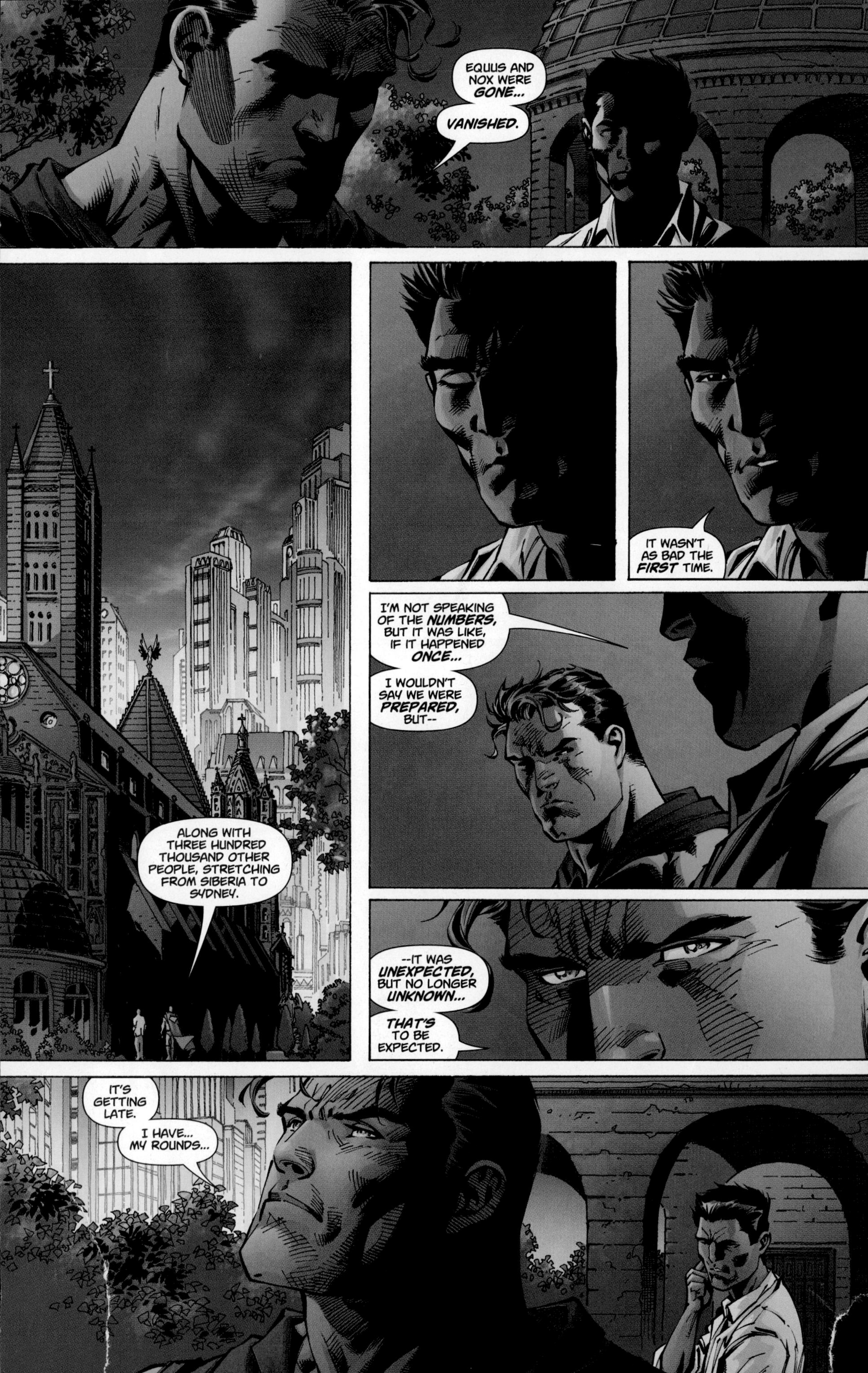
EQUUS AND NOX WERE GONE...
VANISHED.
ALONG WITH THREE HUNDRED THOUSAND OTHER PEOPLE, STRETCHING FROM SIBERIA TO SYDNEY.
IT WASN'T AS BAD THE FIRST TIME.
I'M NOT SPEAKING OF THE NUMBERS, BUT IT WAS LIKE, IF IT HAPPENED ONCE...
I WOULDN'T SAY WE WERE PREPARED, BUT--
--IT WAS UNEXPECTED, BUT NO LONGER UNKNOWN...
THAT'S TO BE EXPECTED.
IT'S GETTING LATE.
I HAVE... MY ROUNDS...

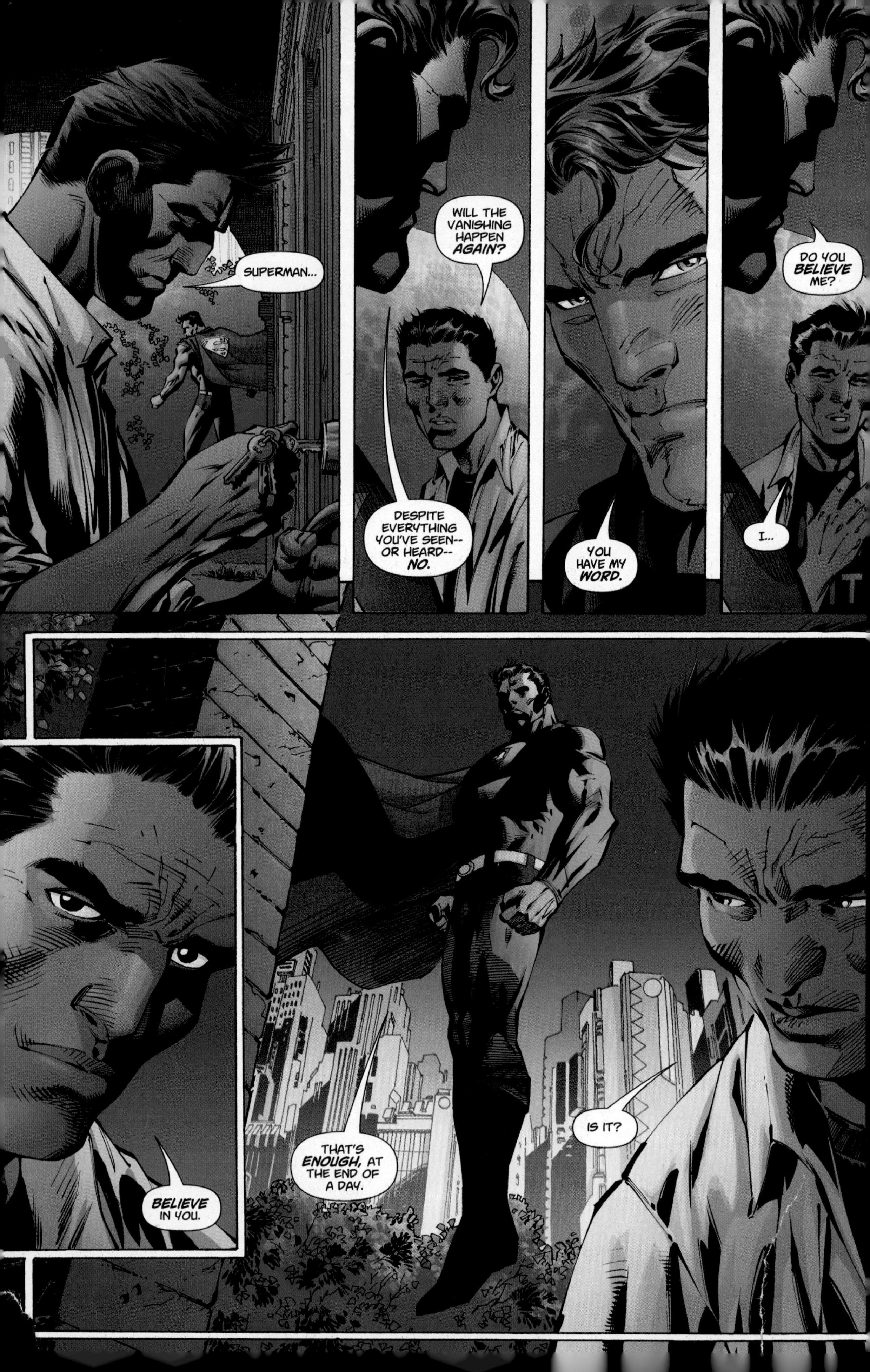
SUPERMAN...
WILL THE VANISHING HAPPEN AGAIN?
DESPITE EVERYTHING YOU'VE SEEN-- OR HEARD-- NO.
YOU HAVE MY WORD.
DO YOU BELIEVE ME?
I...
BELIEVE IN YOU.
THAT'S ENOUGH, AT THE END OF A DAY.
IS IT?

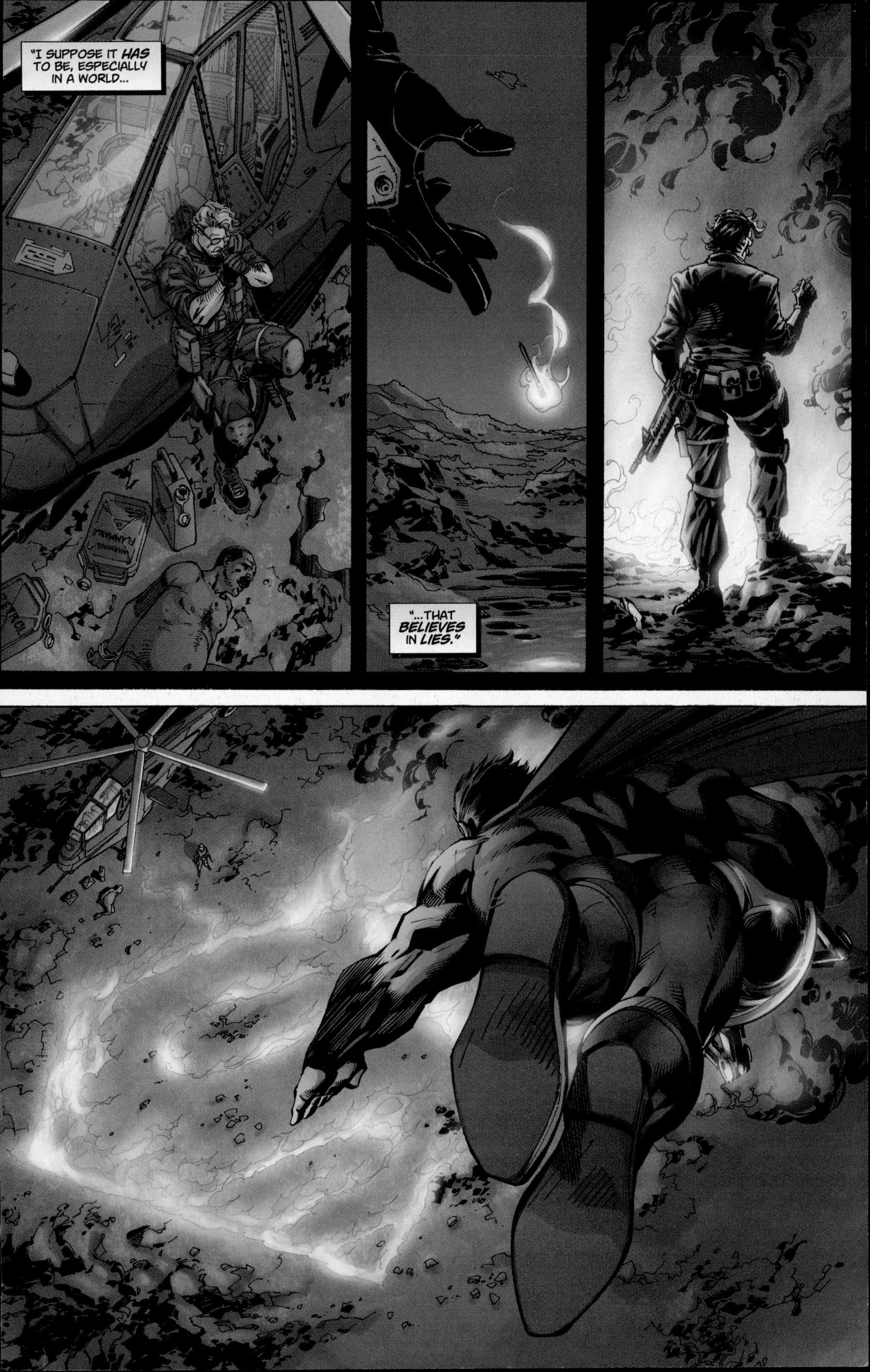
"I SUPPOSE IT HAS TO BE, ESPECIALLY IN A WORLD...
"...THAT BELIEVES IN LIES."

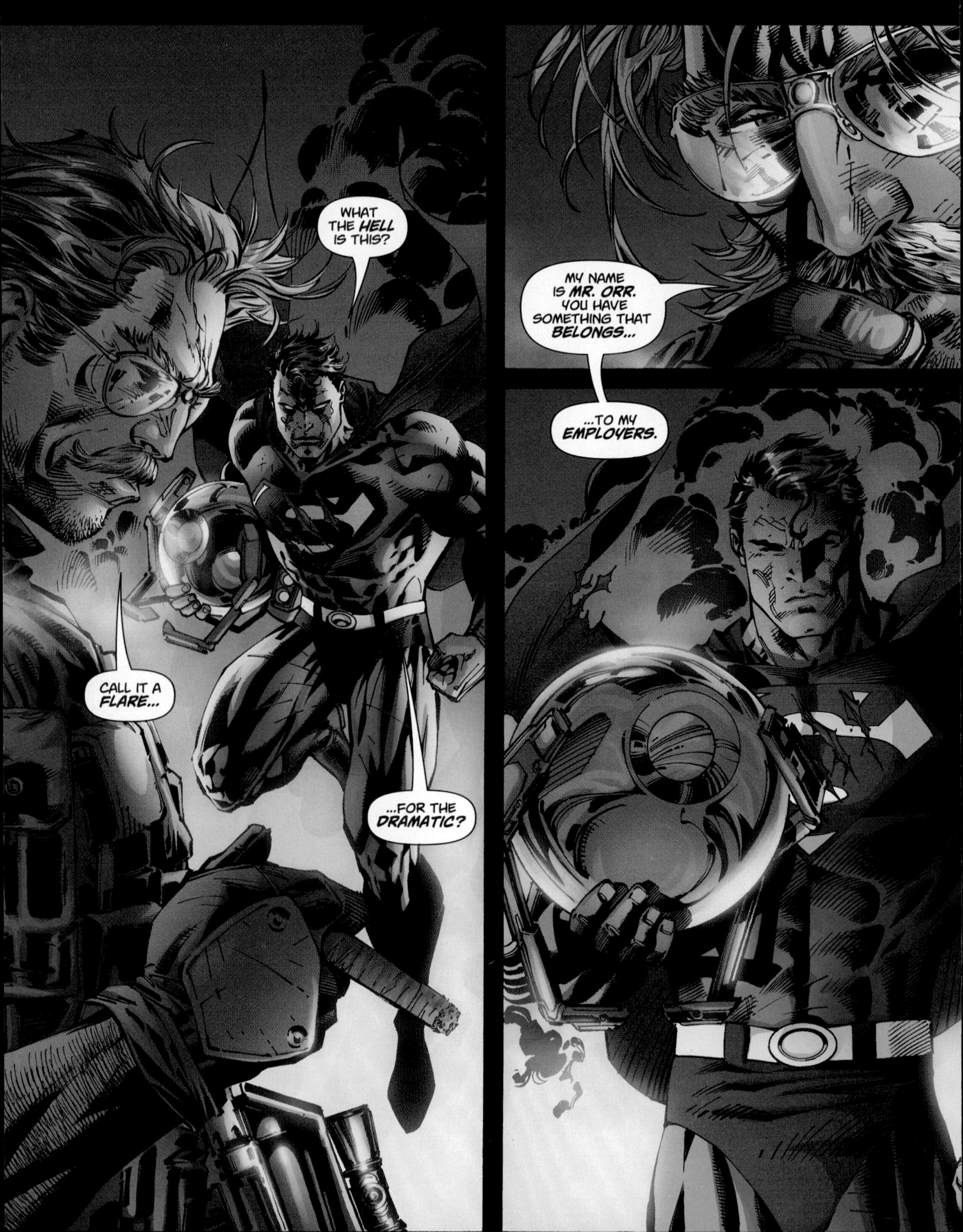
WHAT THE HELL IS THIS?
CALL IT A FLARE...
...FOR THE DRAMATIC?
MY NAME IS MR. ORR. YOU HAVE SOMETHING THAT BELONGS...
...TO MY EMPLOYERS.

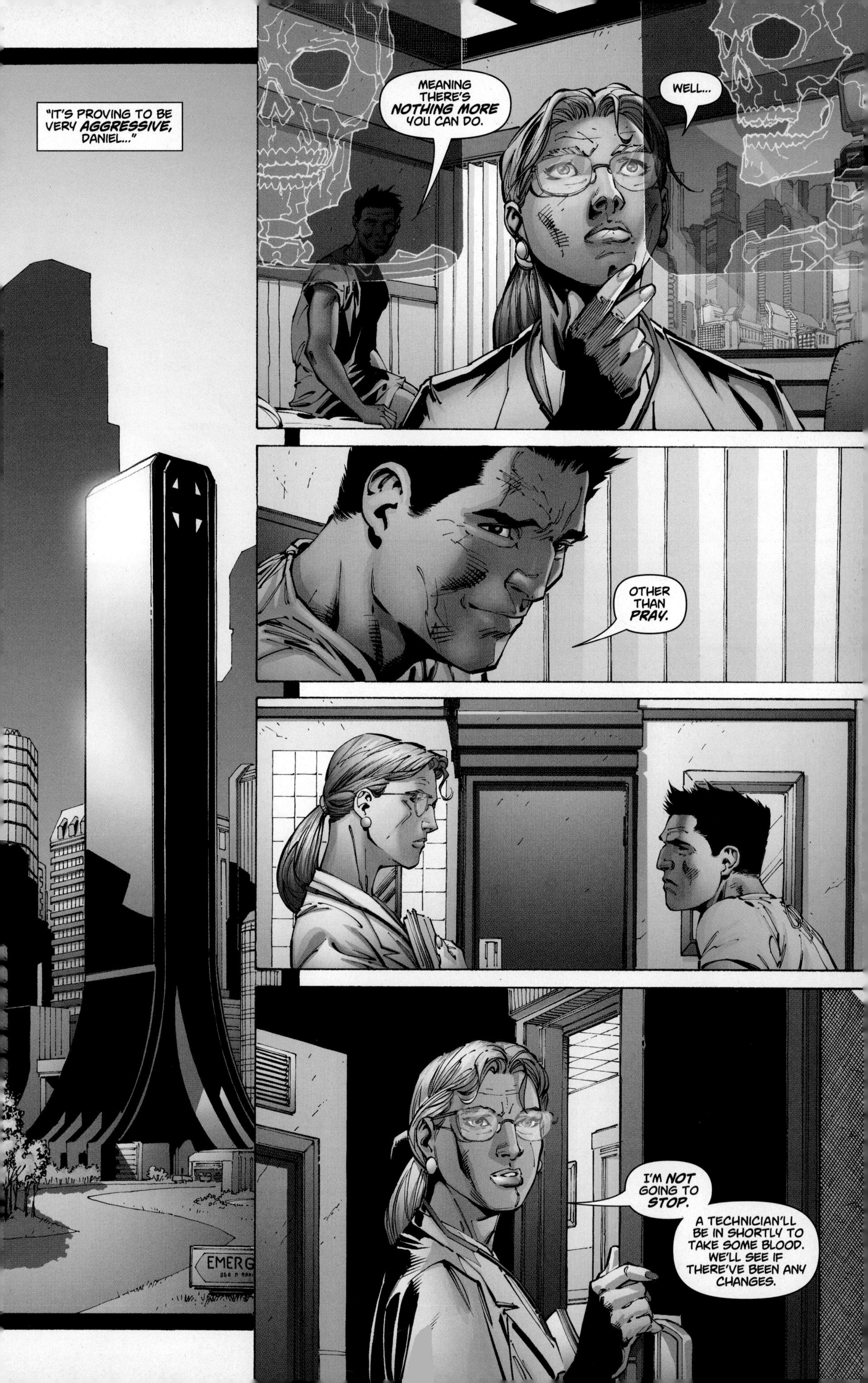
"IT'S PROVING TO BE VERY AGGRESSIVE, DANIEL..."
MEANING THERE'S NOTHING MORE YOU CAN DO.
WELL...
OTHER THAN PRAY.
I'M NOT GOING TO STOP.
A TECHNICIAN'LL BE IN SHORTLY TO TAKE SOME BLOOD. WE'LL SEE IF THERE'VE BEEN ANY CHANGES.
EMERG

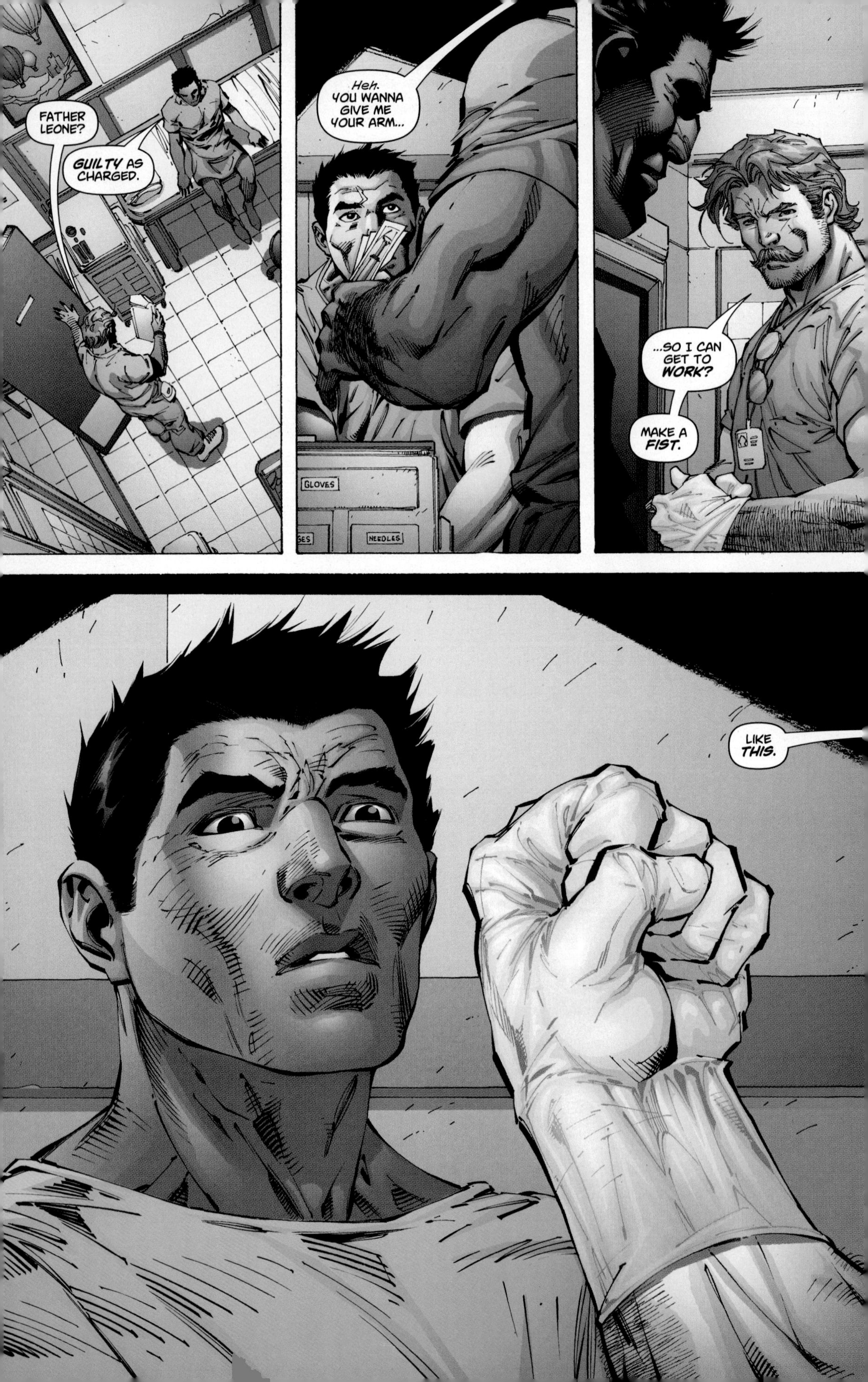
FATHER LEONE?
GUILTY AS CHARGED.
Heh. YOU WANNA GIVE ME YOUR ARM...
...SO I CAN GET TO WORK?
MAKE A FIST.
GLOVES
NEEDLES
LIKE THIS.

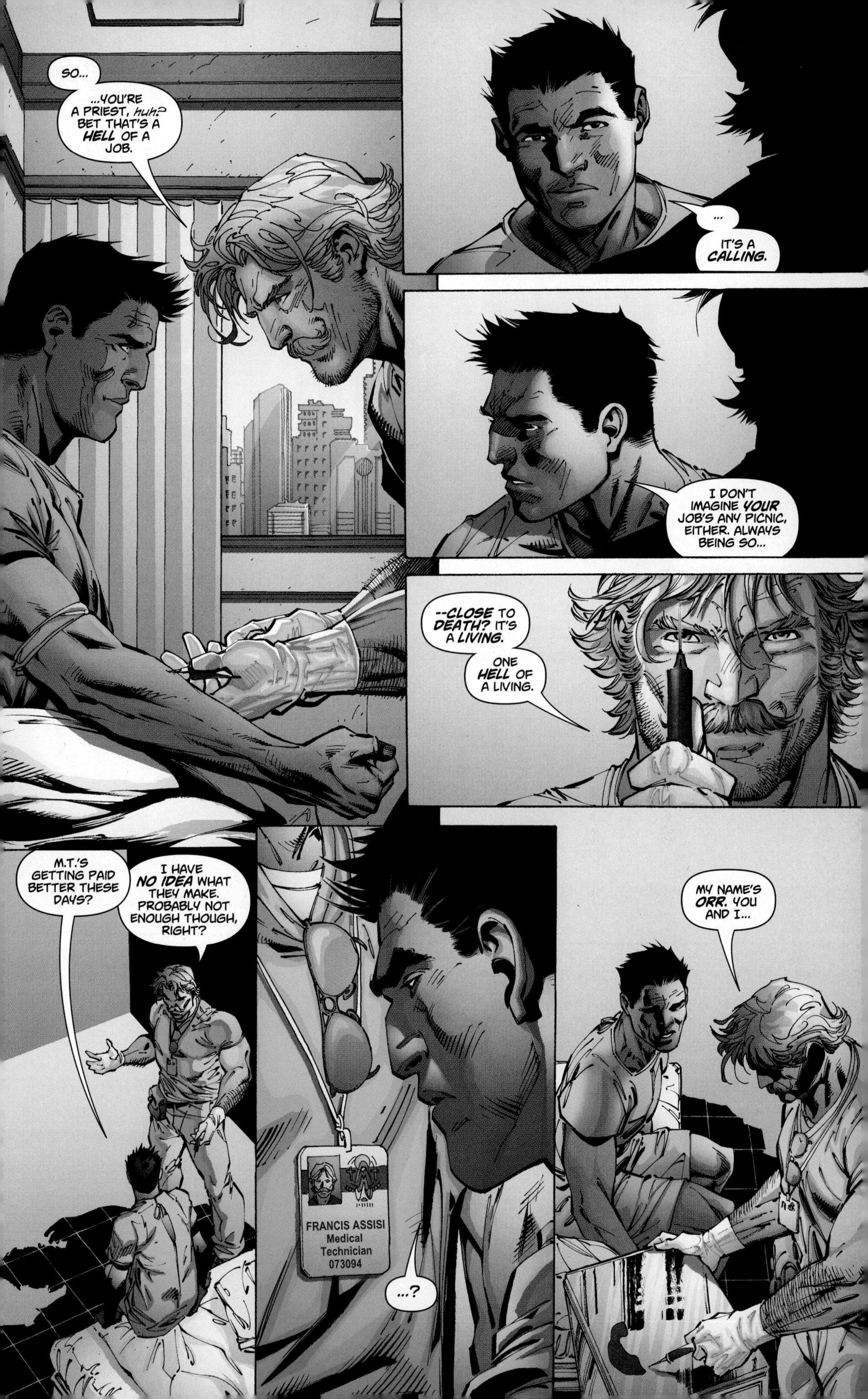
SO...
...YOU'RE A PRIEST, *huh?* BET THAT'S A **HELL** OF A JOB.
... IT'S A **CALLING.**
I DON'T IMAGINE **YOUR** JOB'S ANY PICNIC, EITHER. ALWAYS BEING SO...
--**CLOSE** TO **DEATH?** IT'S A **LIVING.**
ONE **HELL** OF A LIVING.
M.T.'S GETTING PAID BETTER THESE DAYS?
I HAVE **NO IDEA** WHAT THEY MAKE. PROBABLY NOT ENOUGH THOUGH, RIGHT?
FRANCIS ASSISI
Medical
Technician
073094
...?
MY NAME'S **ORR.** YOU AND I...

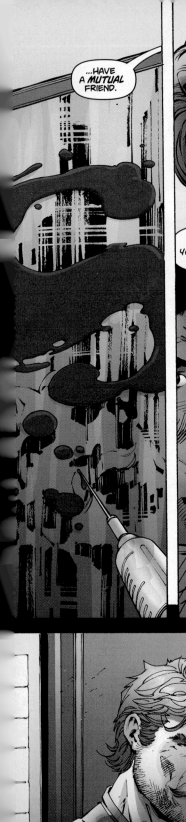

...HAVE A *MUTUAL* FRIEND.

I DON'T KNOW *WHAT* YOU'RE TALKING ABOUT.

YOU CALLIN' ME A *LIAR?* THAT'S NOT VERY *CHRISTIAN* OF YOU.

I SHOULD GO...

NOT JUST YET, YE OF LITTLE FAITH.

HE'S COME TO SEE YOU TWICE, AT YOUR *CHURCH.*

HE CAME TO SEE *ME...*

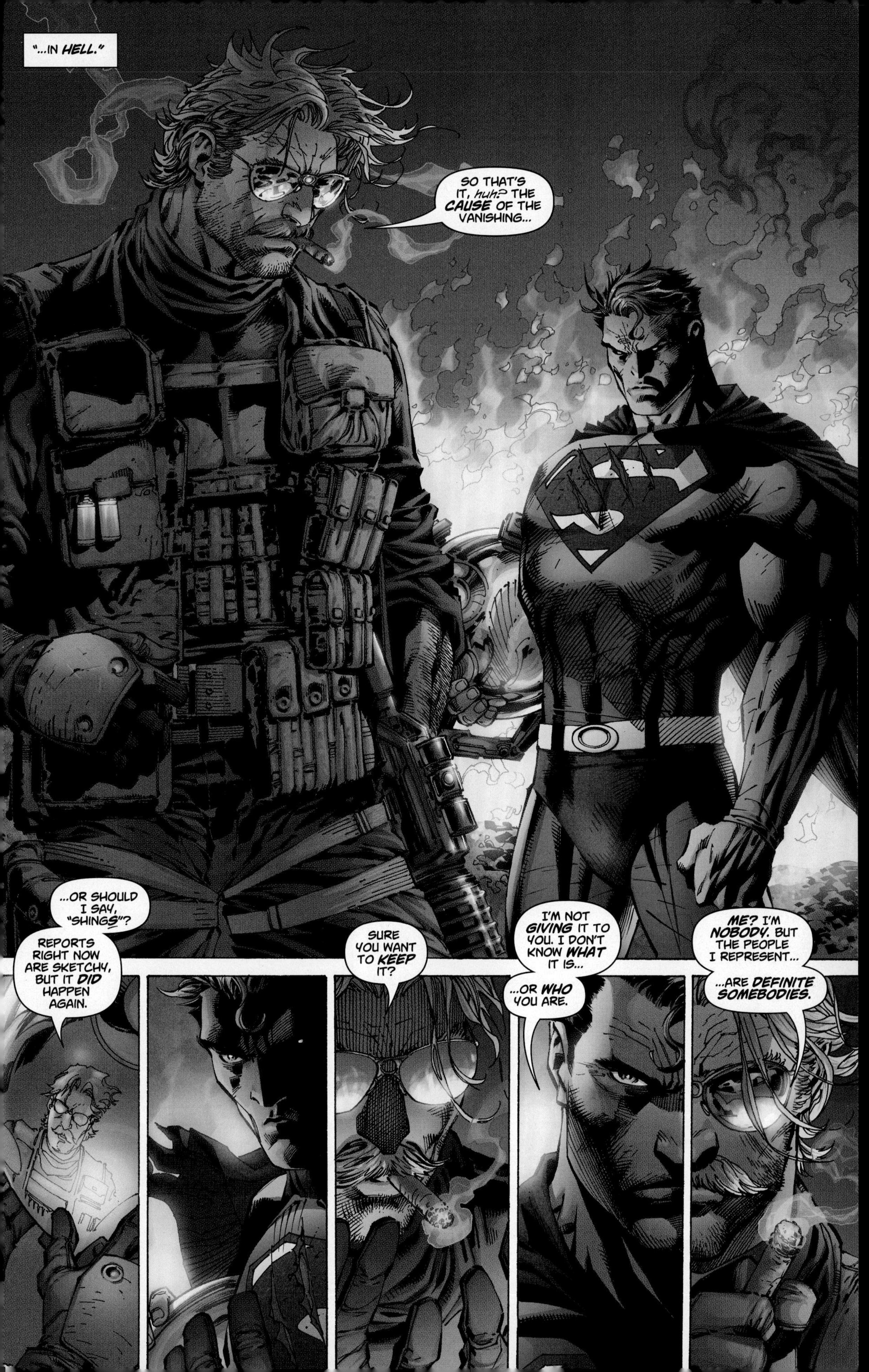
"...IN HELL."
SO THAT'S IT, huh? THE CAUSE OF THE VANISHING...
...OR SHOULD I SAY, "SHINGS"?
REPORTS RIGHT NOW ARE SKETCHY, BUT IT DID HAPPEN AGAIN.
SURE YOU WANT TO KEEP IT?
I'M NOT GIVING IT TO YOU. I DON'T KNOW WHAT IT IS...
...OR WHO YOU ARE.
ME? I'M NOBODY. BUT THE PEOPLE I REPRESENT...
...ARE DEFINITE SOMEBODIES.

THAT'S A COMANCHE STEALTH HELICOPTER.

AMERICAN MILITARY.

I'M NOT. IN *MY BUSINESS*, GOVERNMENTS ARE ON THE PAYROLL.

AND WHAT BUSINESS IS *THAT?*

NONE OF *YOUR* BEESWAX.

...I *DON'T* CARE.

I *DON'T* LIKE YOU...

I WAS HERE TO MONITOR *THINGS.*

WELL...*A* THING. EQUUS. I LOST THE SIGNAL, WHICH MEANS--IMPROBABLE AS IT IS TO BELIEVE, HE'S *DEAD.*

NO, HE ISN'T. THOUGH HE *MIGHT* BE...I CAN'T ACCEPT THAT HE *IS.*

HE VANISHED.

WOW.

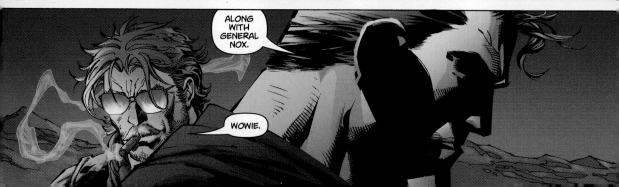

ALONG WITH GENERAL NOX.

WOWIE.

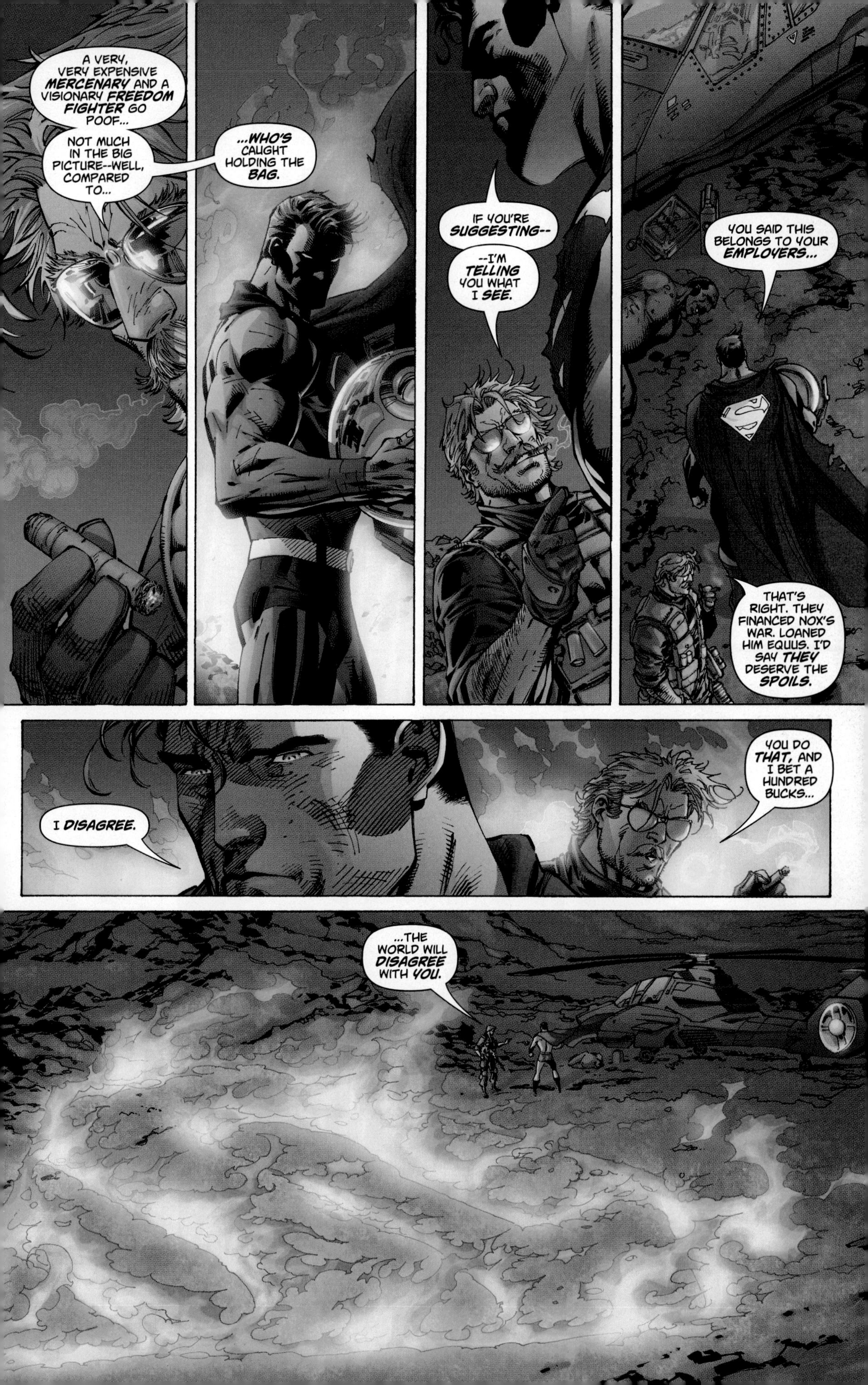
A VERY, VERY EXPENSIVE MERCENARY AND A VISIONARY FREEDOM FIGHTER GO POOF...
NOT MUCH IN THE BIG PICTURE--WELL, COMPARED TO...
...WHO'S CAUGHT HOLDING THE BAG.
IF YOU'RE SUGGESTING--
--I'M TELLING YOU WHAT I SEE.
YOU SAID THIS BELONGS TO YOUR EMPLOYERS...
THAT'S RIGHT. THEY FINANCED NOX'S WAR. LOANED HIM EQUUS. I'D SAY THEY DESERVE THE SPOILS.
I DISAGREE.
YOU DO THAT, AND I BET A HUNDRED BUCKS...
...THE WORLD WILL DISAGREE WITH YOU.

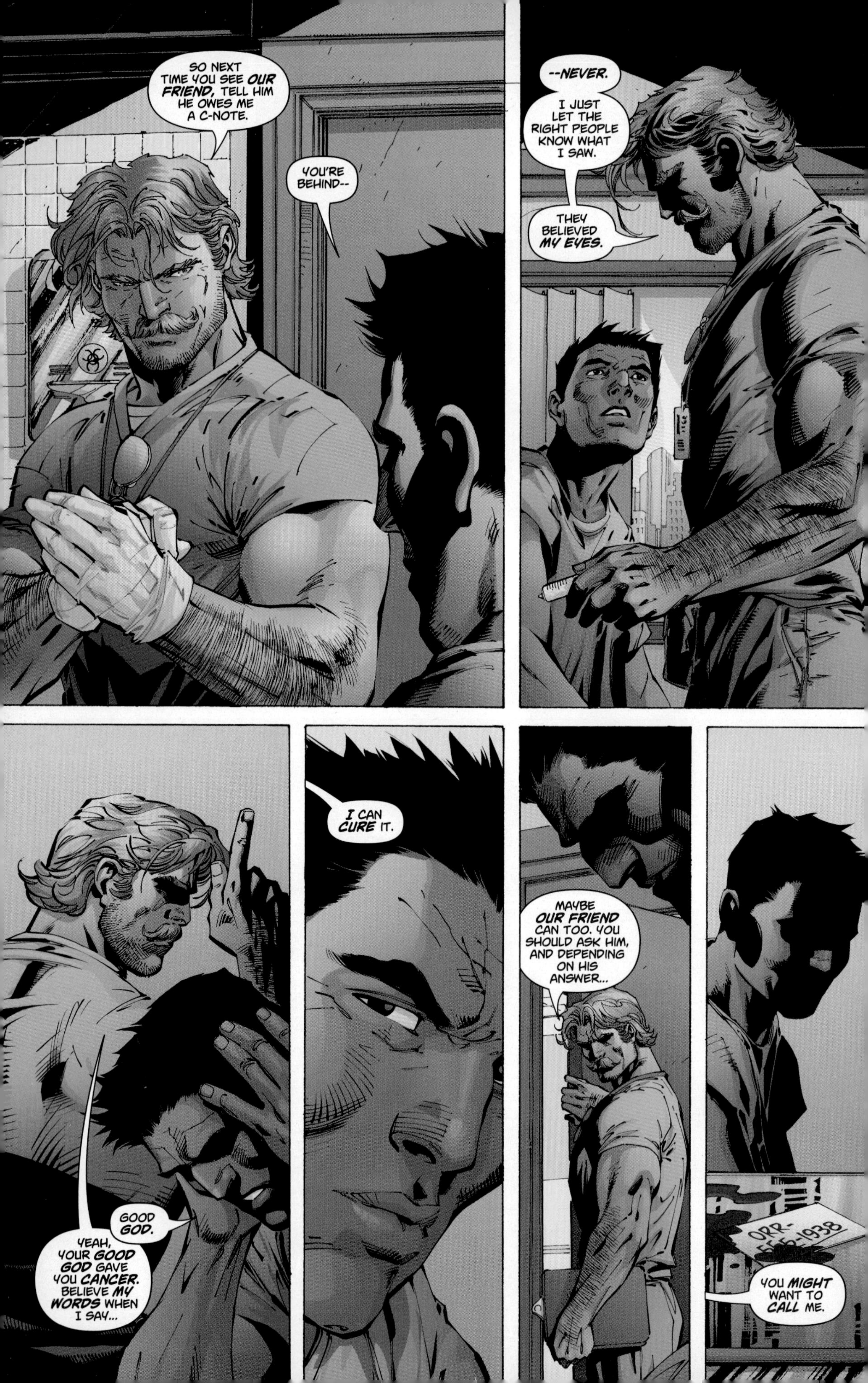
SO NEXT TIME YOU SEE OUR FRIEND, TELL HIM HE OWES ME A C-NOTE.
YOU'RE BEHIND--
--NEVER.
I JUST LET THE RIGHT PEOPLE KNOW WHAT I SAW.
THEY BELIEVED MY EYES.
GOOD GOD.
YEAH, YOUR GOOD GOD GAVE YOU CANCER. BELIEVE MY WORDS WHEN I SAY...
I CAN CURE IT.
MAYBE OUR FRIEND CAN TOO. YOU SHOULD ASK HIM, AND DEPENDING ON HIS ANSWER...
ORR-555-1938
YOU MIGHT WANT TO CALL ME.

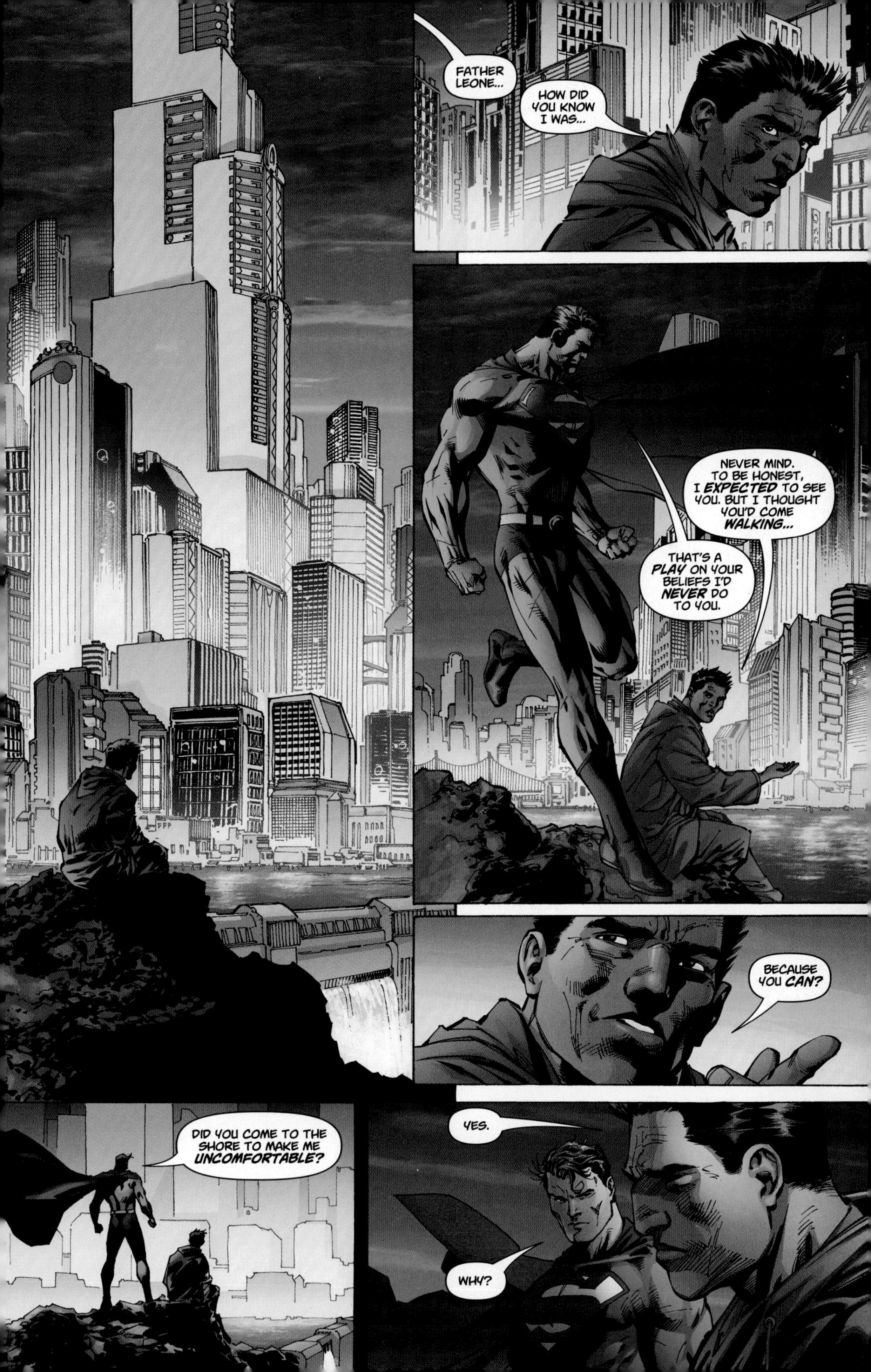
FATHER LEONE...
HOW DID YOU KNOW I WAS...
NEVER MIND. TO BE HONEST, I EXPECTED TO SEE YOU. BUT I THOUGHT YOU'D COME WALKING...
THAT'S A PLAY ON YOUR BELIEFS I'D NEVER DO TO YOU.
BECAUSE YOU CAN?
DID YOU COME TO THE SHORE TO MAKE ME UNCOMFORTABLE?
YES.
WHY?

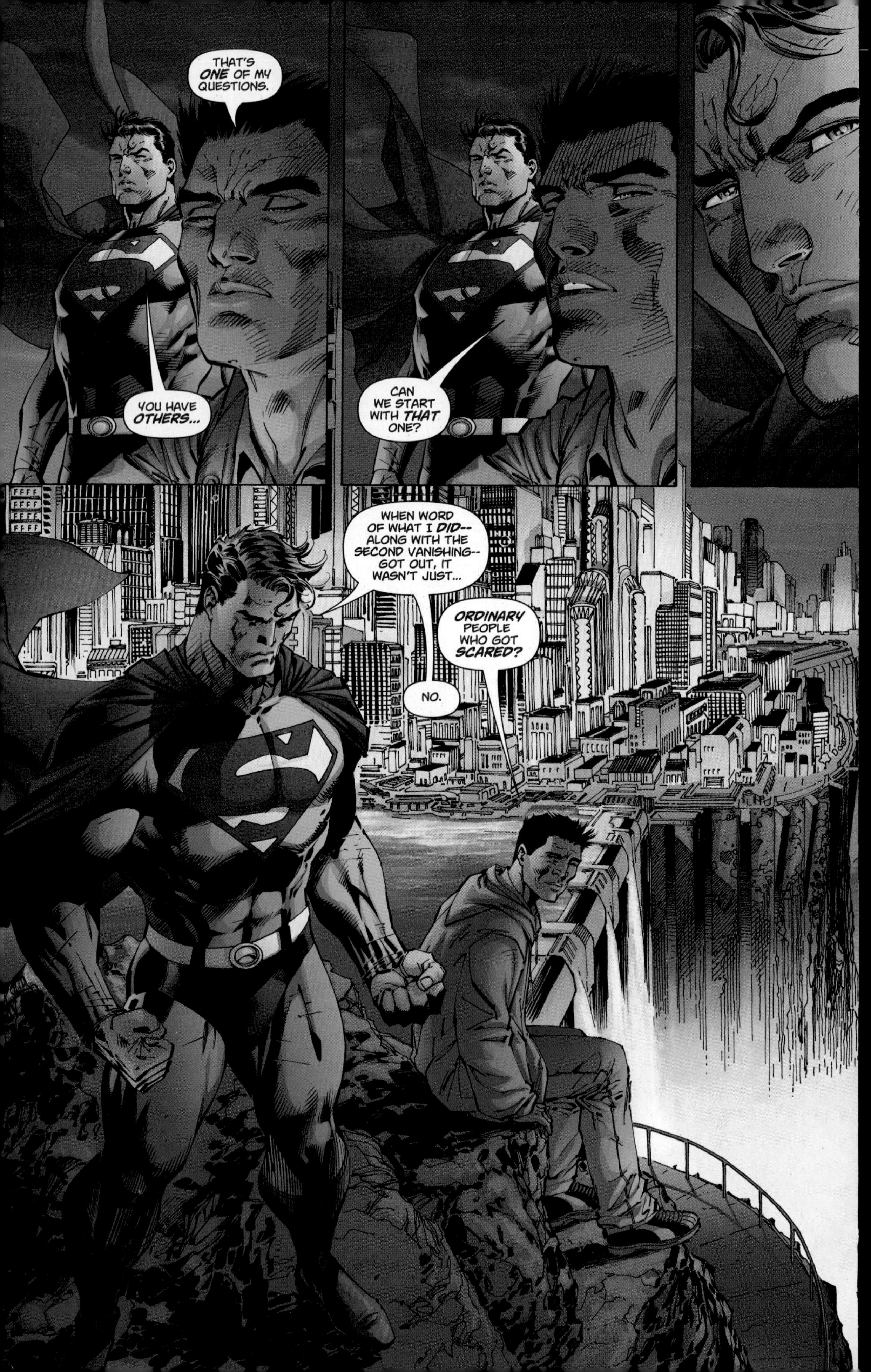
THAT'S *ONE* OF MY QUESTIONS.
YOU HAVE *OTHERS...*
CAN WE START WITH *THAT* ONE?
WHEN WORD OF WHAT I *DID--* ALONG WITH THE SECOND VANISHING-- GOT OUT, IT WASN'T JUST...
*ORDINARY* PEOPLE WHO GOT *SCARED?*
NO.

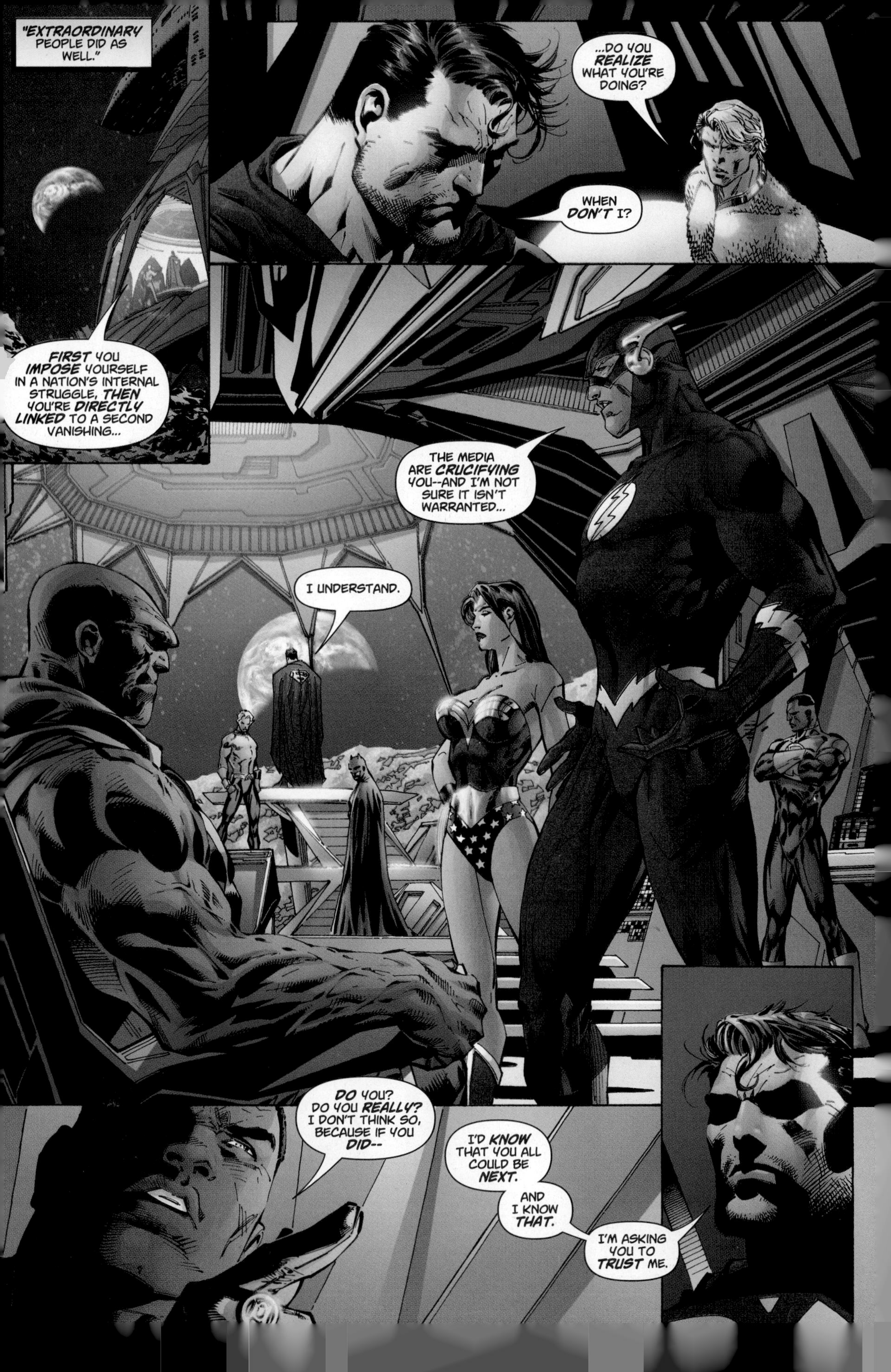
"EXTRAORDINARY PEOPLE DID AS WELL."
...DO YOU REALIZE WHAT YOU'RE DOING?
WHEN DON'T I?
FIRST YOU IMPOSE YOURSELF IN A NATION'S INTERNAL STRUGGLE, THEN YOU'RE DIRECTLY LINKED TO A SECOND VANISHING...
THE MEDIA ARE CRUCIFYING YOU--AND I'M NOT SURE IT ISN'T WARRANTED...
I UNDERSTAND.
DO YOU? DO YOU REALLY? I DON'T THINK SO, BECAUSE IF YOU DID--
I'D KNOW THAT YOU ALL COULD BE NEXT.
AND I KNOW THAT.
I'M ASKING YOU TO TRUST ME.

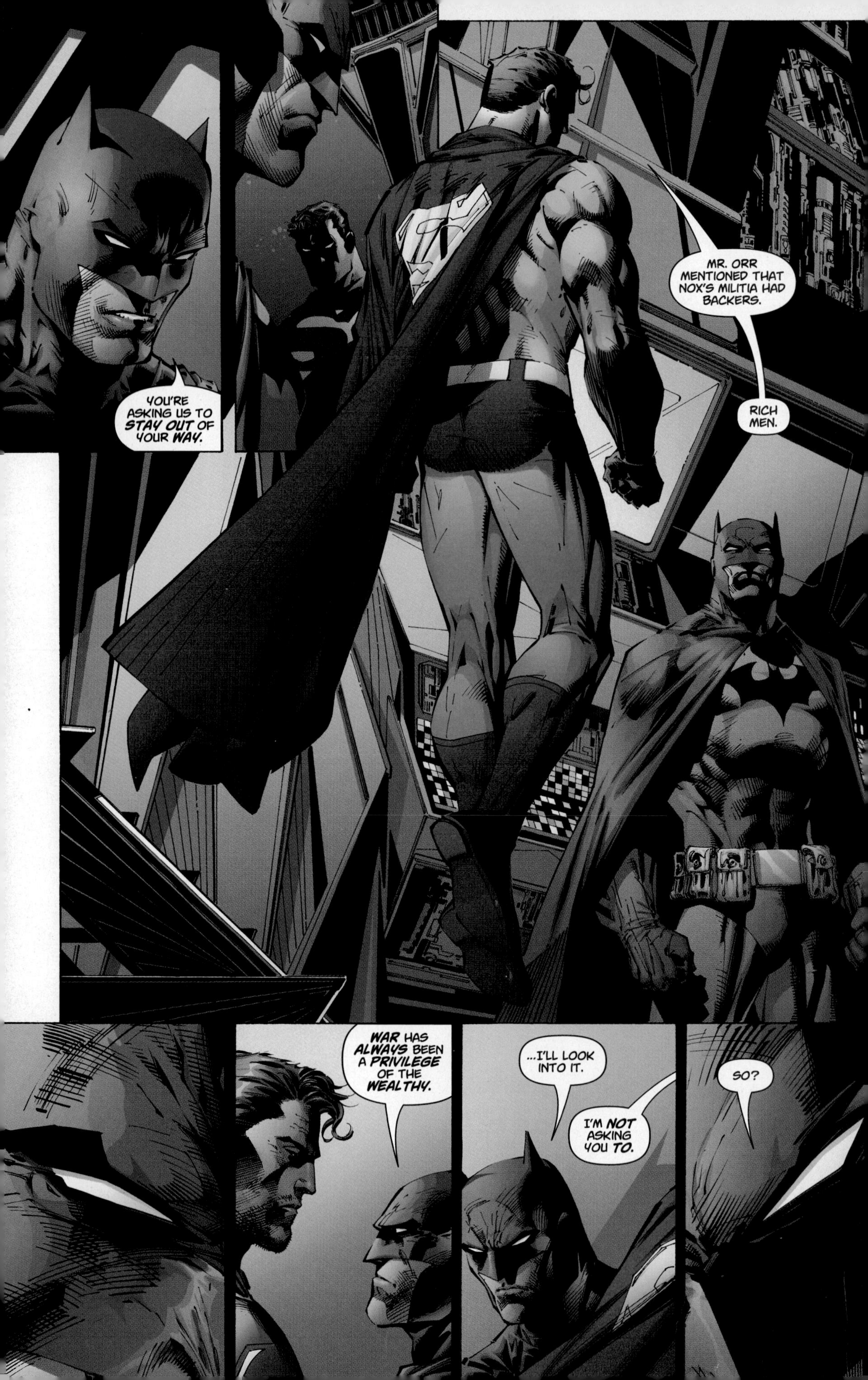
YOU'RE ASKING US TO STAY OUT OF YOUR WAY.
MR. ORR MENTIONED THAT NOX'S MILITIA HAD BACKERS.
RICH MEN.
WAR HAS ALWAYS BEEN A PRIVILEGE OF THE WEALTHY.
...I'LL LOOK INTO IT.
I'M NOT ASKING YOU TO.
SO?

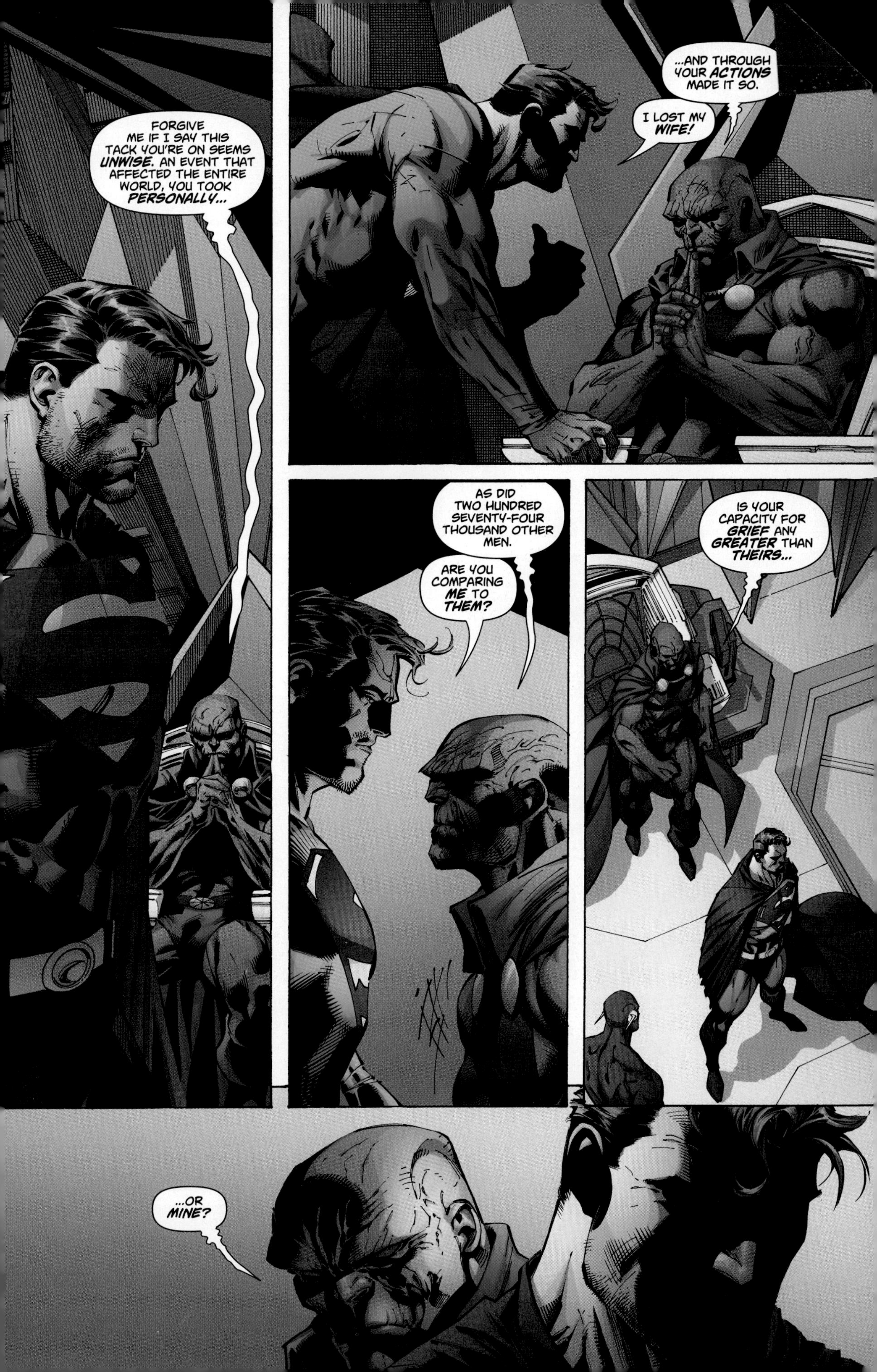
FORGIVE ME IF I SAY THIS TACK YOU'RE ON SEEMS UNWISE. AN EVENT THAT AFFECTED THE ENTIRE WORLD, YOU TOOK PERSONALLY...
...AND THROUGH YOUR ACTIONS MADE IT SO.
I LOST MY WIFE!
AS DID TWO HUNDRED SEVENTY-FOUR THOUSAND OTHER MEN.
ARE YOU COMPARING ME TO THEM?
IS YOUR CAPACITY FOR GRIEF ANY GREATER THAN THEIRS...
...OR MINE?

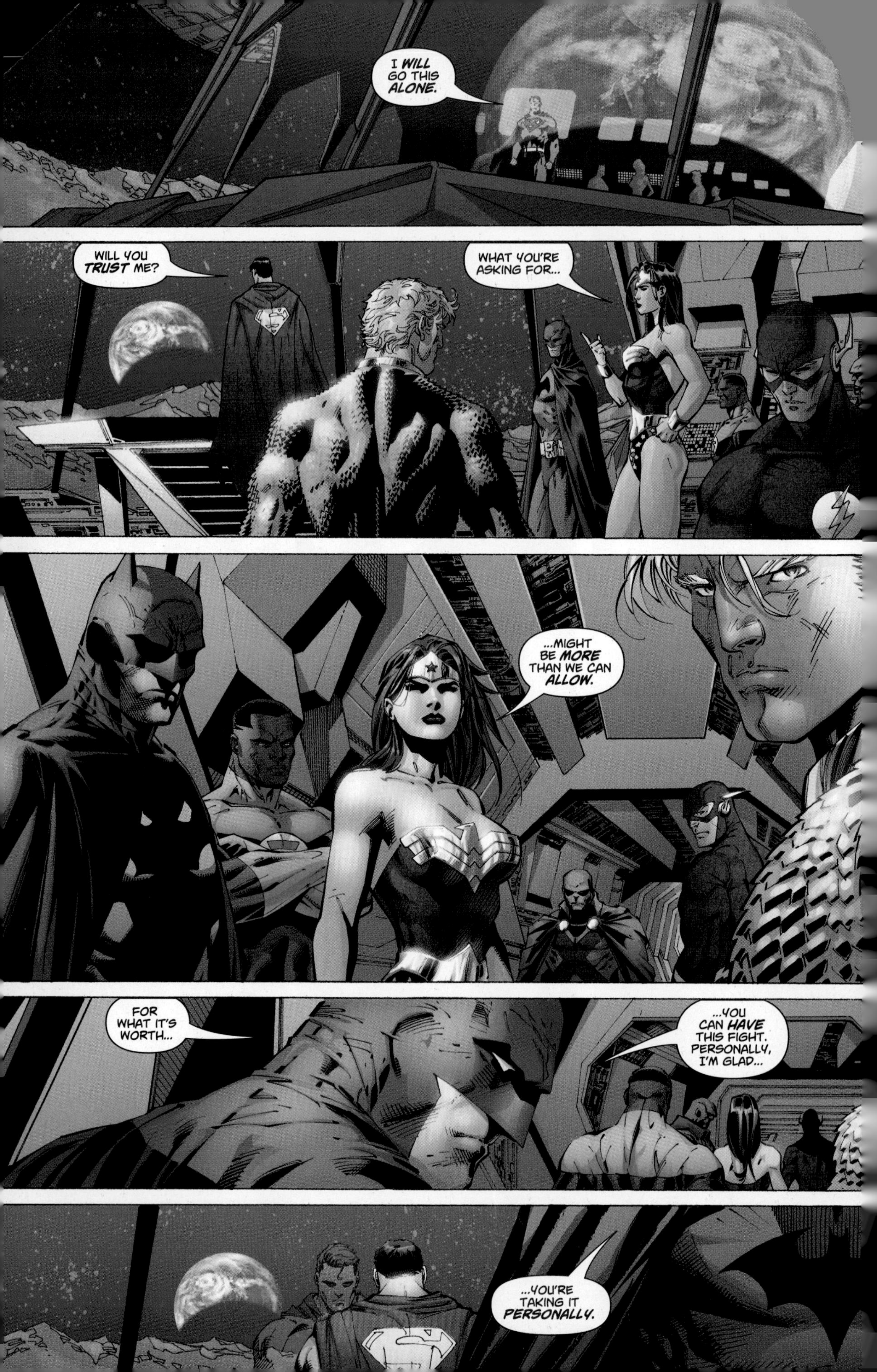

I WILL GO THIS ALONE.
WILL YOU TRUST ME?
WHAT YOU'RE ASKING FOR...
...MIGHT BE MORE THAN WE CAN ALLOW.
FOR WHAT IT'S WORTH...
...YOU CAN HAVE THIS FIGHT. PERSONALLY, I'M GLAD...
...YOU'RE TAKING IT PERSONALLY.

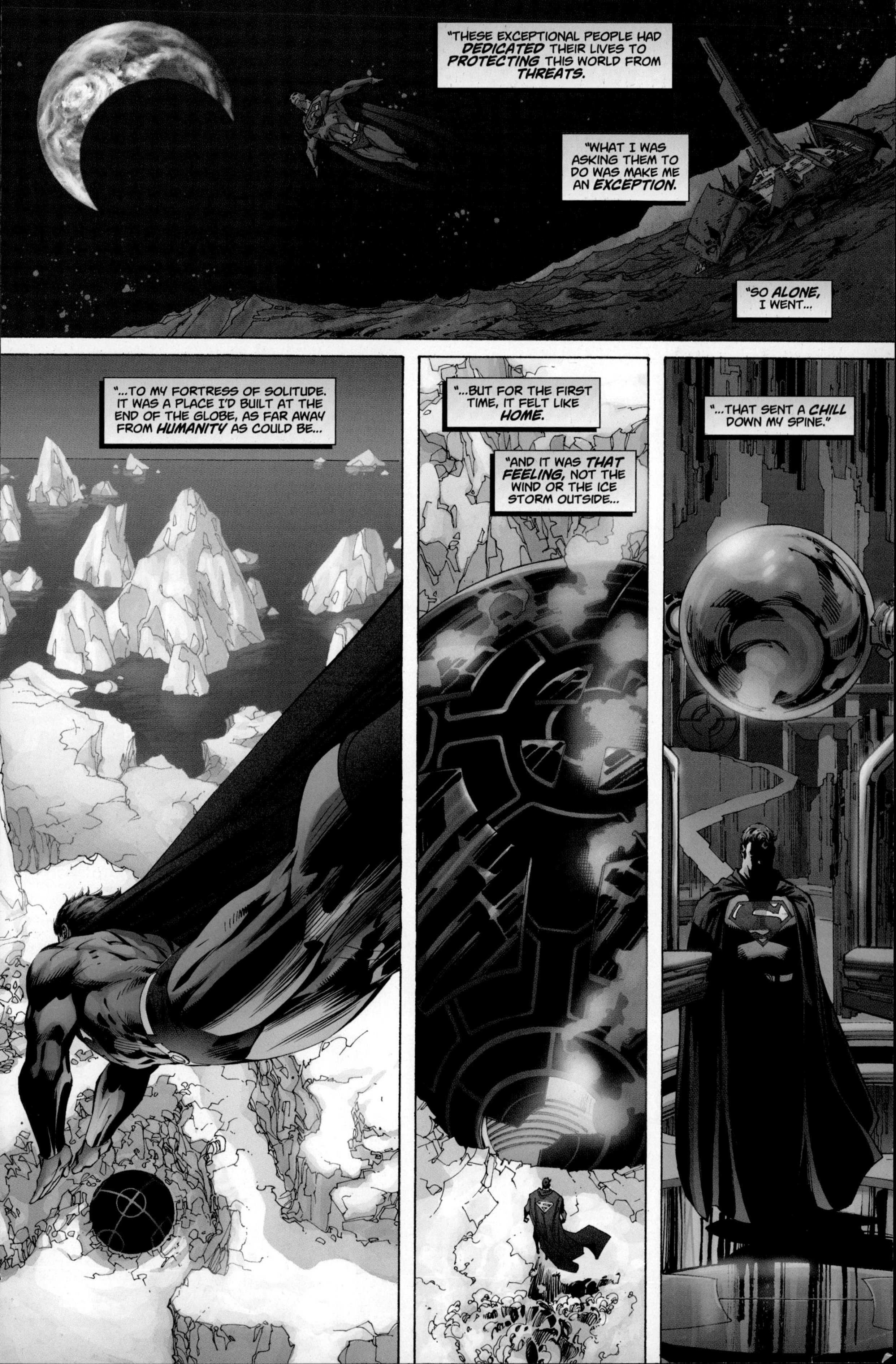
"THESE EXCEPTIONAL PEOPLE HAD DEDICATED THEIR LIVES TO PROTECTING THIS WORLD FROM THREATS.
"WHAT I WAS ASKING THEM TO DO WAS MAKE ME AN EXCEPTION.
"SO ALONE, I WENT...
"...TO MY FORTRESS OF SOLITUDE. IT WAS A PLACE I'D BUILT AT THE END OF THE GLOBE, AS FAR AWAY FROM HUMANITY AS COULD BE...
"...BUT FOR THE FIRST TIME, IT FELT LIKE HOME.
"AND IT WAS THAT FEELING, NOT THE WIND OR THE ICE STORM OUTSIDE...
"...THAT SENT A CHILL DOWN MY SPINE."

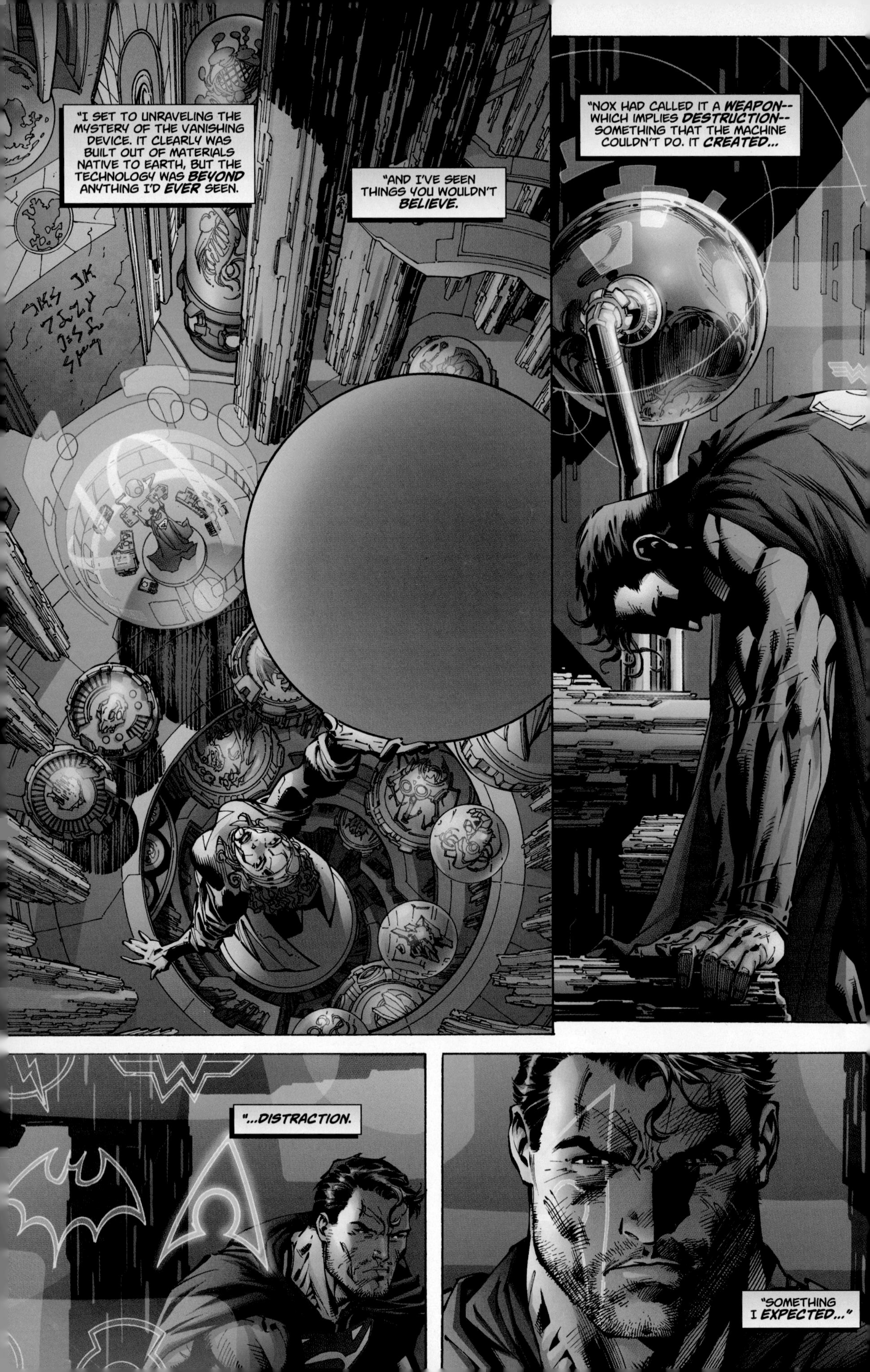
"I SET TO UNRAVELING THE MYSTERY OF THE VANISHING DEVICE. IT CLEARLY WAS BUILT OUT OF MATERIALS NATIVE TO EARTH, BUT THE TECHNOLOGY WAS BEYOND ANYTHING I'D EVER SEEN.
"AND I'VE SEEN THINGS YOU WOULDN'T BELIEVE.
"NOX HAD CALLED IT A WEAPON-- WHICH IMPLIES DESTRUCTION-- SOMETHING THAT THE MACHINE COULDN'T DO. IT CREATED...
"...DISTRACTION.
"SOMETHING I EXPECTED..."

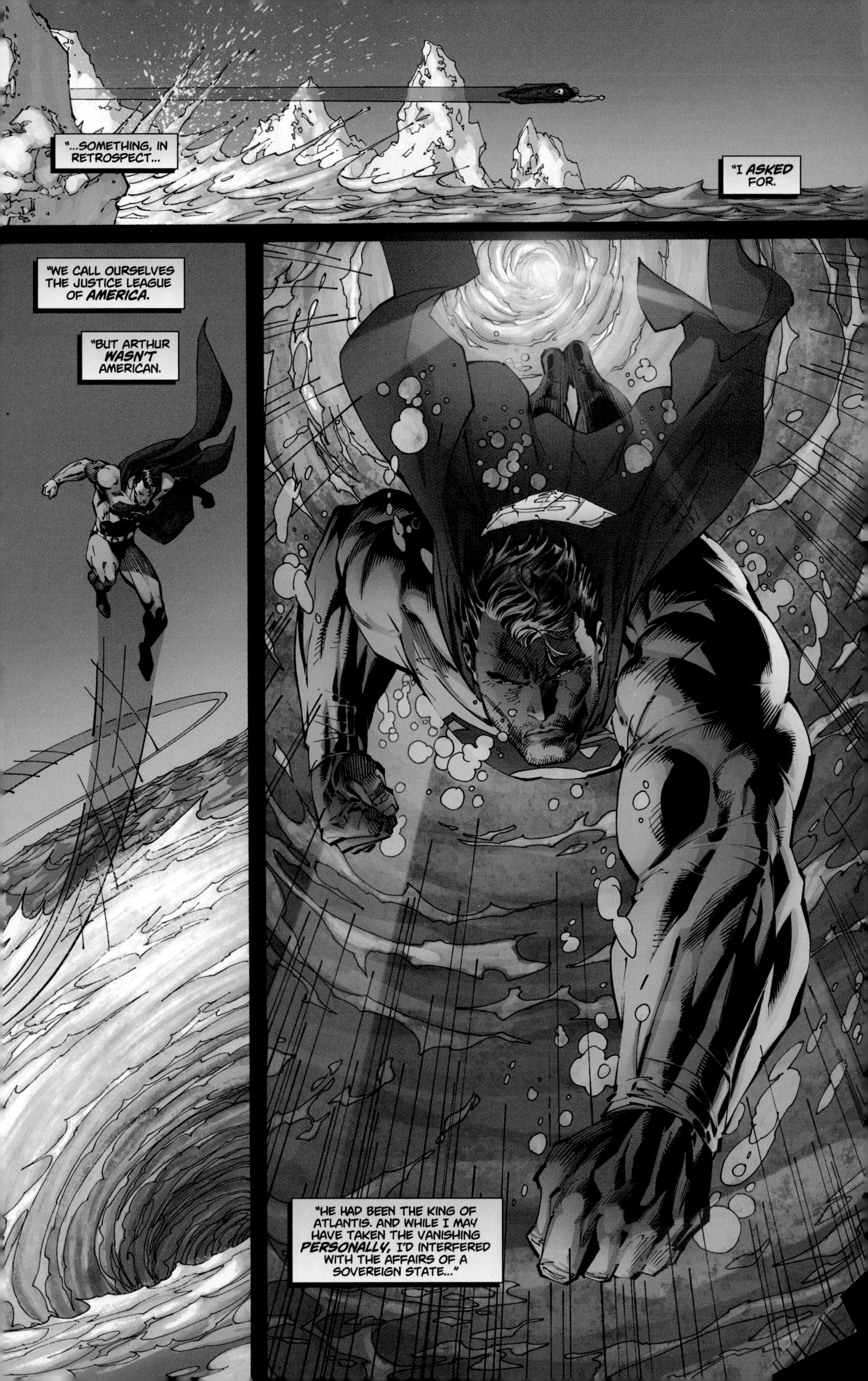
"...SOMETHING, IN RETROSPECT...
"I ASKED FOR.
"WE CALL OURSELVES THE JUSTICE LEAGUE OF AMERICA.
"BUT ARTHUR WASN'T AMERICAN.
"HE HAD BEEN THE KING OF ATLANTIS. AND WHILE I MAY HAVE TAKEN THE VANISHING PERSONALLY, I'D INTERFERED WITH THE AFFAIRS OF A SOVEREIGN STATE..."

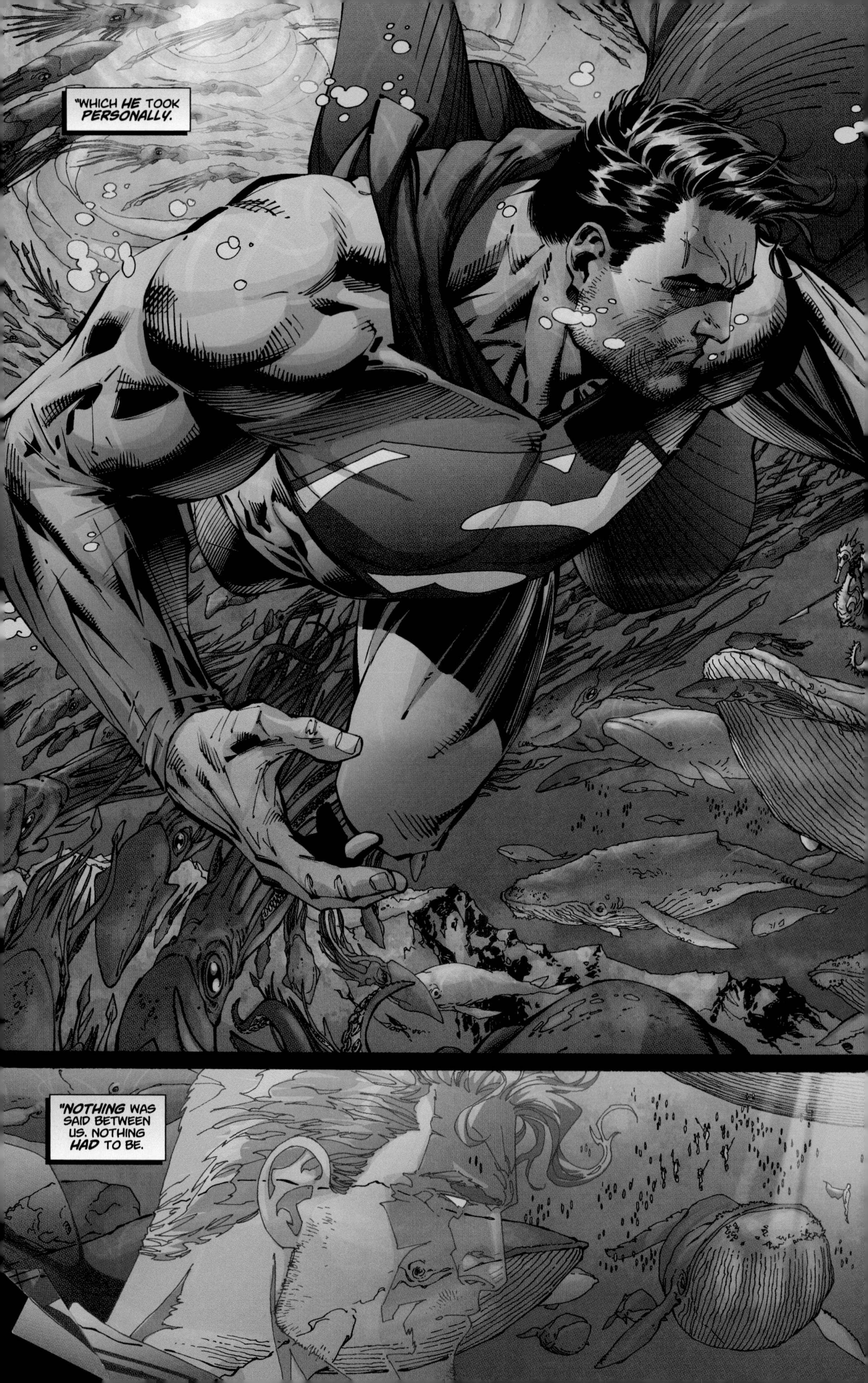
"WHICH HE TOOK PERSONALLY.
"NOTHING WAS SAID BETWEEN US. NOTHING HAD TO BE.

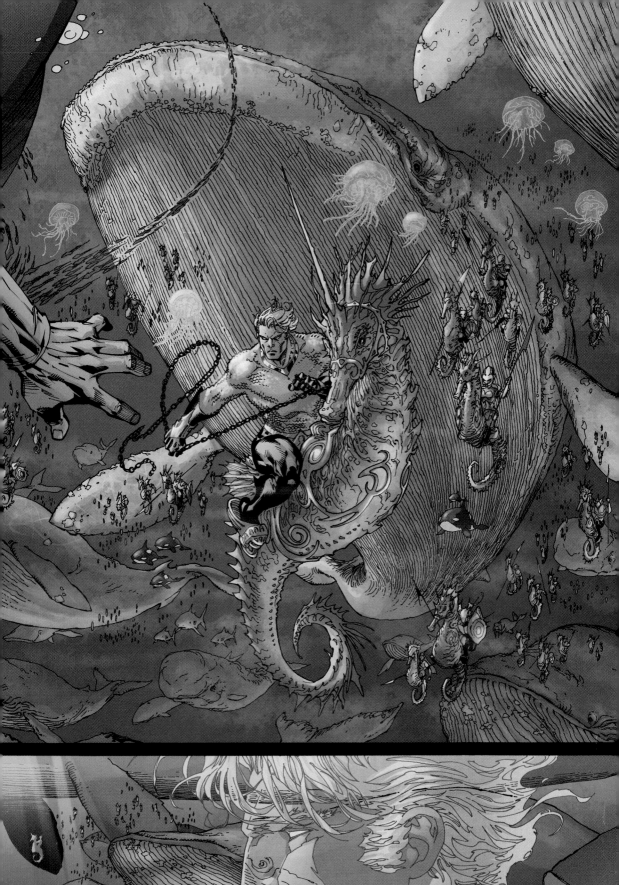

"HIS *MESSAGE* WAS CLEAR..."

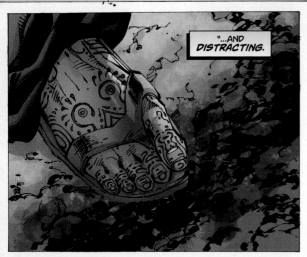

"...AND **DISTRACTING.**

"I'D ALWAYS BELIEVED THAT MY ROLE IN THE WORLD WAS *REACTIVE.* LIKE THE LEAGUE, I WAS HERE TO PROTECT THE WORLD FROM THREATS.

"TO *STOP* SOMETHING BEFORE IT GOT ANY *WORSE.*

"BUT *MY REACTION* TO THE VANISHING HAD *STARTED* SOMETHING IN THE WORLD."

PTOO*

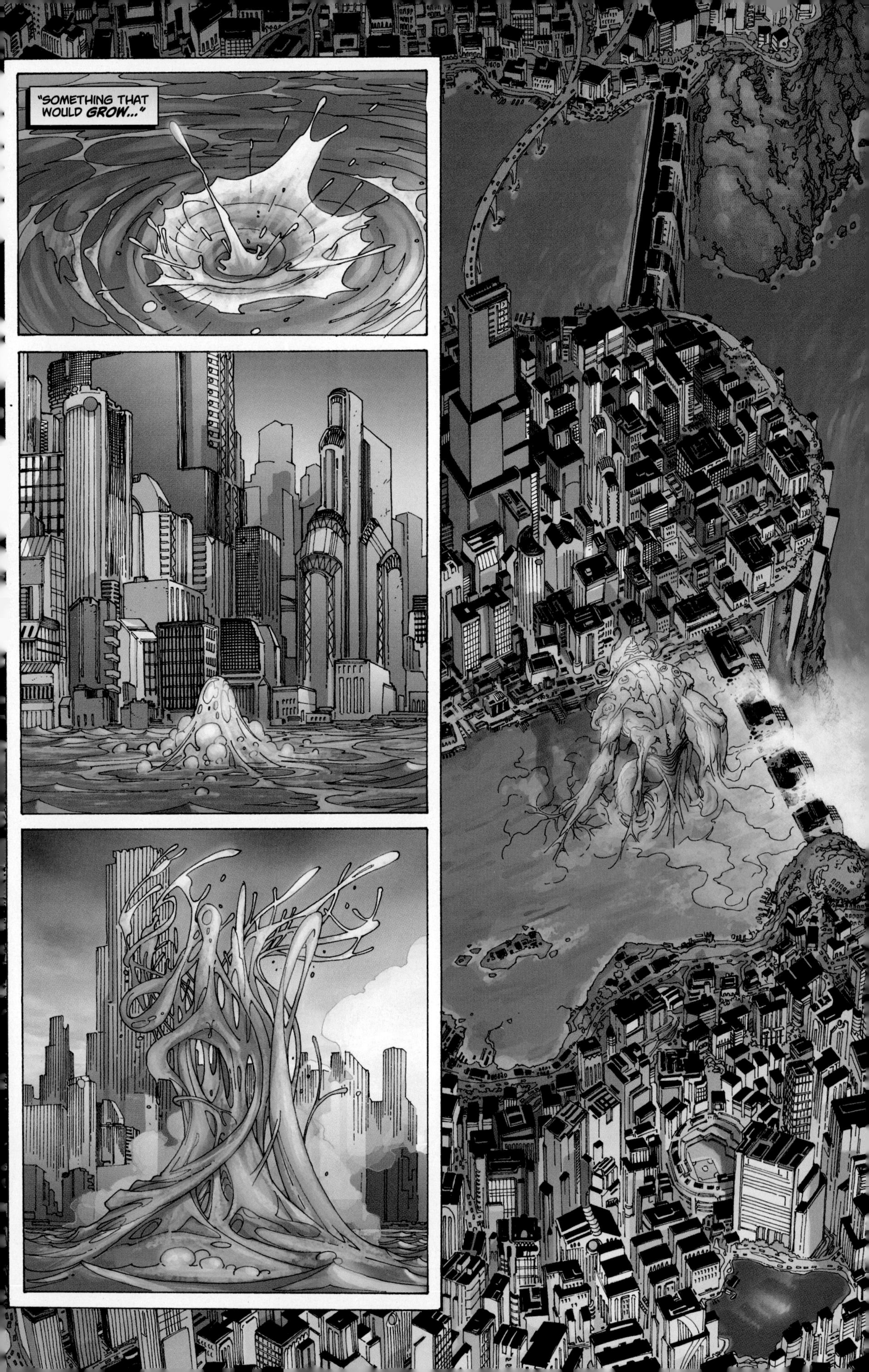
"SOMETHING THAT WOULD GROW..."

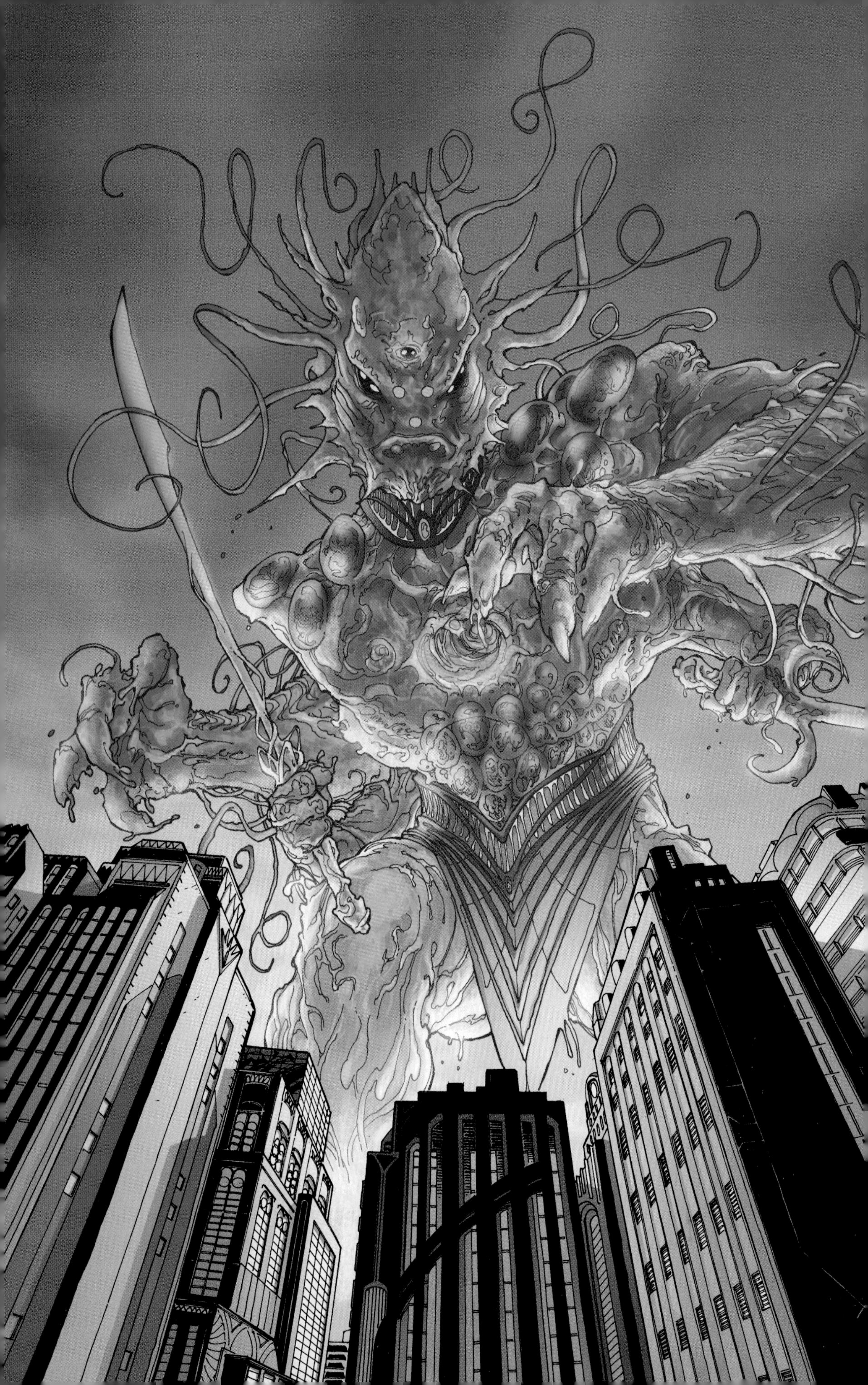

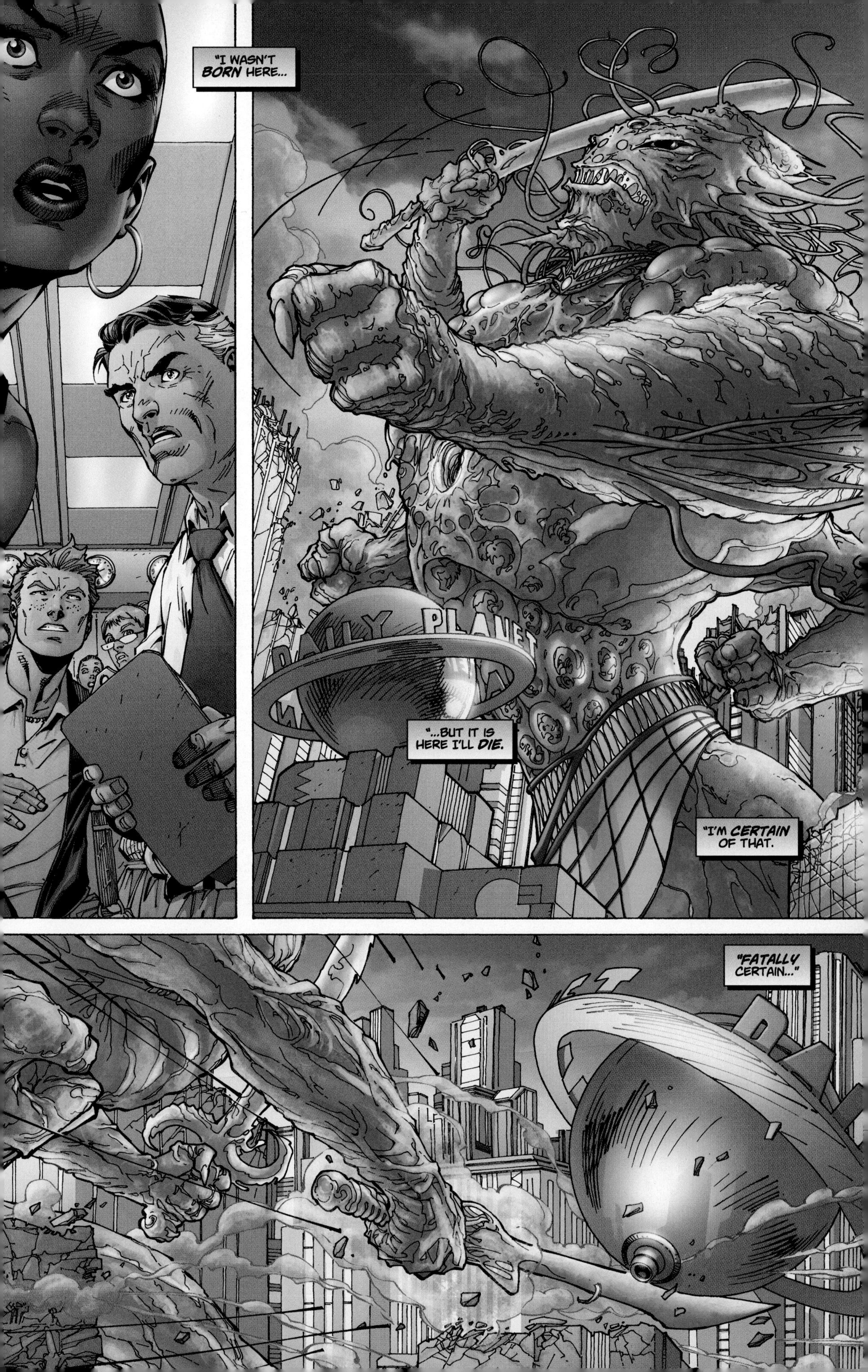
"I WASN'T BORN HERE...
"...BUT IT IS HERE I'LL DIE.
"I'M CERTAIN OF THAT.
"FATALLY CERTAIN..."

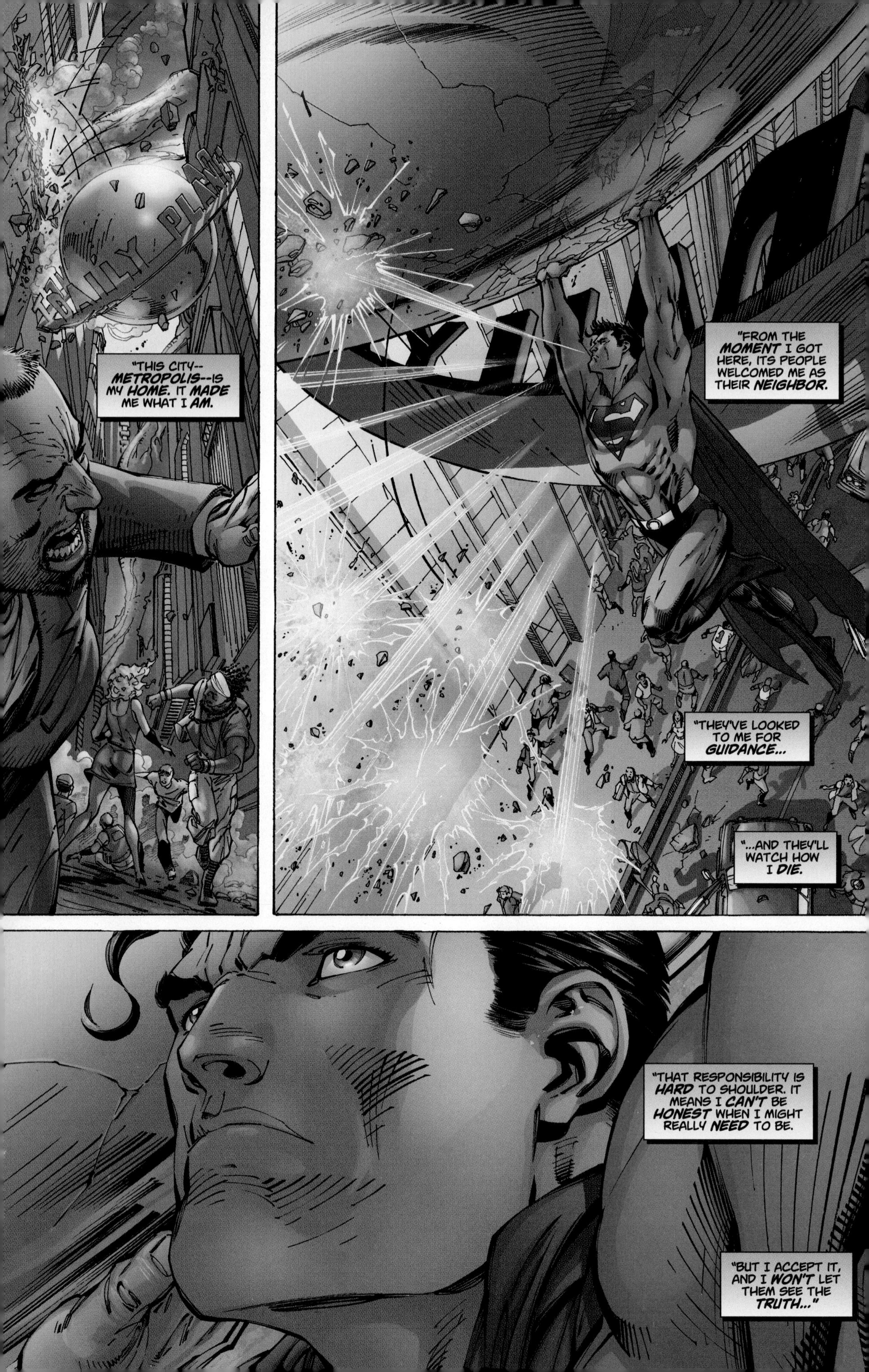
"THIS CITY-- METROPOLIS--IS MY HOME. IT MADE ME WHAT I AM.
"FROM THE MOMENT I GOT HERE, ITS PEOPLE WELCOMED ME AS THEIR NEIGHBOR.
"THEY'VE LOOKED TO ME FOR GUIDANCE...
"...AND THEY'LL WATCH HOW I DIE.
"THAT RESPONSIBILITY IS HARD TO SHOULDER. IT MEANS I CAN'T BE HONEST WHEN I MIGHT REALLY NEED TO BE.
"BUT I ACCEPT IT, AND I WON'T LET THEM SEE THE TRUTH..."

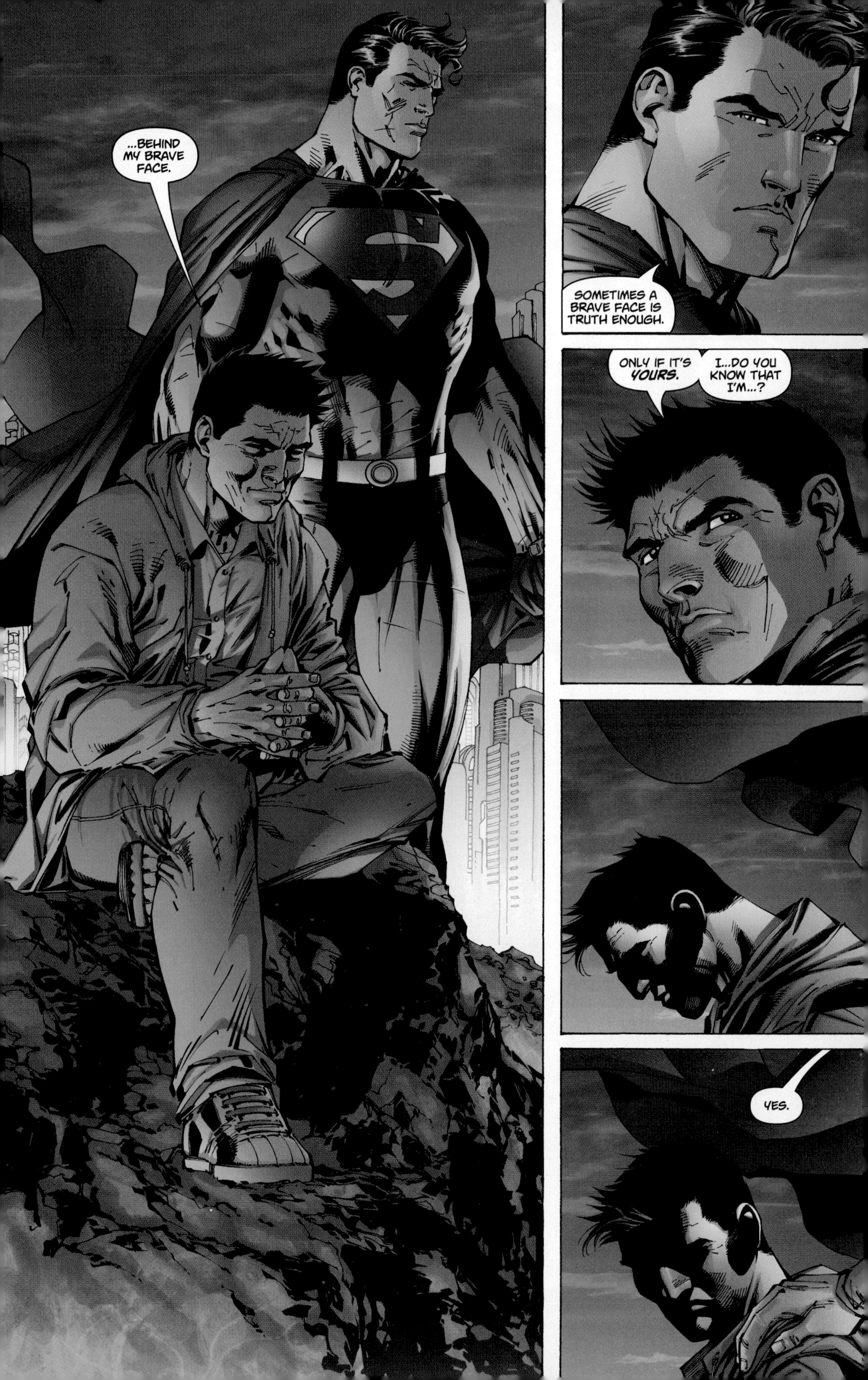
...BEHIND MY BRAVE FACE.
SOMETIMES A BRAVE FACE IS TRUTH ENOUGH.
ONLY IF IT'S *YOURS.*
I...DO YOU KNOW THAT I'M...?
YES.

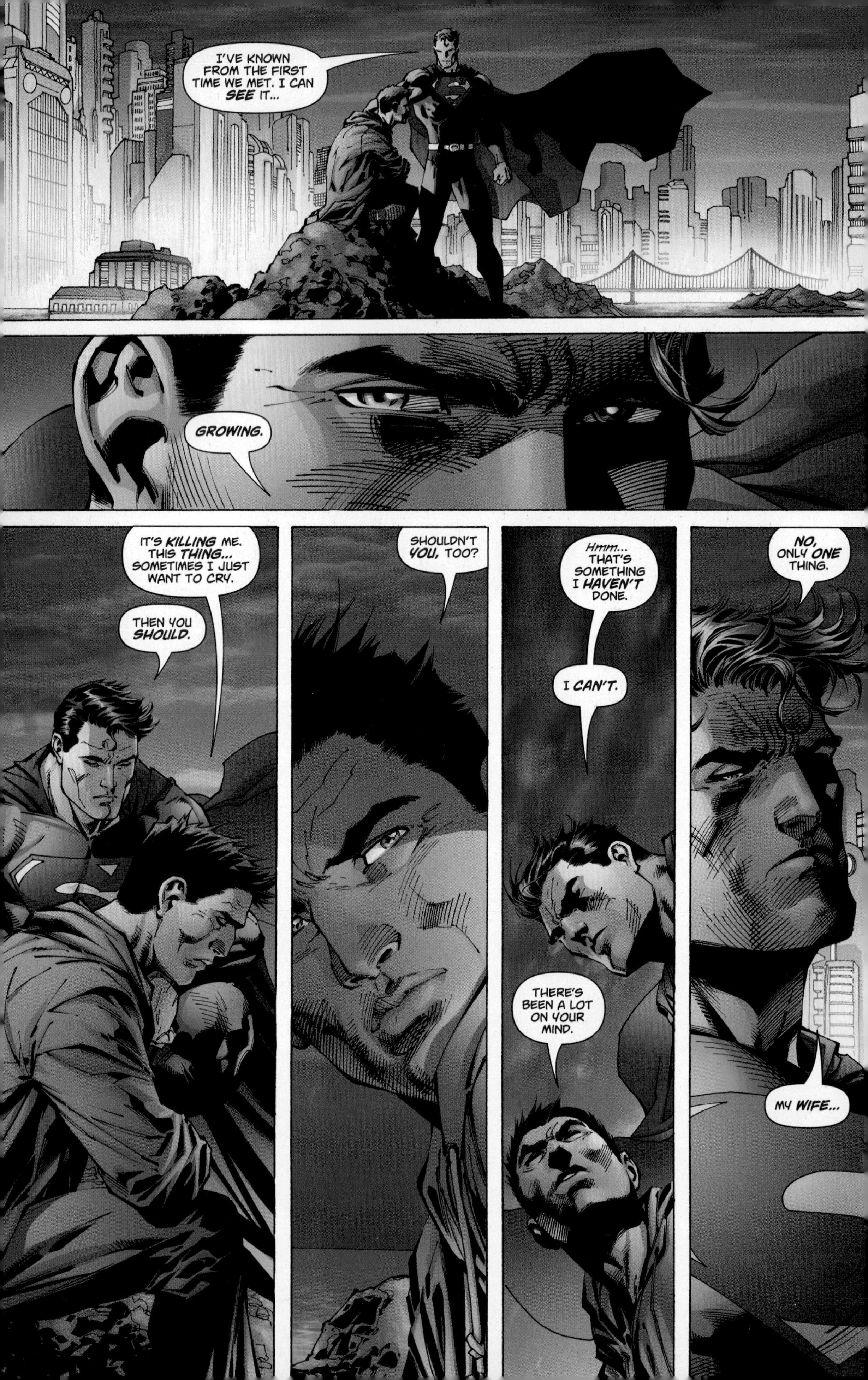
I'VE KNOWN FROM THE FIRST TIME WE MET. I CAN SEE IT...
GROWING.
IT'S KILLING ME. THIS THING... SOMETIMES I JUST WANT TO CRY.
THEN YOU SHOULD.
SHOULDN'T YOU, TOO?
Hmm... THAT'S SOMETHING I HAVEN'T DONE.
I CAN'T.
THERE'S BEEN A LOT ON YOUR MIND.
NO, ONLY ONE THING.
MY WIFE...

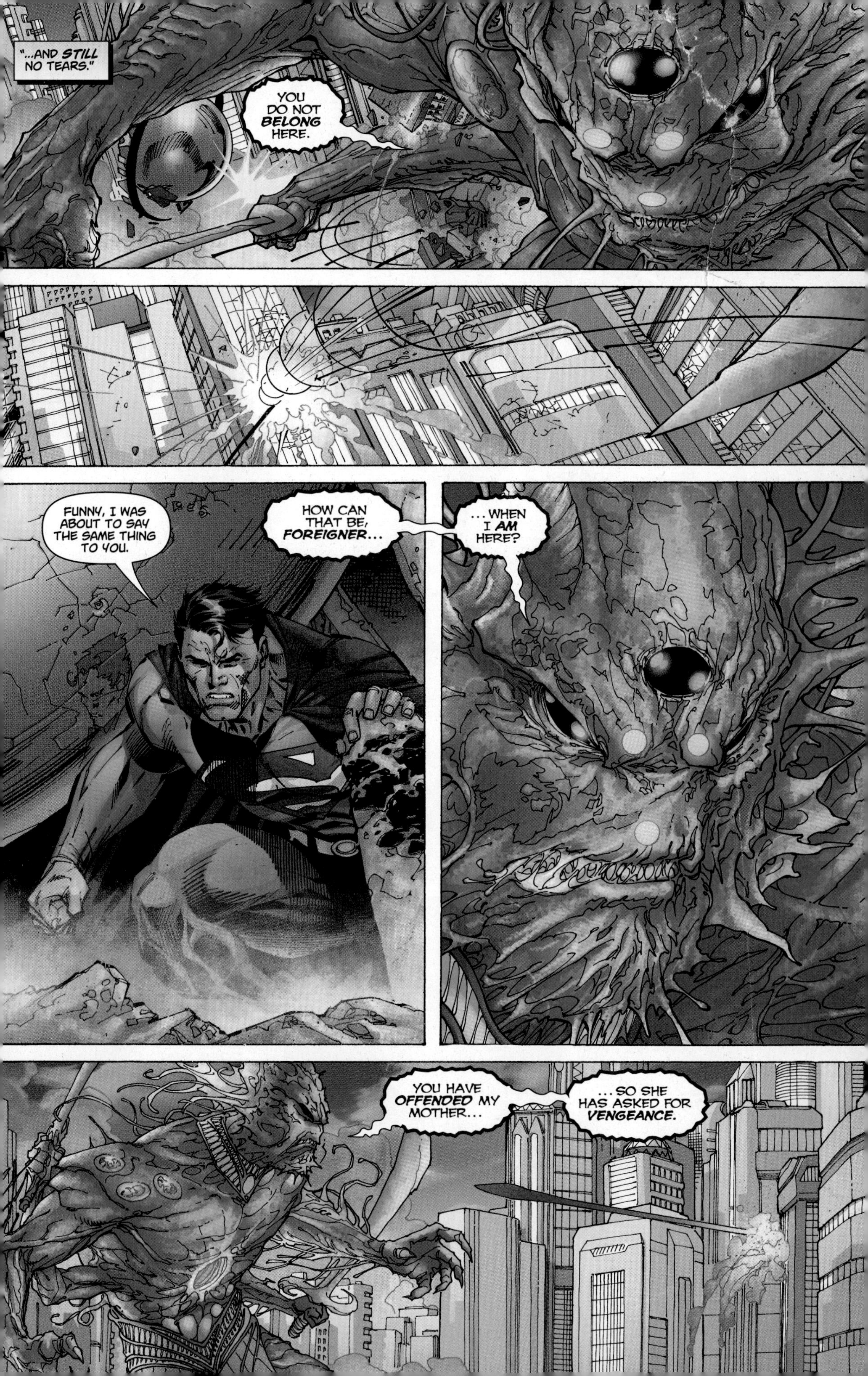
"...AND STILL NO TEARS."
YOU DO NOT BELONG HERE.
FUNNY, I WAS ABOUT TO SAY THE SAME THING TO YOU.
HOW CAN THAT BE, FOREIGNER...
...WHEN I AM HERE?
YOU HAVE OFFENDED MY MOTHER...
...SO SHE HAS ASKED FOR VENGEANCE.

"MY FIRST REACTION TO THIS CREATURE WAS THAT IT WAS ARTHUR'S DOING--THAT THE SEA *BELONGS* TO HIM...

"...AND THIS HAD SPRUNG FROM THE *DEPTHS* OF HIS *SILENCE.*

"BUT I WAS *WRONG.*

"AGAIN."

MY BROTHERS AND I *DEMAND* ONE THING...

YOUR *EXILE.*

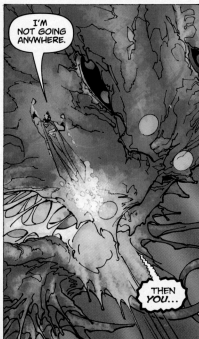

I'M NOT GOING ANYWHERE.

THEN *YOU*...

...AND THE *DOGS* THAT HAVE *ACCEPTED* YOU AS ONE OF THEM...

...WILL BE *SLAUGHTERED.*

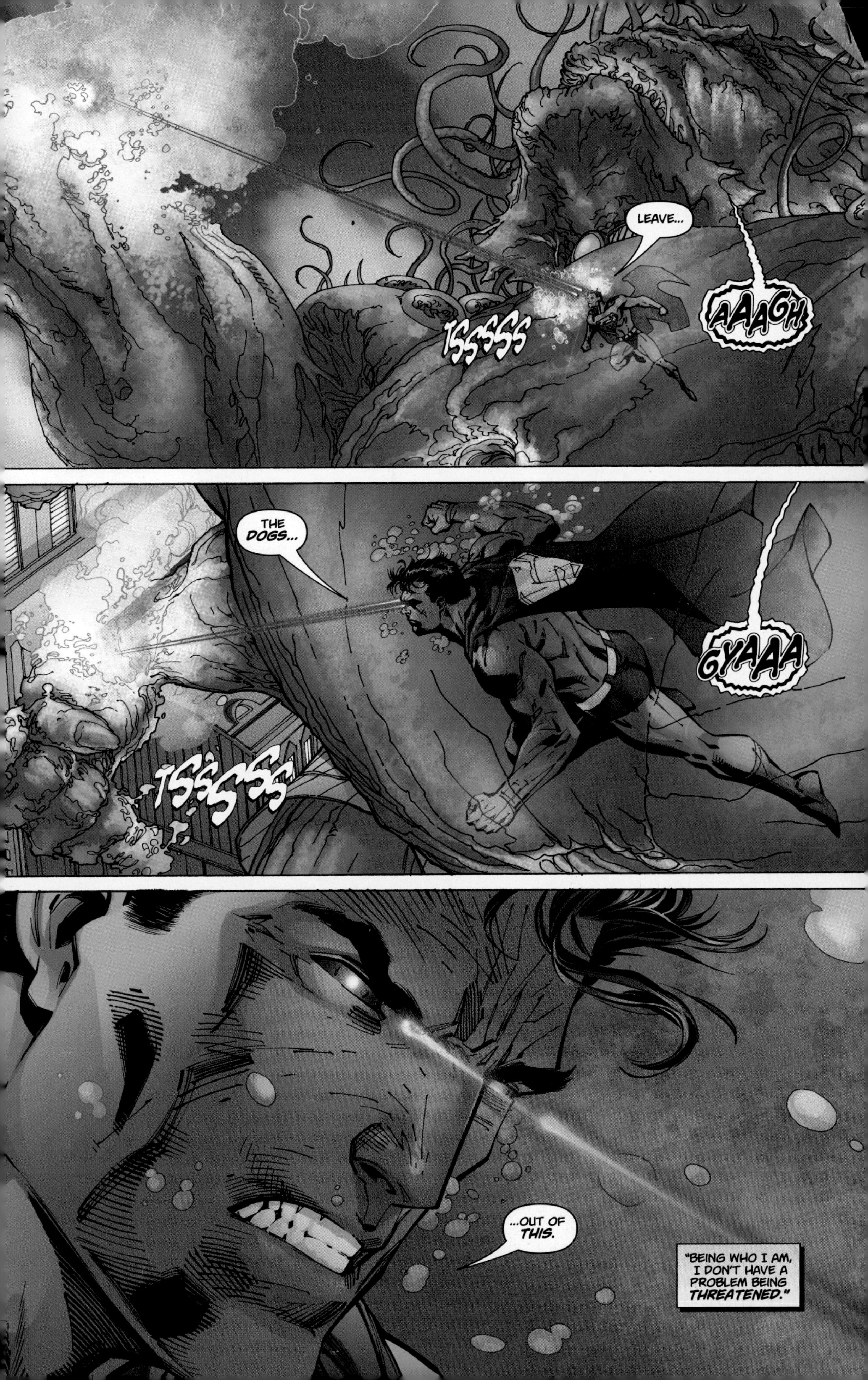
LEAVE...
AAAGH
TSSSSS
THE DOGS...
GYAAA
TSSSSS
...OUT OF THIS.
"BEING WHO I AM, I DON'T HAVE A PROBLEM BEING THREATENED."

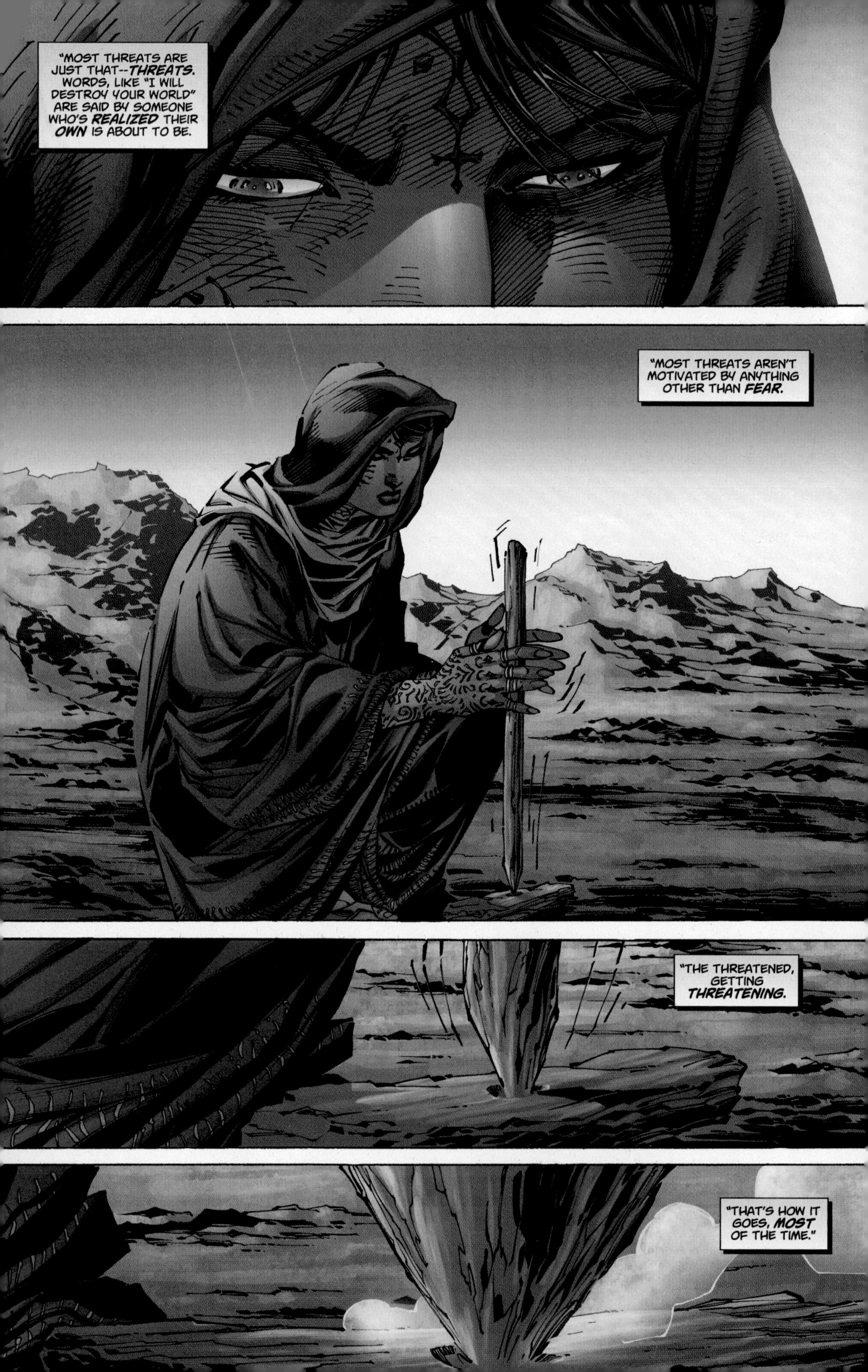
"MOST THREATS ARE JUST THAT--THREATS. WORDS, LIKE "I WILL DESTROY YOUR WORLD" ARE SAID BY SOMEONE WHO'S REALIZED THEIR OWN IS ABOUT TO BE.
"MOST THREATS AREN'T MOTIVATED BY ANYTHING OTHER THAN FEAR.
"THE THREATENED, GETTING THREATENING.
"THAT'S HOW IT GOES, MOST OF THE TIME."

"BUT NOT ALL."

SSSSSS

AAAHH

FFFF...

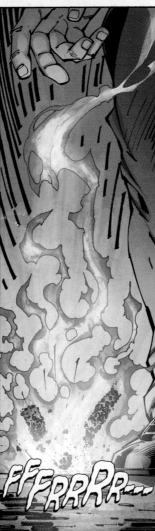

FFFRRRR...

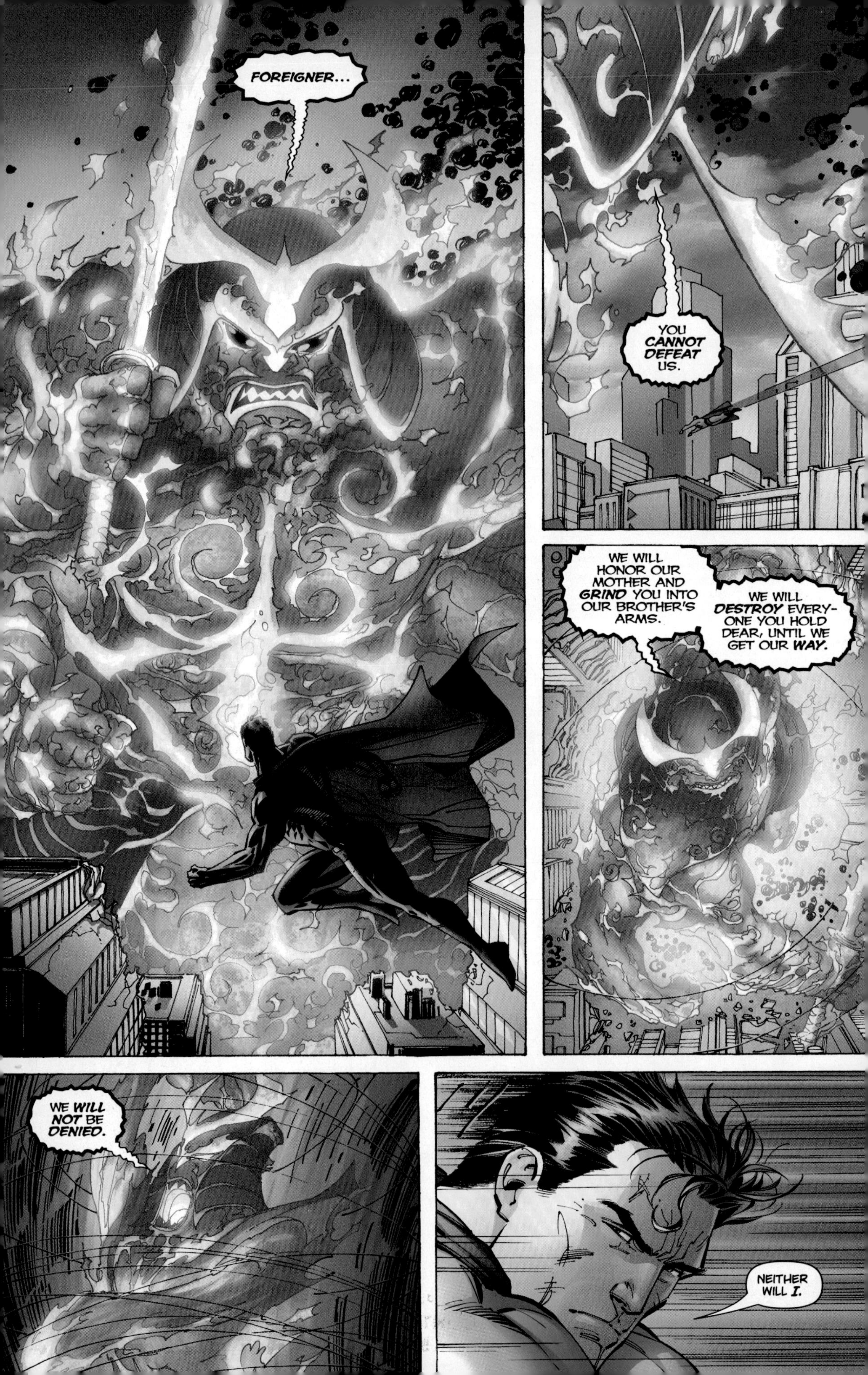
FOREIGNER...
YOU CANNOT DEFEAT US.
WE WILL HONOR OUR MOTHER AND GRIND YOU INTO OUR BROTHER'S ARMS.
WE WILL DESTROY EVERY-ONE YOU HOLD DEAR, UNTIL WE GET OUR WAY.
WE WILL NOT BE DENIED.
NEITHER WILL I.

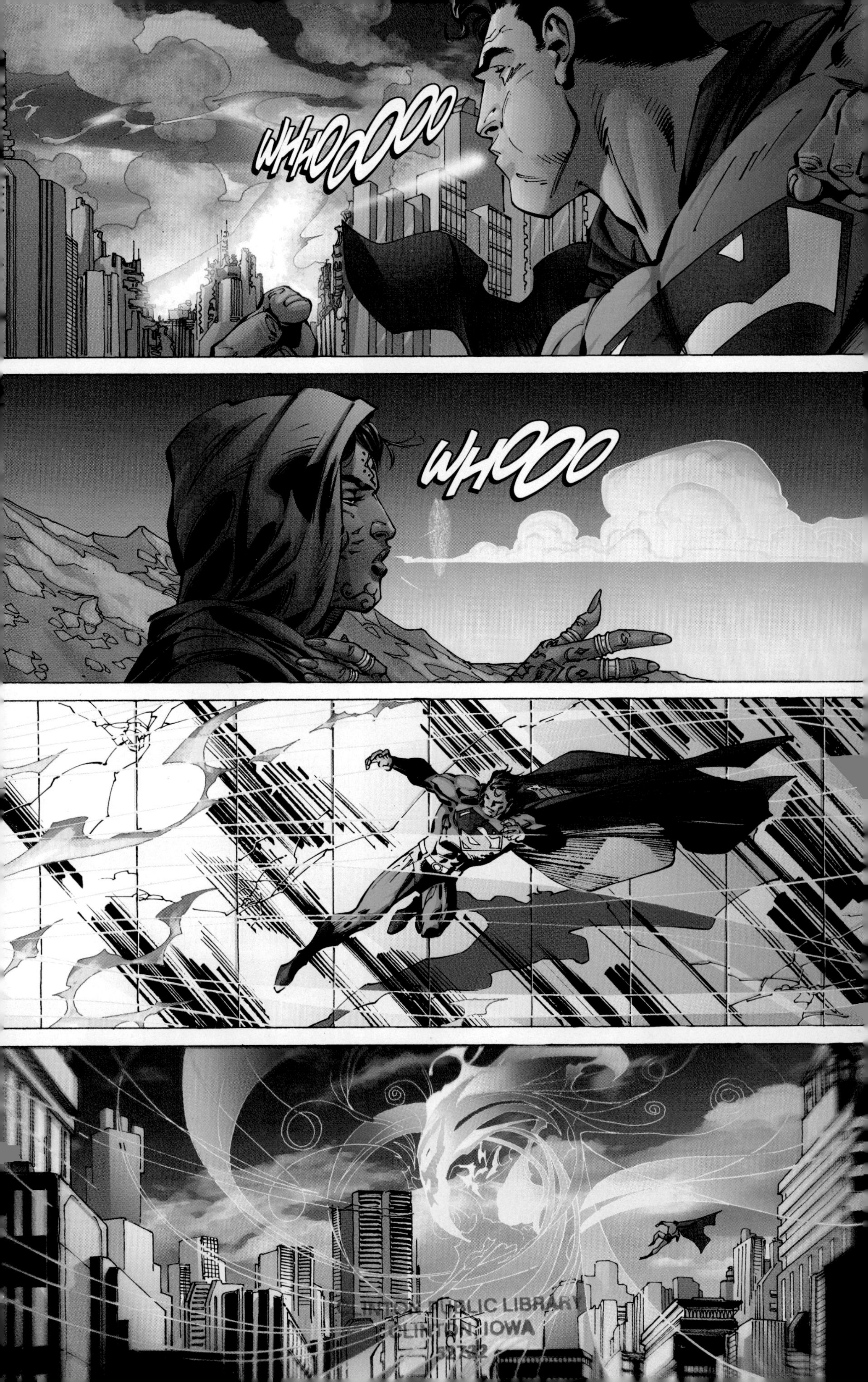
WHHOOOOOO
WHOOO

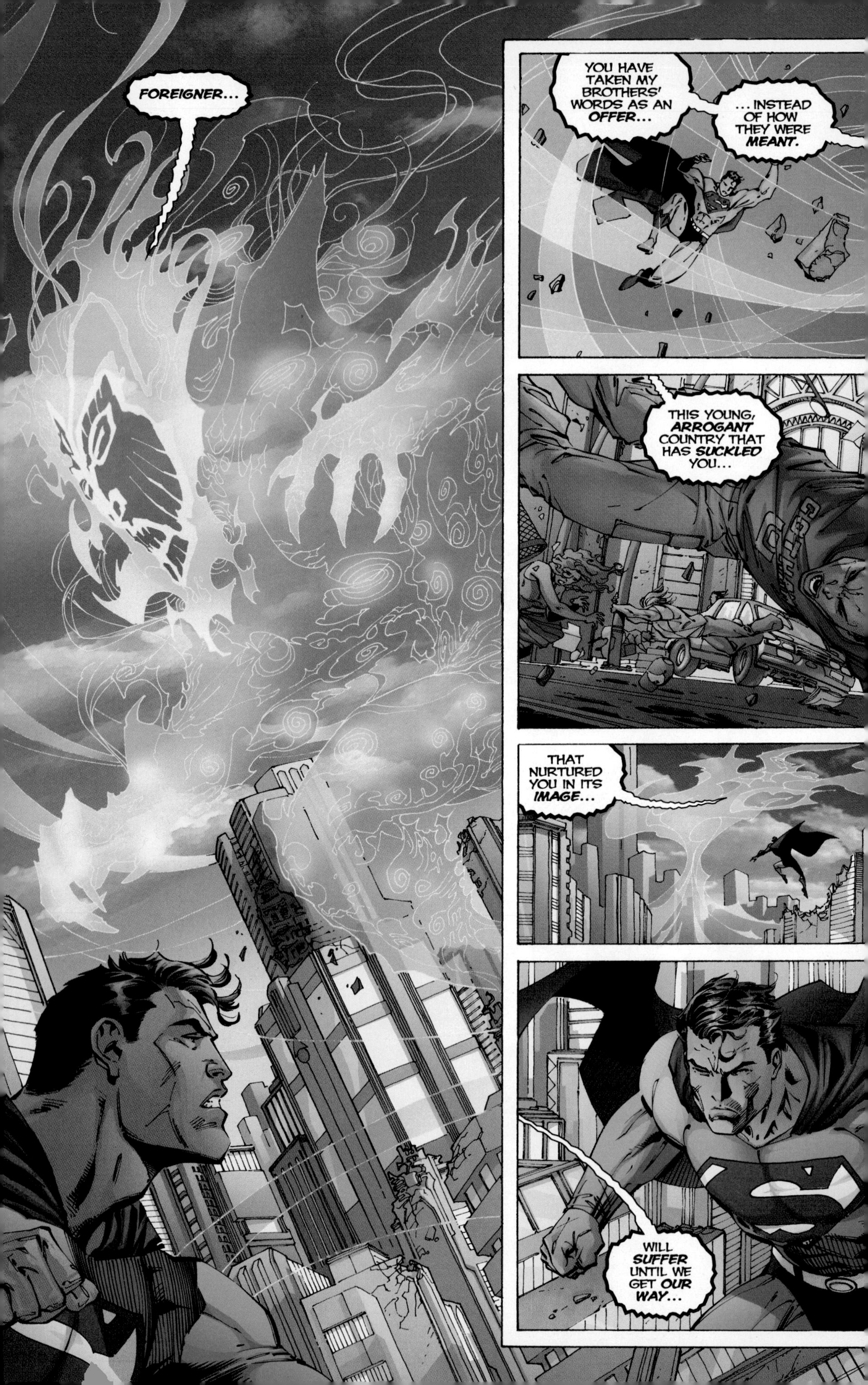
FOREIGNER...
YOU HAVE TAKEN MY BROTHERS' WORDS AS AN OFFER...
...INSTEAD OF HOW THEY WERE MEANT.
THIS YOUNG, ARROGANT COUNTRY THAT HAS SUCKLED YOU...
THAT NURTURED YOU IN ITS IMAGE...
WILL SUFFER UNTIL WE GET OUR WAY...

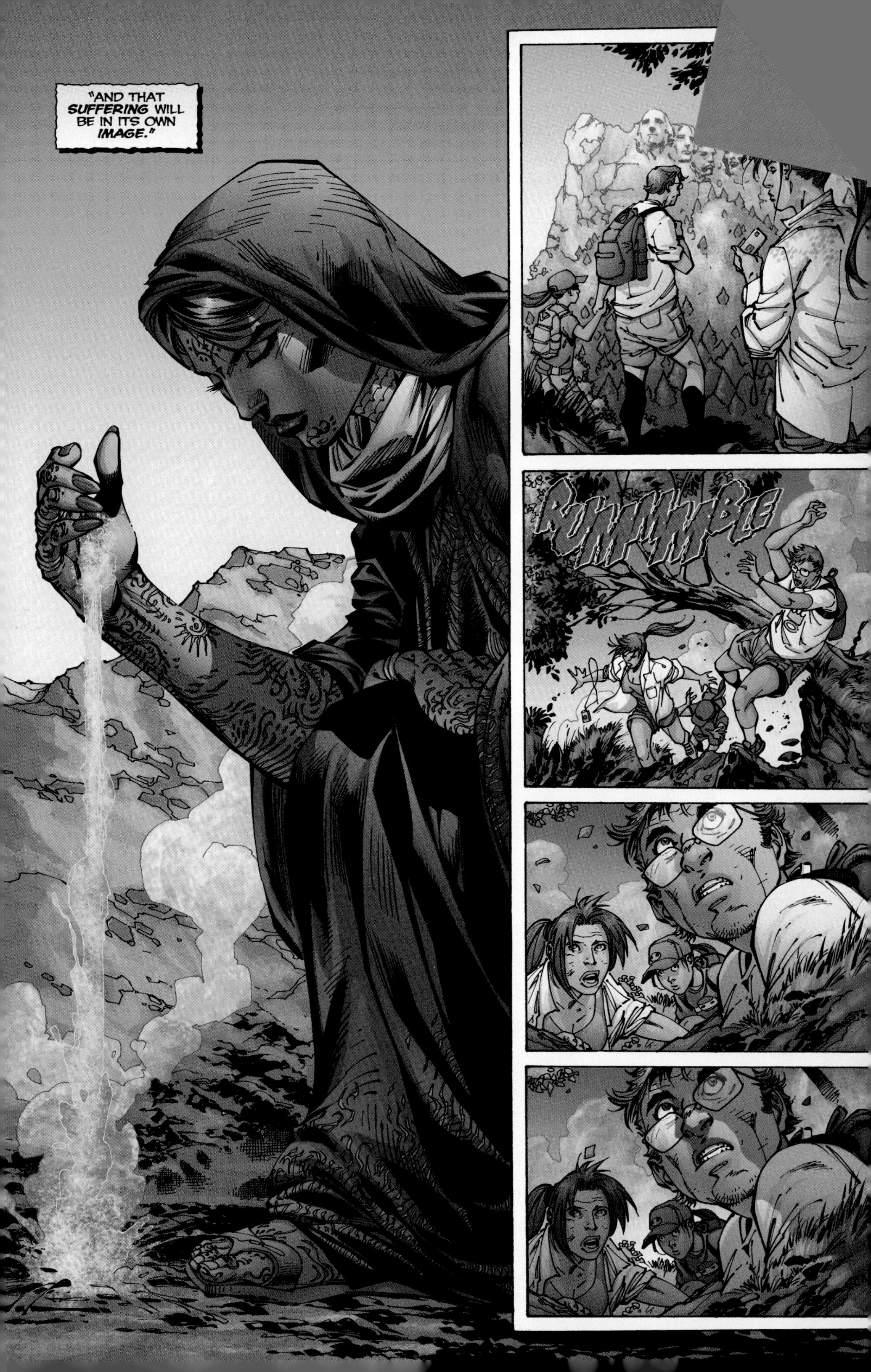
"AND THAT SUFFERING WILL BE IN ITS OWN IMAGE."
RUMMMMBLE

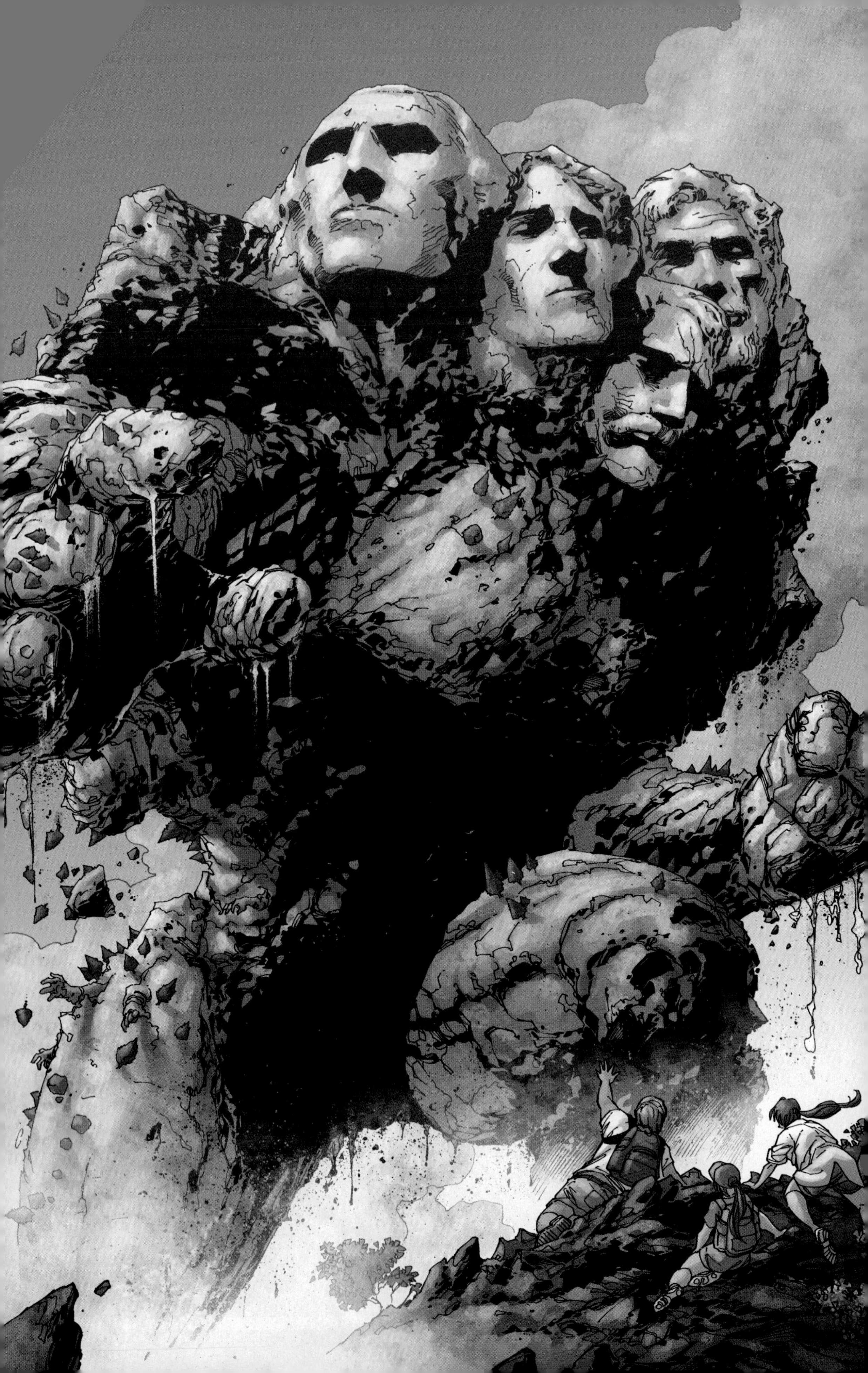

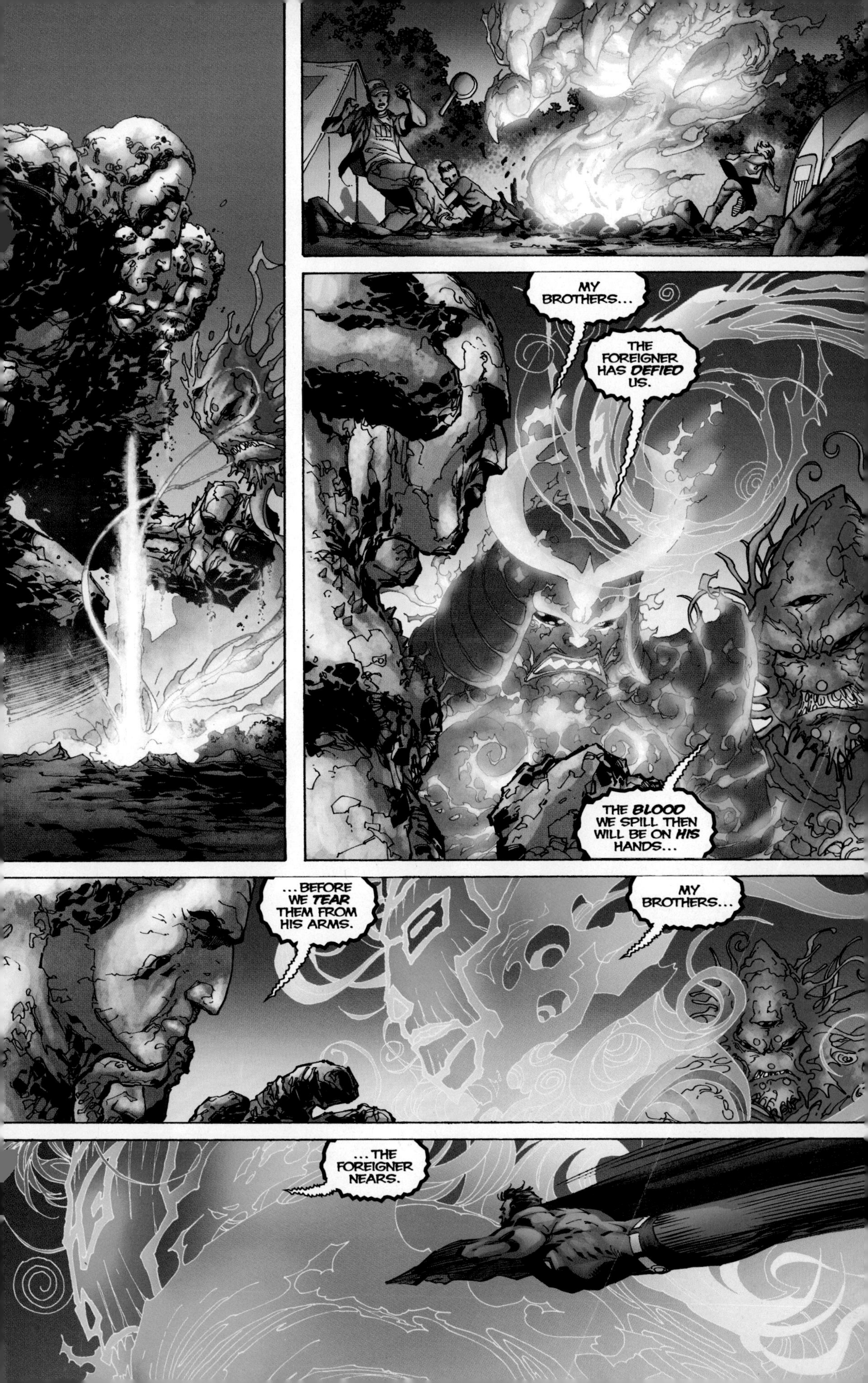
MY BROTHERS...
THE FOREIGNER HAS DEFIED US.
THE BLOOD WE SPILL THEN WILL BE ON HIS HANDS...
...BEFORE WE TEAR THEM FROM HIS ARMS.
MY BROTHERS...
...THE FOREIGNER NEARS.

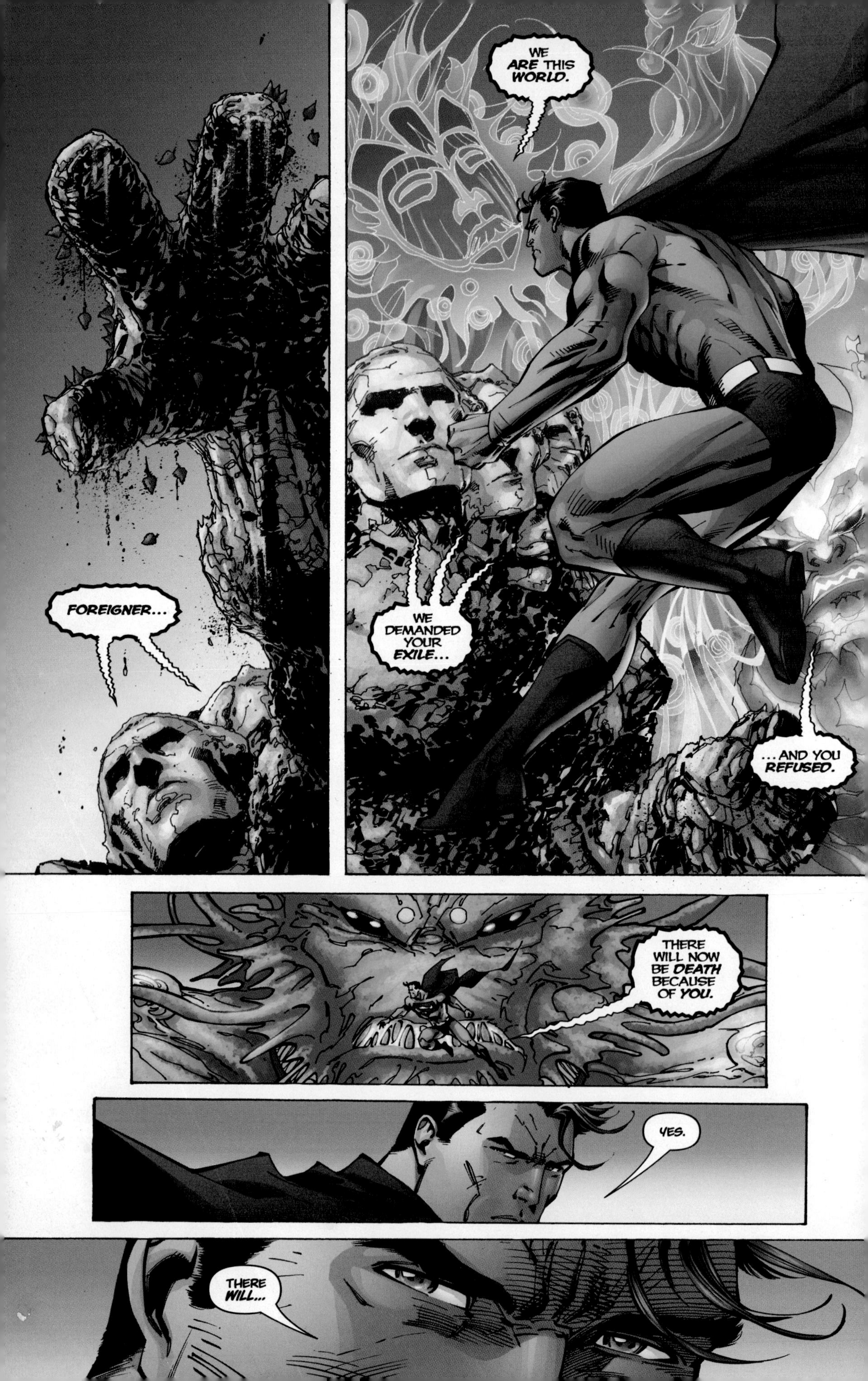
FOREIGNER...
WE ARE THIS WORLD.
WE DEMANDED YOUR EXILE...
...AND YOU REFUSED.
THERE WILL NOW BE DEATH BECAUSE OF YOU.
YES.
THERE WILL...

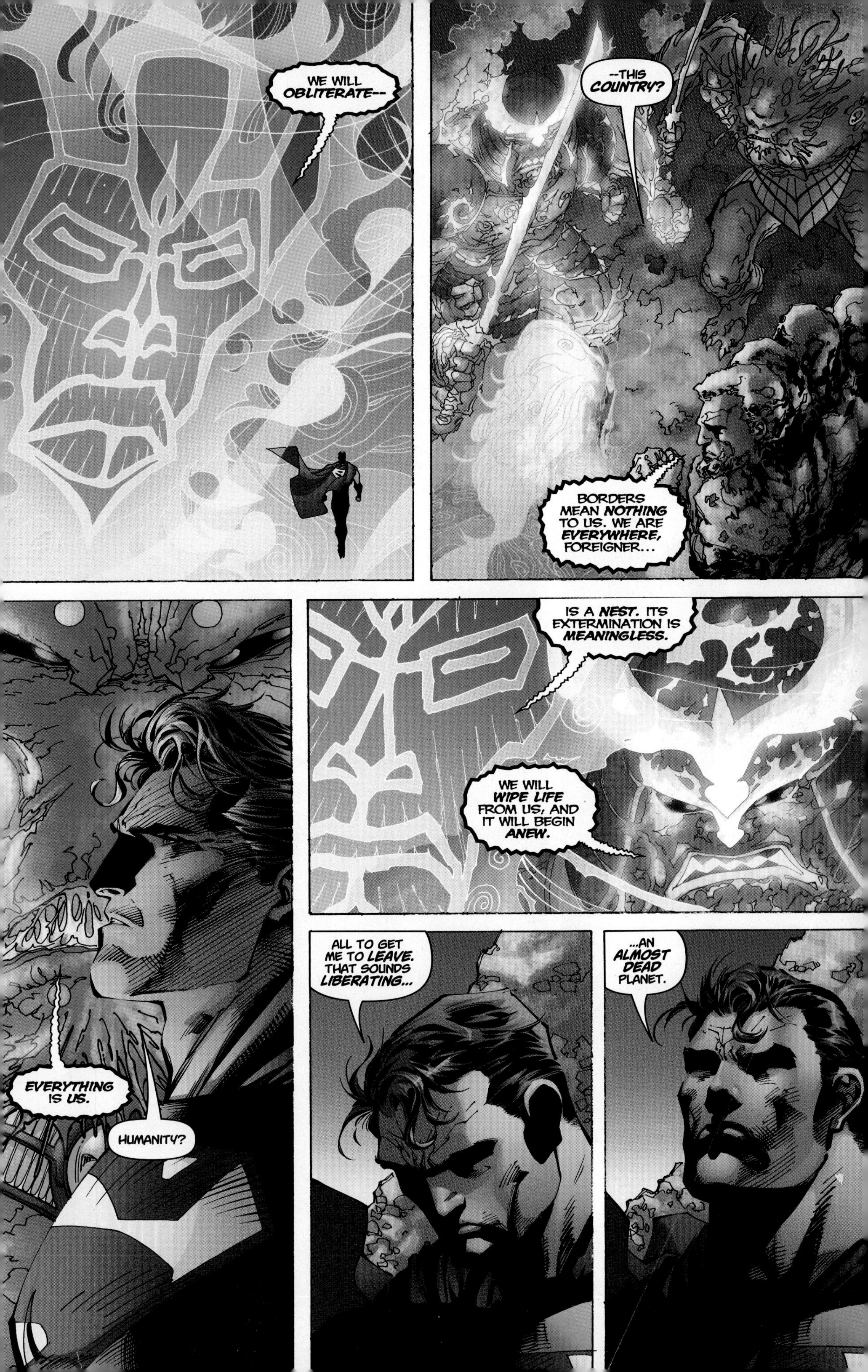
WE WILL OBLITERATE--
--THIS COUNTRY?
BORDERS MEAN NOTHING TO US. WE ARE EVERYWHERE, FOREIGNER...
IS A NEST. ITS EXTERMINATION IS MEANINGLESS.
WE WILL WIPE LIFE FROM US, AND IT WILL BEGIN ANEW.
EVERYTHING IS US.
HUMANITY?
ALL TO GET ME TO LEAVE. THAT SOUNDS LIBERATING...
...AN ALMOST DEAD PLANET.

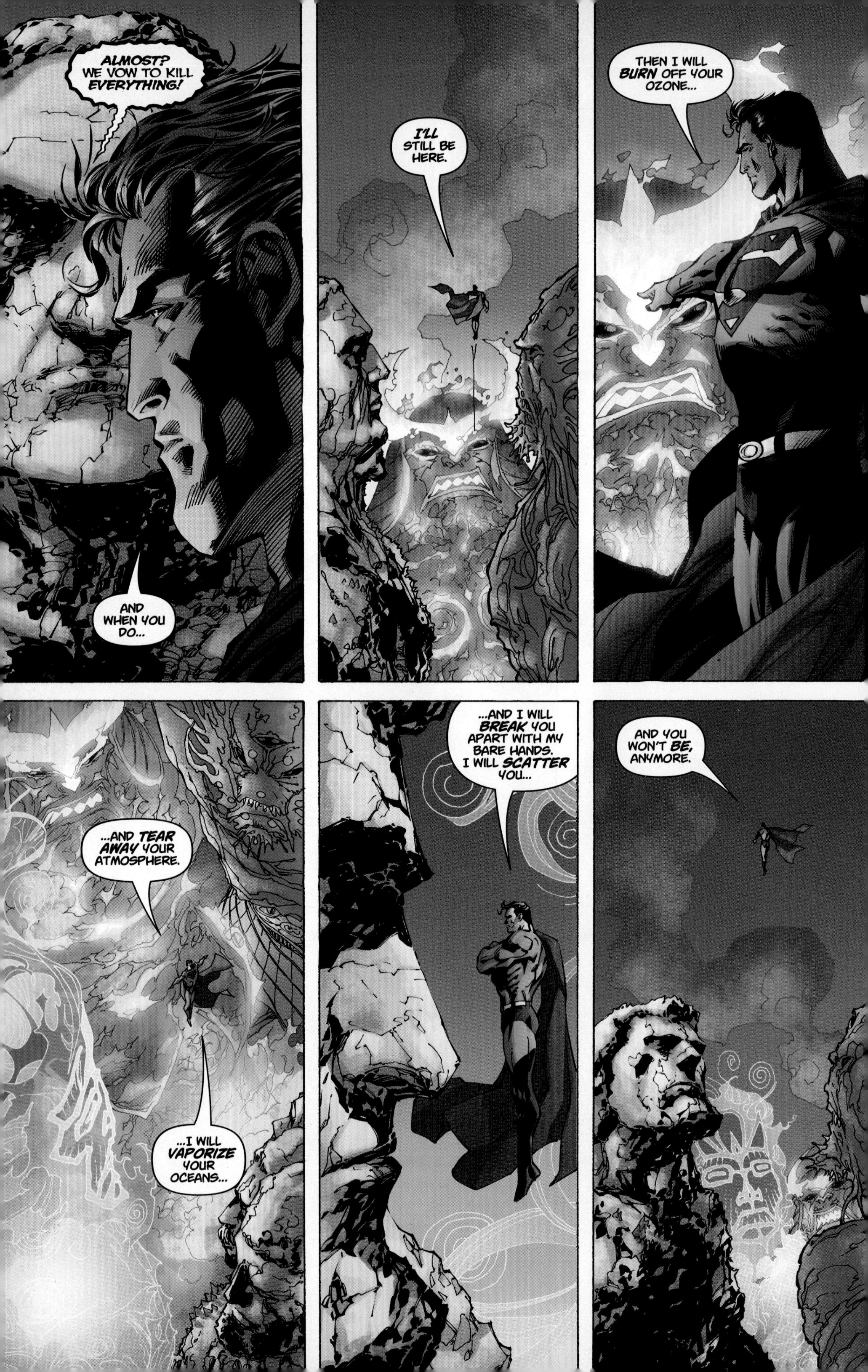
ALMOST? WE VOW TO KILL EVERYTHING!
AND WHEN YOU DO...
I'LL STILL BE HERE.
THEN I WILL BURN OFF YOUR OZONE...
...AND TEAR AWAY YOUR ATMOSPHERE.
...I WILL VAPORIZE YOUR OCEANS...
...AND I WILL BREAK YOU APART WITH MY BARE HANDS. I WILL SCATTER YOU...
AND YOU WON'T BE, ANYMORE.

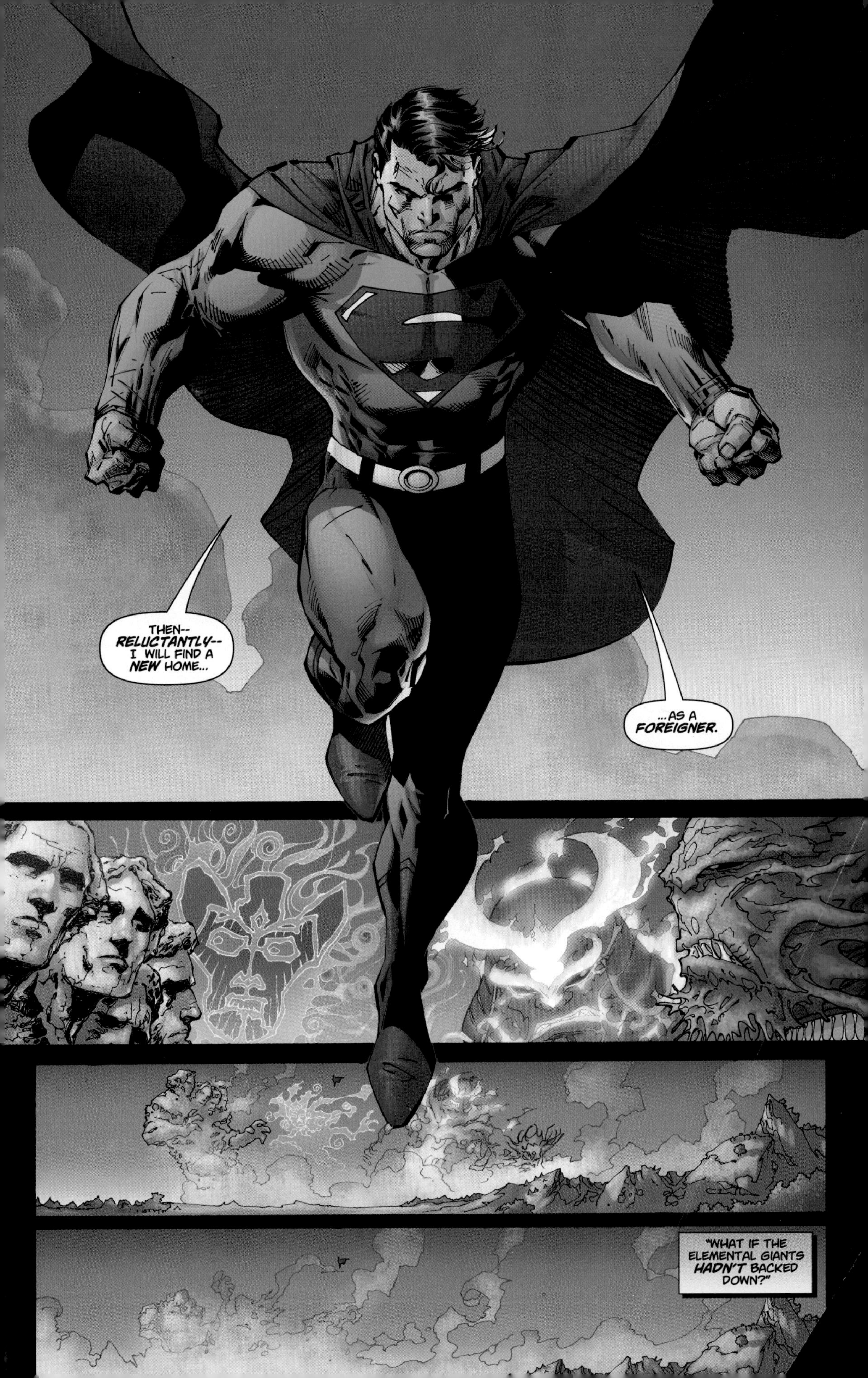
THEN-- RELUCTANTLY-- I WILL FIND A NEW HOME...
...AS A FOREIGNER.
"WHAT IF THE ELEMENTAL GIANTS HADN'T BACKED DOWN?"

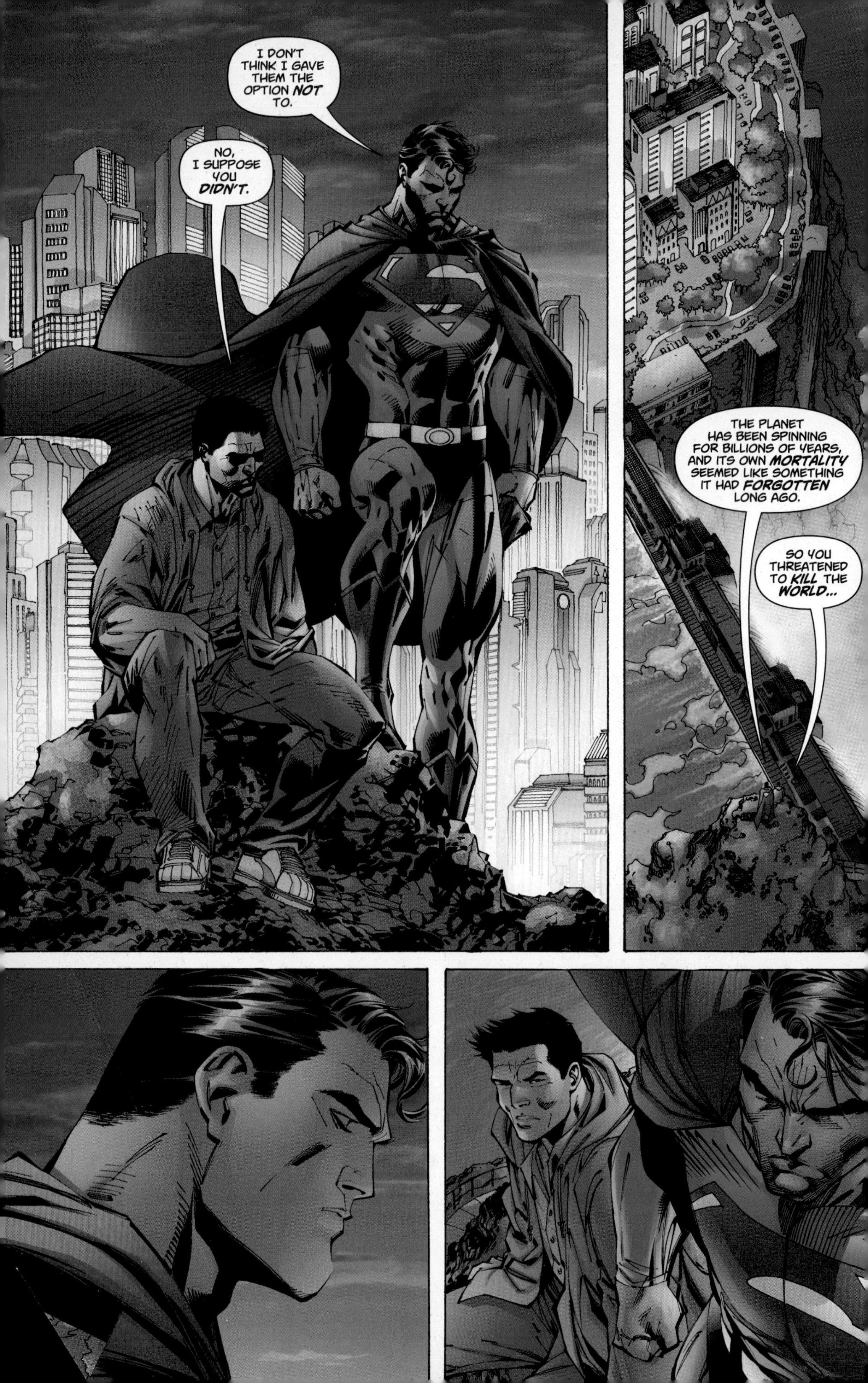
I DON'T THINK I GAVE THEM THE OPTION NOT TO.
NO, I SUPPOSE YOU DIDN'T.
THE PLANET HAS BEEN SPINNING FOR BILLIONS OF YEARS, AND ITS OWN MORTALITY SEEMED LIKE SOMETHING IT HAD FORGOTTEN LONG AGO.
SO YOU THREATENED TO KILL THE WORLD...

"...WOULD YOU HAVE DONE IT?"

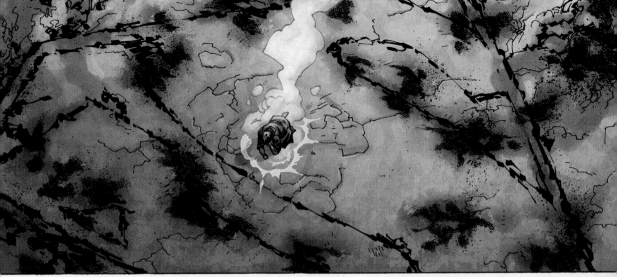

SISTER...

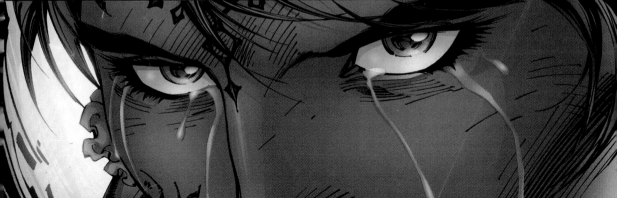

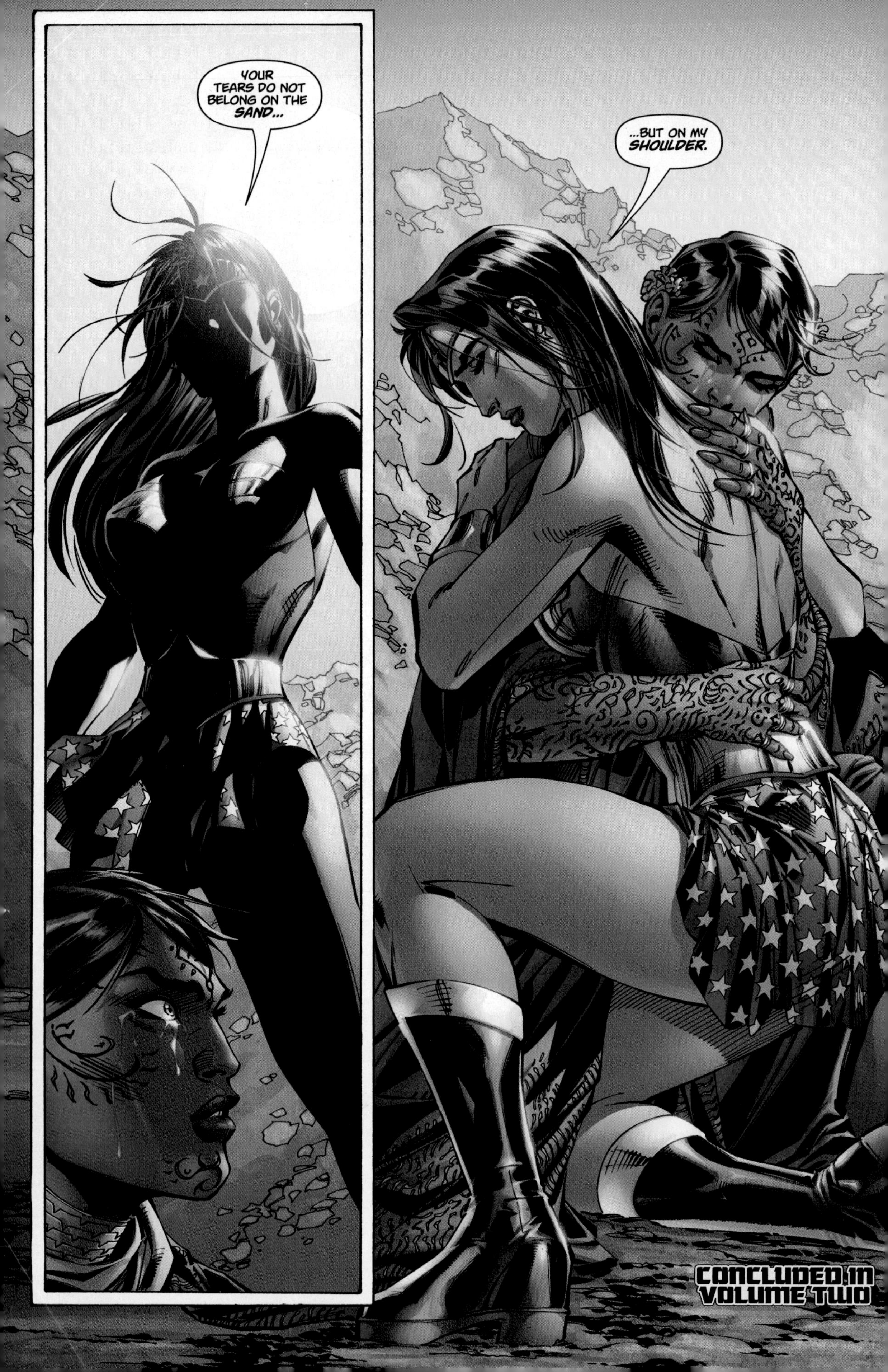
YOUR TEARS DO NOT BELONG ON THE SAND...
...BUT ON MY SHOULDER.
CONCLUDED IN VOLUME TWO

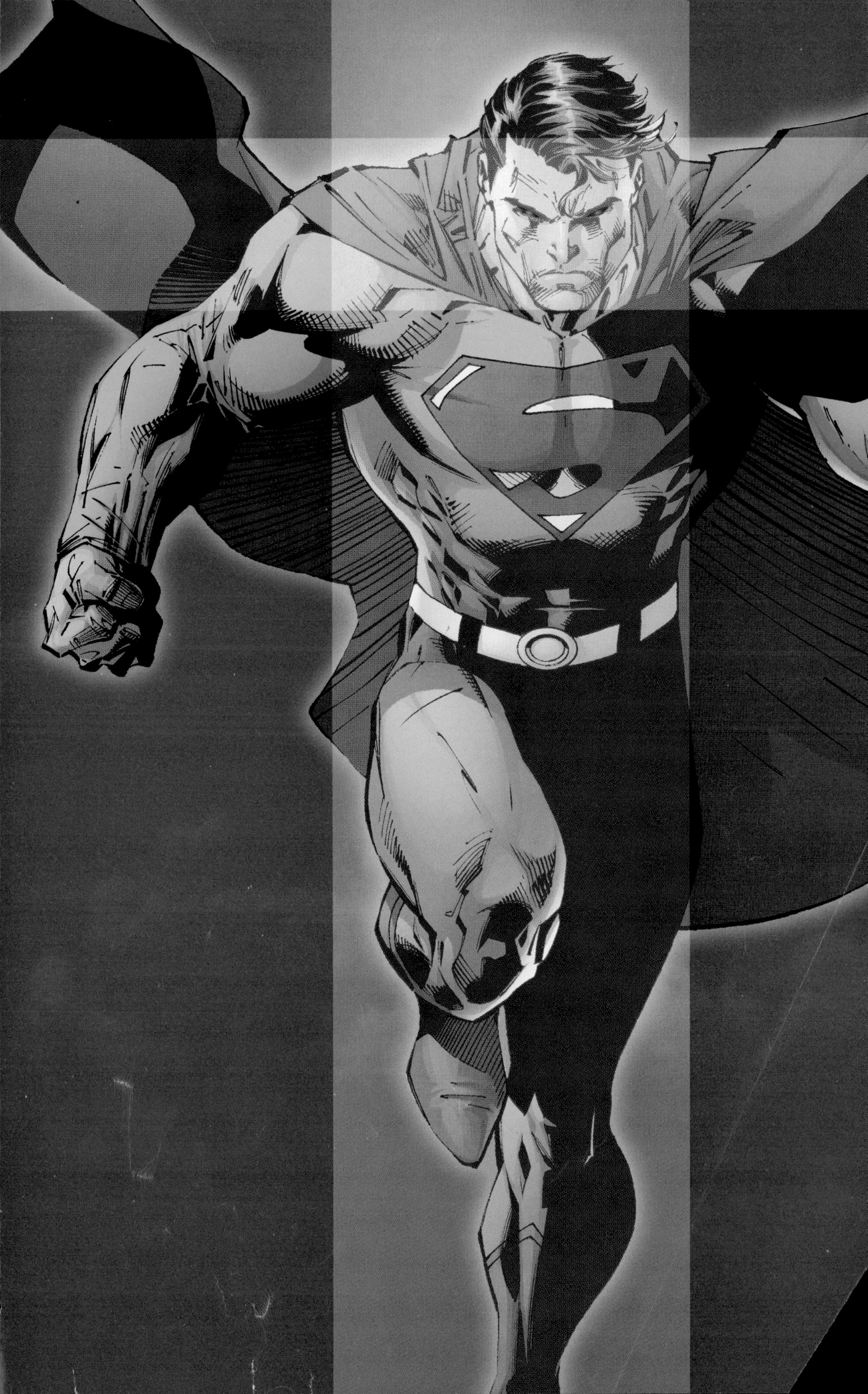

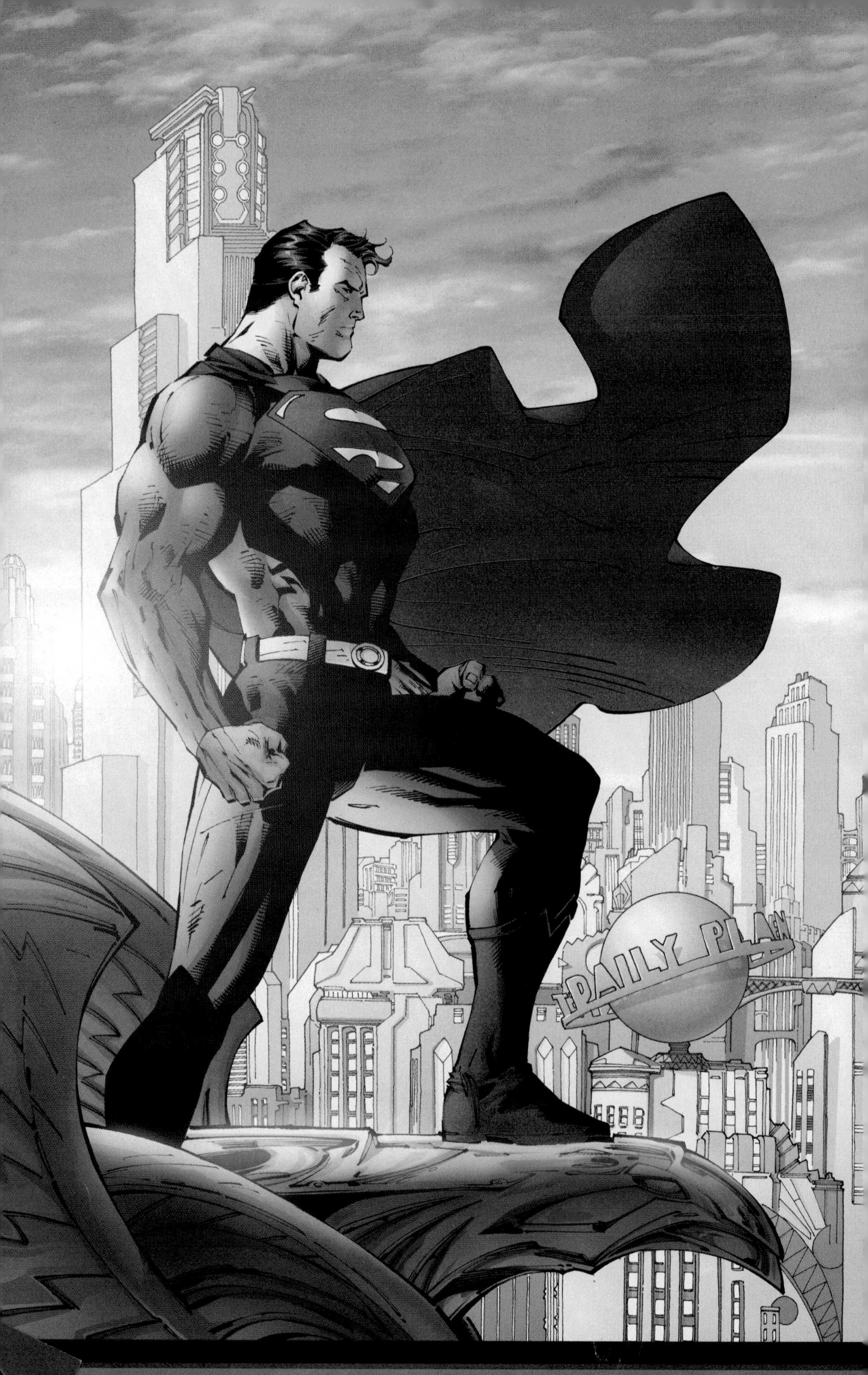
DAILY

ERMAN #204 ★ ART BY JIM LEE & SCOTT WILLIAMS WITH ALEX SINCLAIR

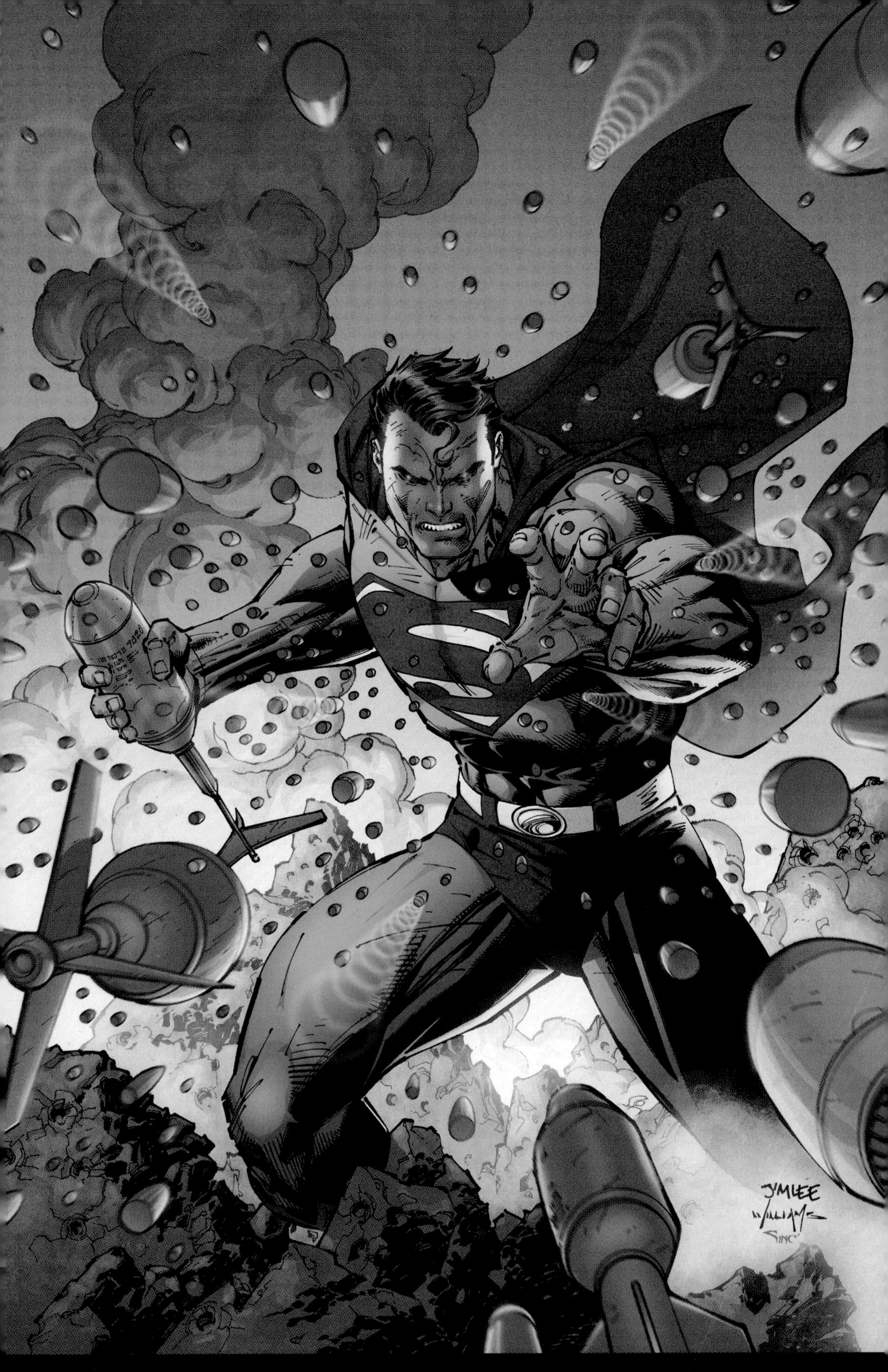

SUPERMAN #205 ★ ART BY JIM LEE & SCOTT WILLIAMS WITH ALEX SINCLAIR

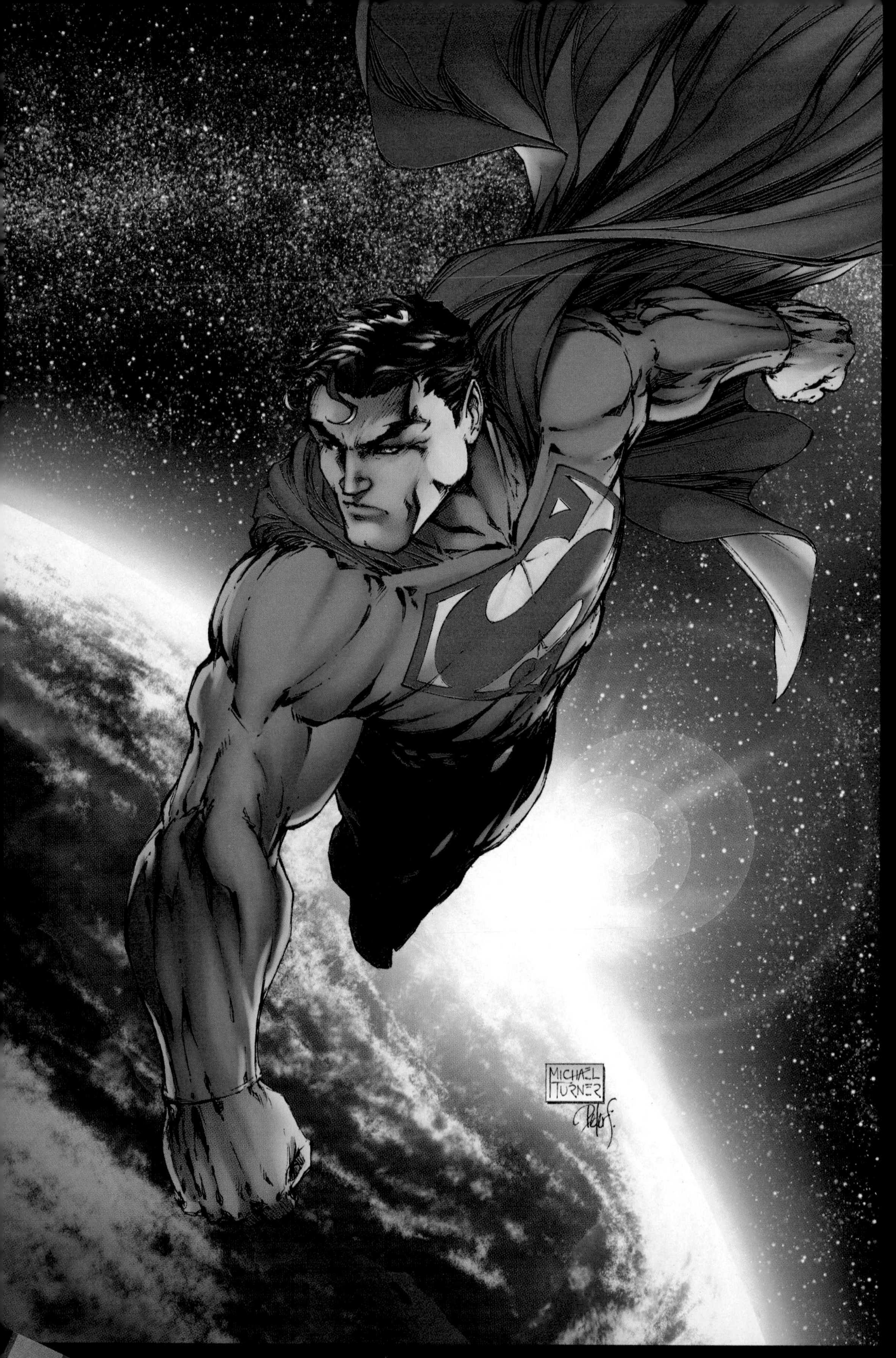
MICHAEL TURNER

RMAN #205 VARIANT COVER ★ ART BY MICHAEL TURNER WITH PETER STEIGERWALD

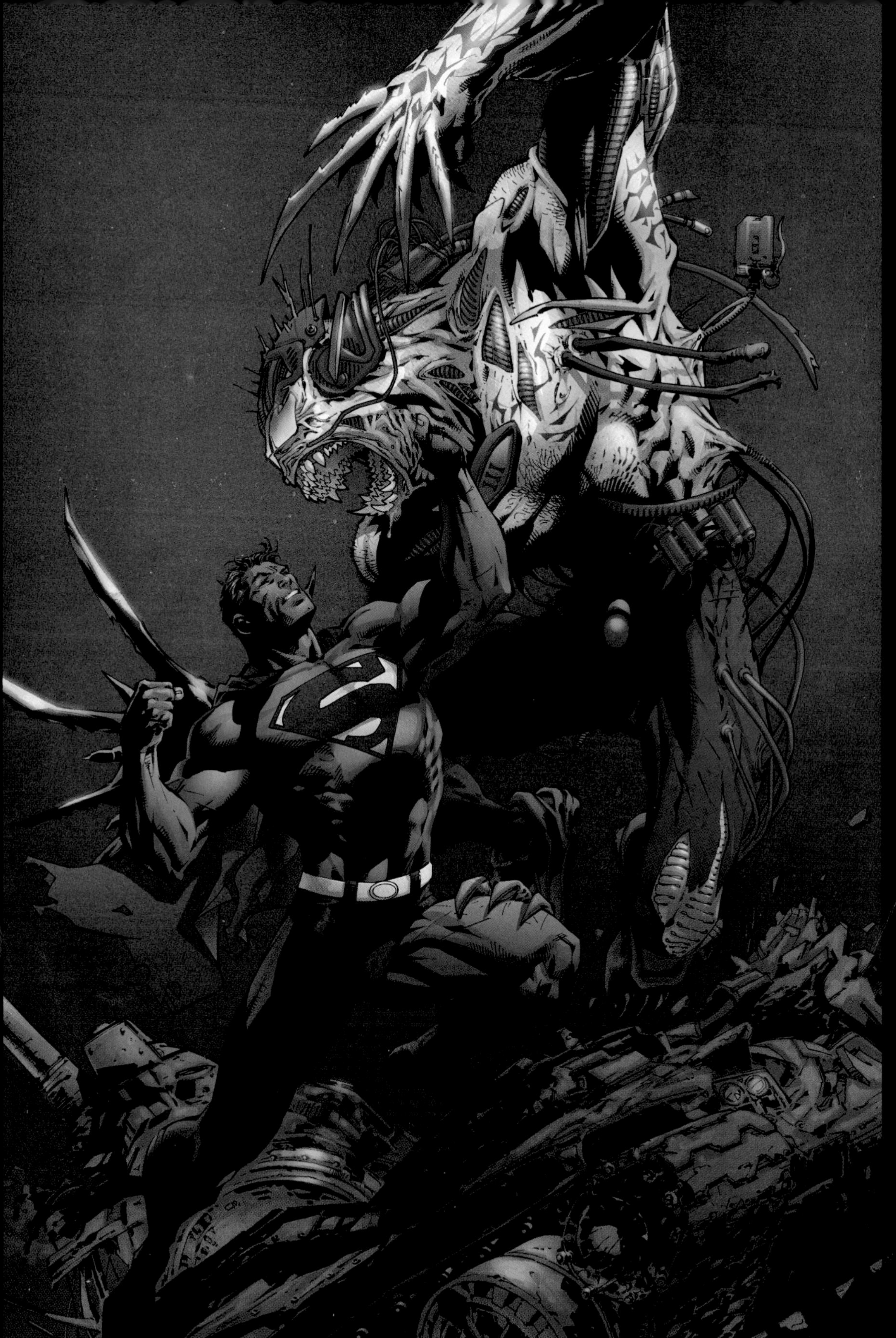

SUPERMAN #206 ★ ART BY JIM LEE & SCOTT WILLIAMS WITH ALEX SINCLAIR

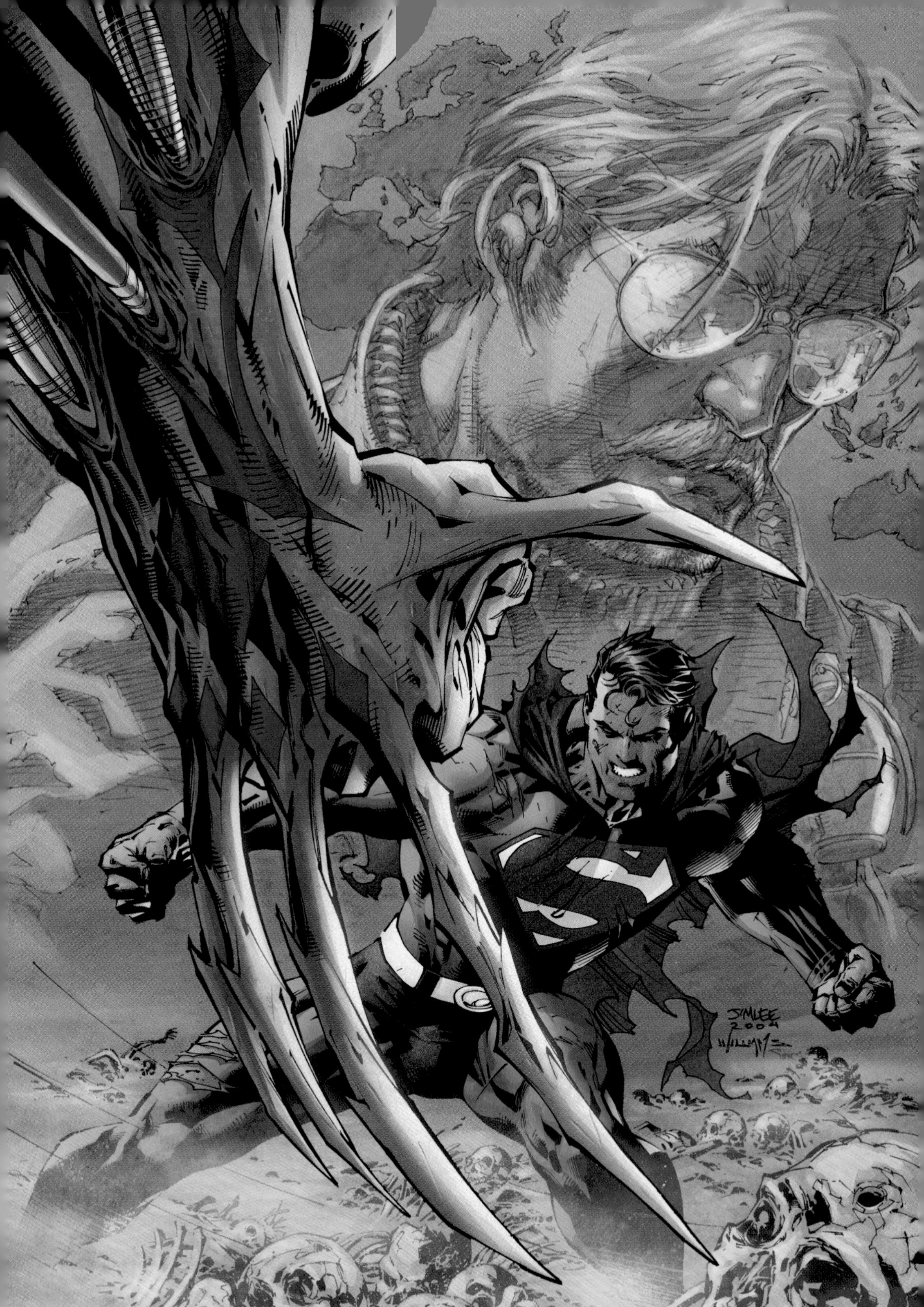
JIMLEE 2004

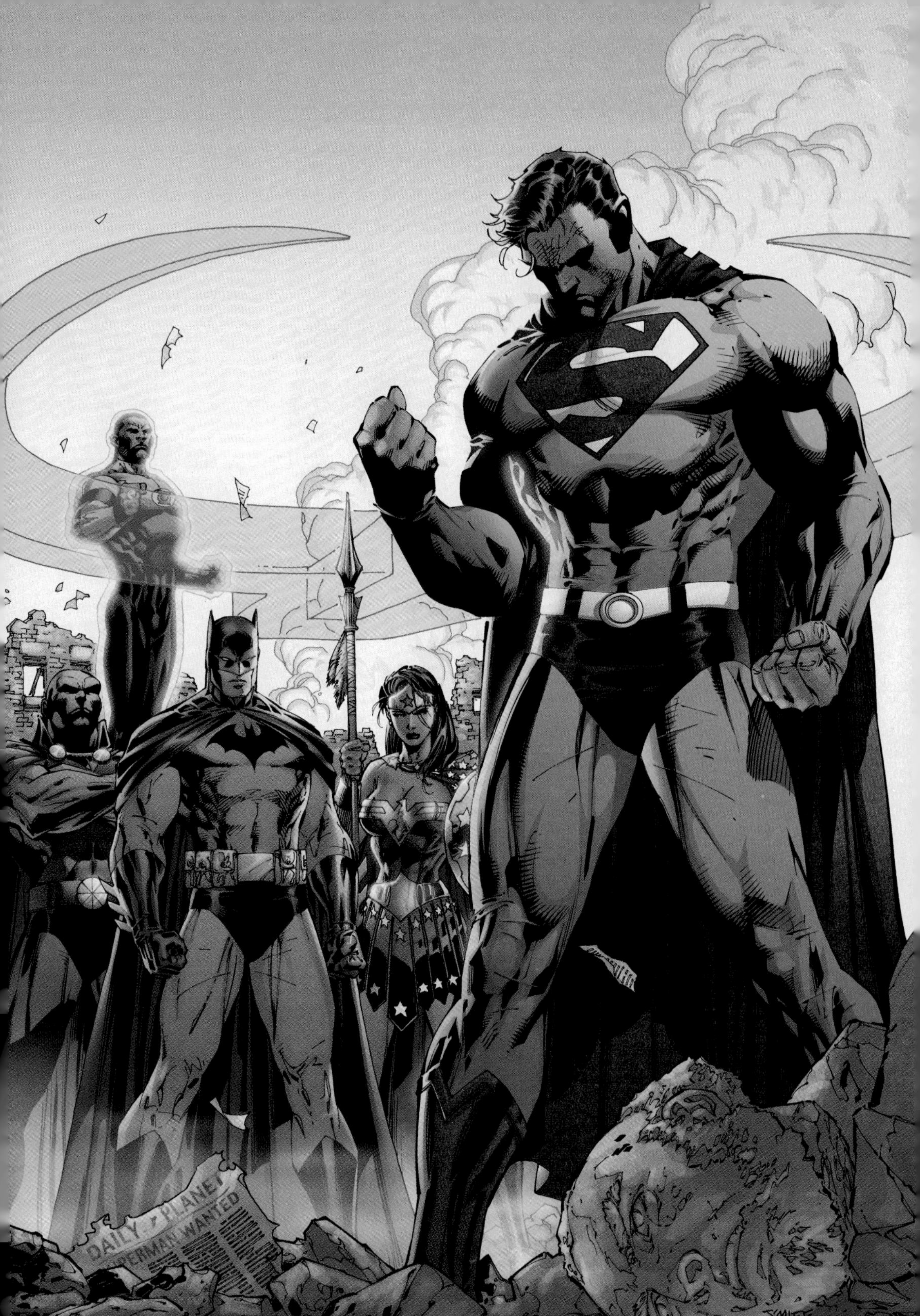
DAILY PLANET
WANTED

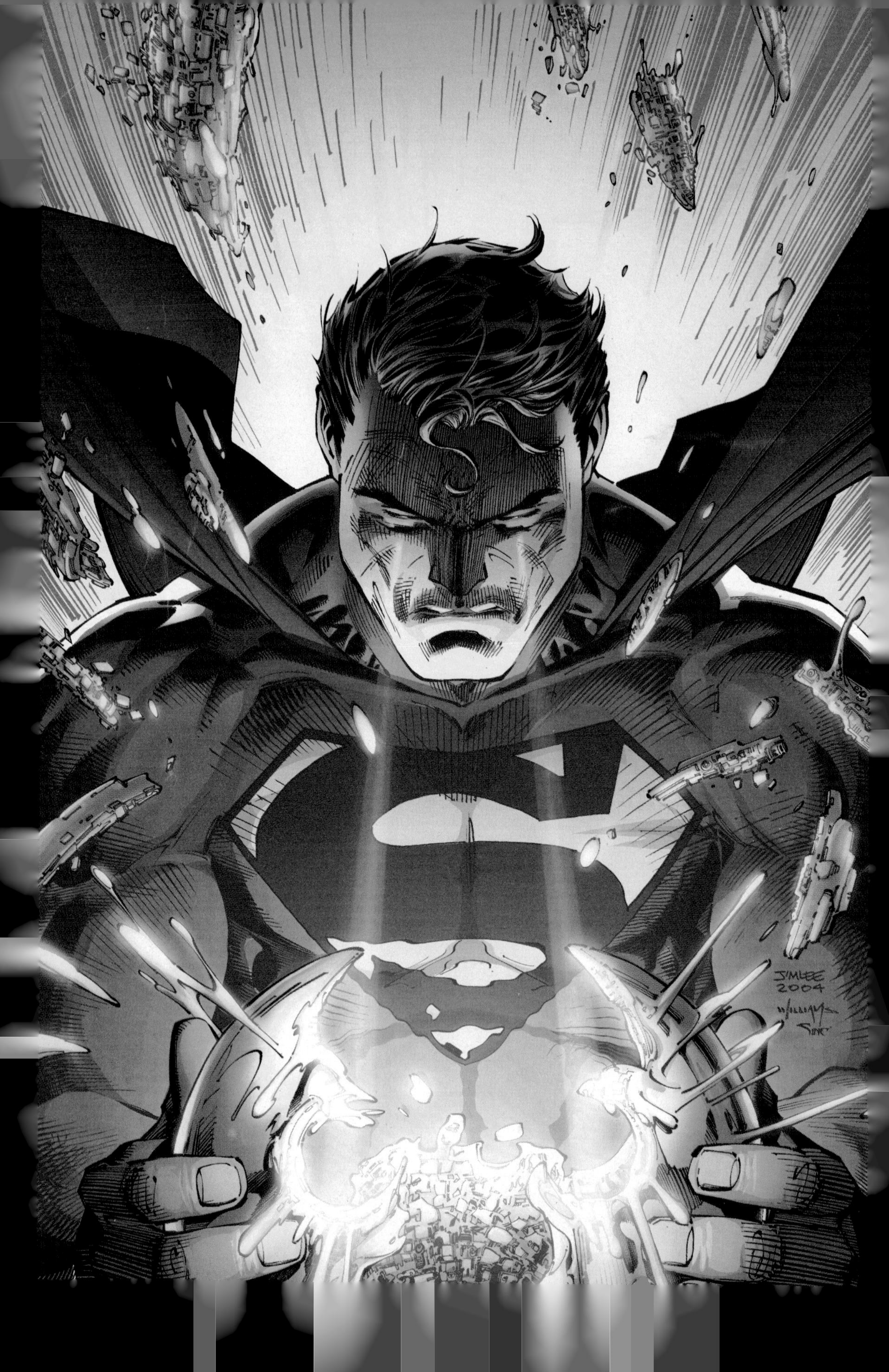
JIMLEE
2004

# SKETCHBOOK

## BY JIM LEE

During the BATMAN: HUSH run, I had a chance to draw Superman but I didn't always feel comfortable working with the character. Working up sketches before diving into sequential work gives me a chance to ask different questions and explore different answers. In other words, it's a chance to experiment with different looks, different takes on the character before making the final decisions on the pages themselves. His costume is more challenging to draw than, say, Batman because of the primary colors and because it's fairly unadorned with gadgets or doohickeys. Big belts, collars and masks make it easier to draw characters because they hide seamlines, hide details and give the artist more elements to play with.

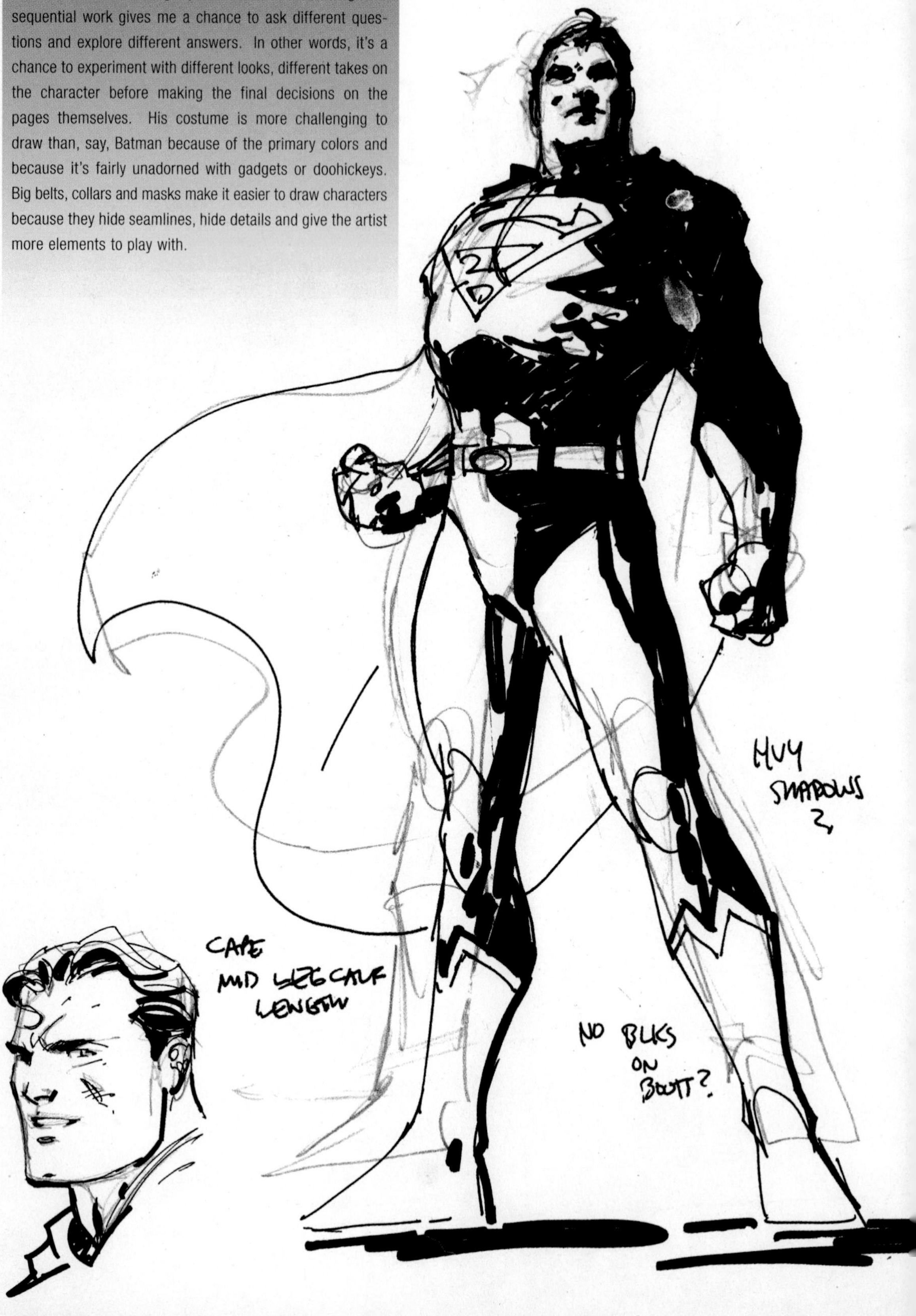
HVY SHADOWS ?
CAPE
MID LEG CALF
LENGTH
NO BLKS ON BOOT?

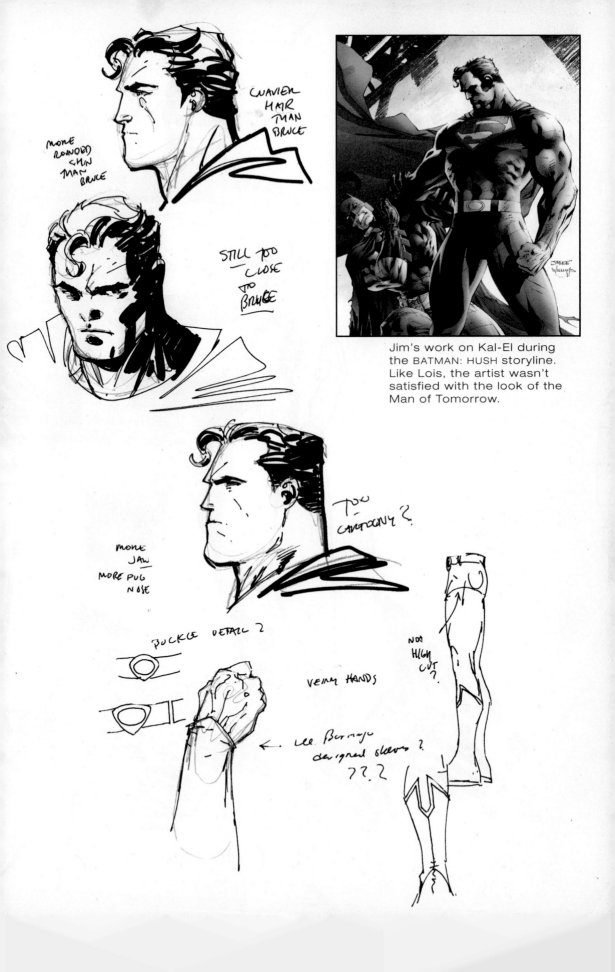

CURLIER HAIR THAN BRUCE

MORE ROUNDED CHIN THAN BRUCE

STILL TOO CLOSE TO BRUCE

Jim's work on Kal-El during the BATMAN: HUSH storyline. Like Lois, the artist wasn't satisfied with the look of the Man of Tomorrow.

TOO CARTOONY?

MORE JAW MORE PUG NOSE

BUCKLE DETAIL?

VEINY HANDS

NOT HIGH CUT?

← Lee Bermejo designed sleeves? ??.?

For the most part, Superman's costume is a nude body with lines at the wrist, collar, waist, legs and thighs. The cape is the only element you get to play with, either as a hiding element or to create a different overall silhouette for the character. In any design or drawing, if you are going to add shadows, you have to decide whether the shadow only affects certain colors — say, Superman's blues or his blues and reds — or if it will be more like real-life shadows and cut across any and all elements — for example, Superman's chest emblem. The problem with the latter is that you are then obscuring his world-famous chest symbol which is probably the most powerful element of his costume.

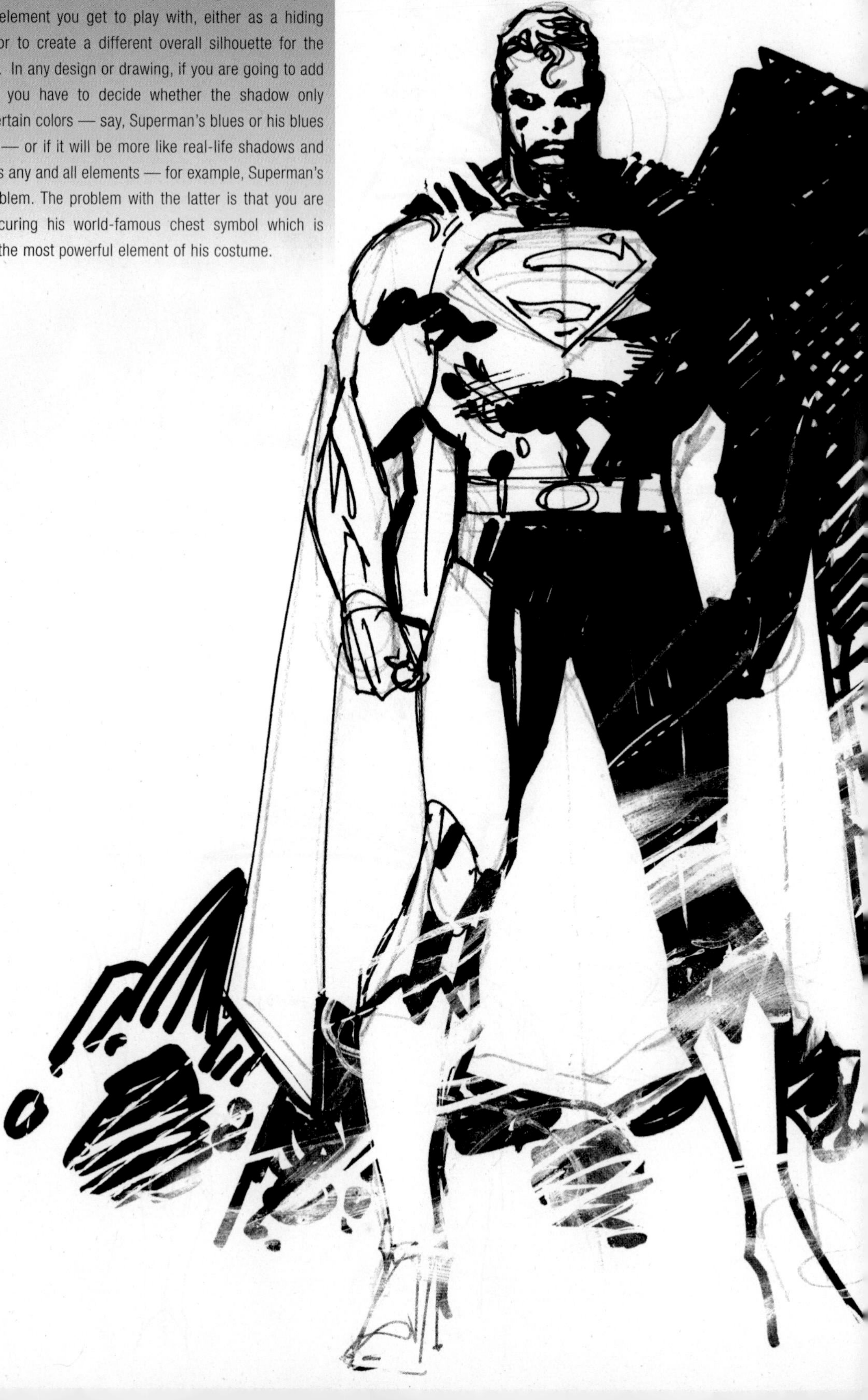

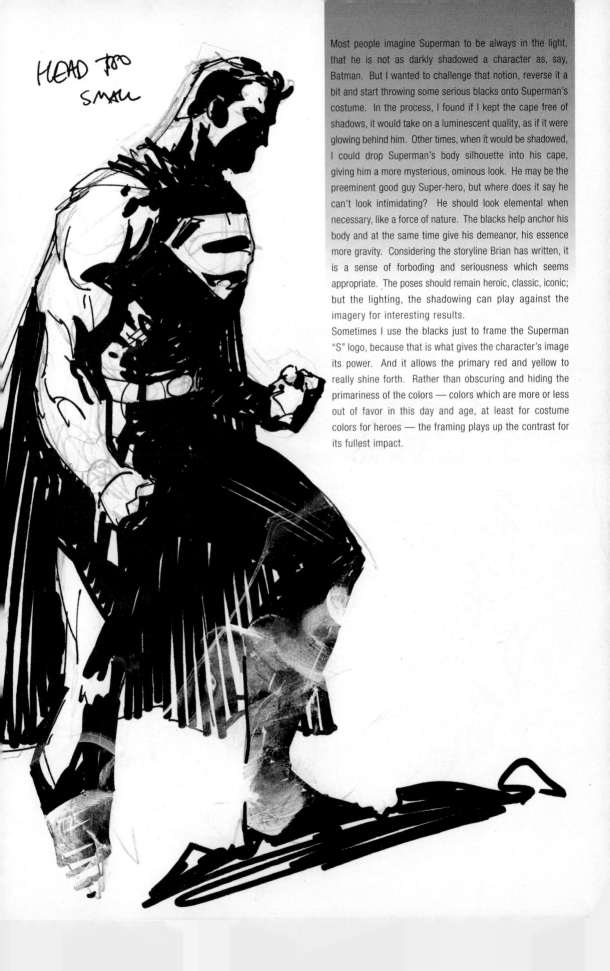

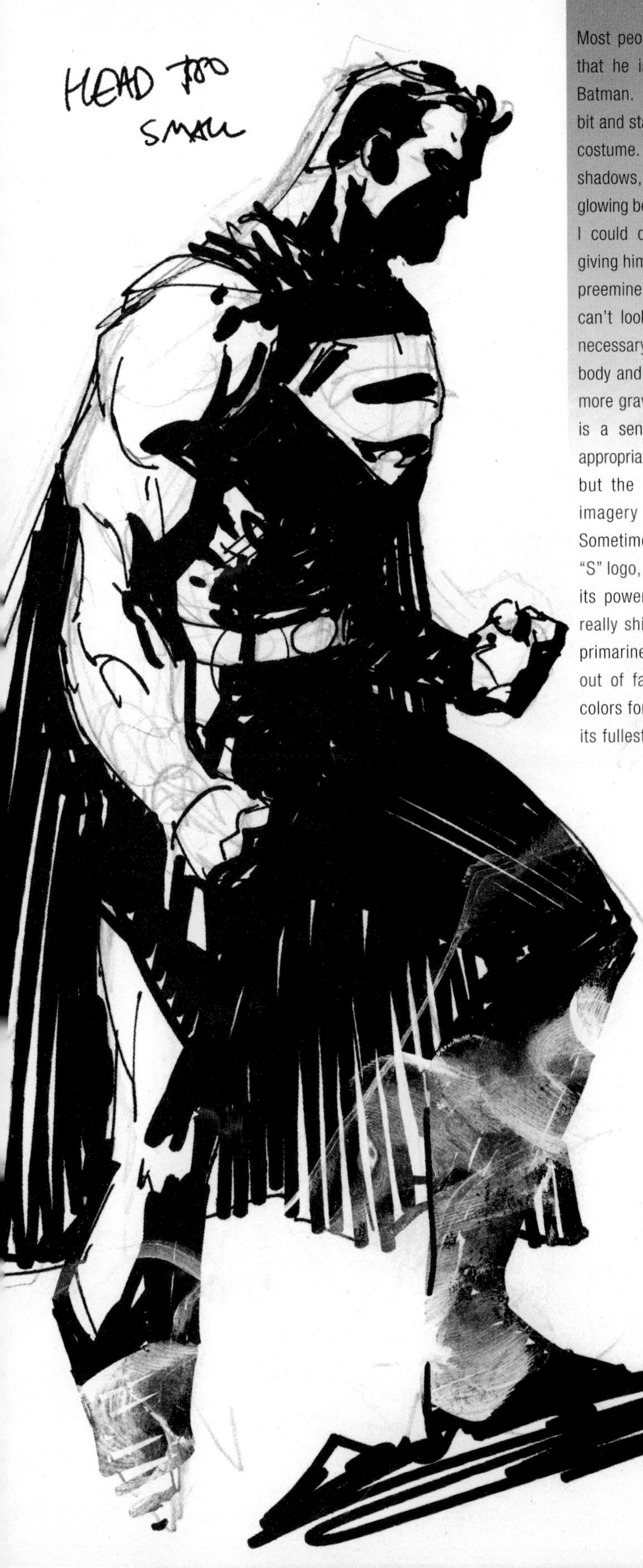
HEAD TOO
SMALL

Most people imagine Superman to be always in the light, that he is not as darkly shadowed a character as, say, Batman. But I wanted to challenge that notion, reverse it a bit and start throwing some serious blacks onto Superman's costume. In the process, I found if I kept the cape free of shadows, it would take on a luminescent quality, as if it were glowing behind him. Other times, when it would be shadowed, I could drop Superman's body silhouette into his cape, giving him a more mysterious, ominous look. He may be the preeminent good guy Super-hero, but where does it say he can't look intimidating? He should look elemental when necessary, like a force of nature. The blacks help anchor his body and at the same time give his demeanor, his essence more gravity. Considering the storyline Brian has written, it is a sense of forboding and seriousness which seems appropriate. The poses should remain heroic, classic, iconic; but the lighting, the shadowing can play against the imagery for interesting results.

Sometimes I use the blacks just to frame the Superman "S" logo, because that is what gives the character's image its power. And it allows the primary red and yellow to really shine forth. Rather than obscuring and hiding the primariness of the colors — colors which are more or less out of favor in this day and age, at least for costume colors for heroes — the framing plays up the contrast for its fullest impact.

I also tinkered around with certain elements of his costume which I may gradually modify over the course of the run. Rather than start with these slight modifications, they may happen more organically as the series progresses. Just like in HUSH, I imagine the Superman I draw in the final chapter will be very different from the first. Not just costumewise but in terms of the body's proportions, his sense of mass and in his lines.

It's part of the fun in working on a regular book — finding the character as you do the work. In many ways, he actually finds you as the creative process unfolds.

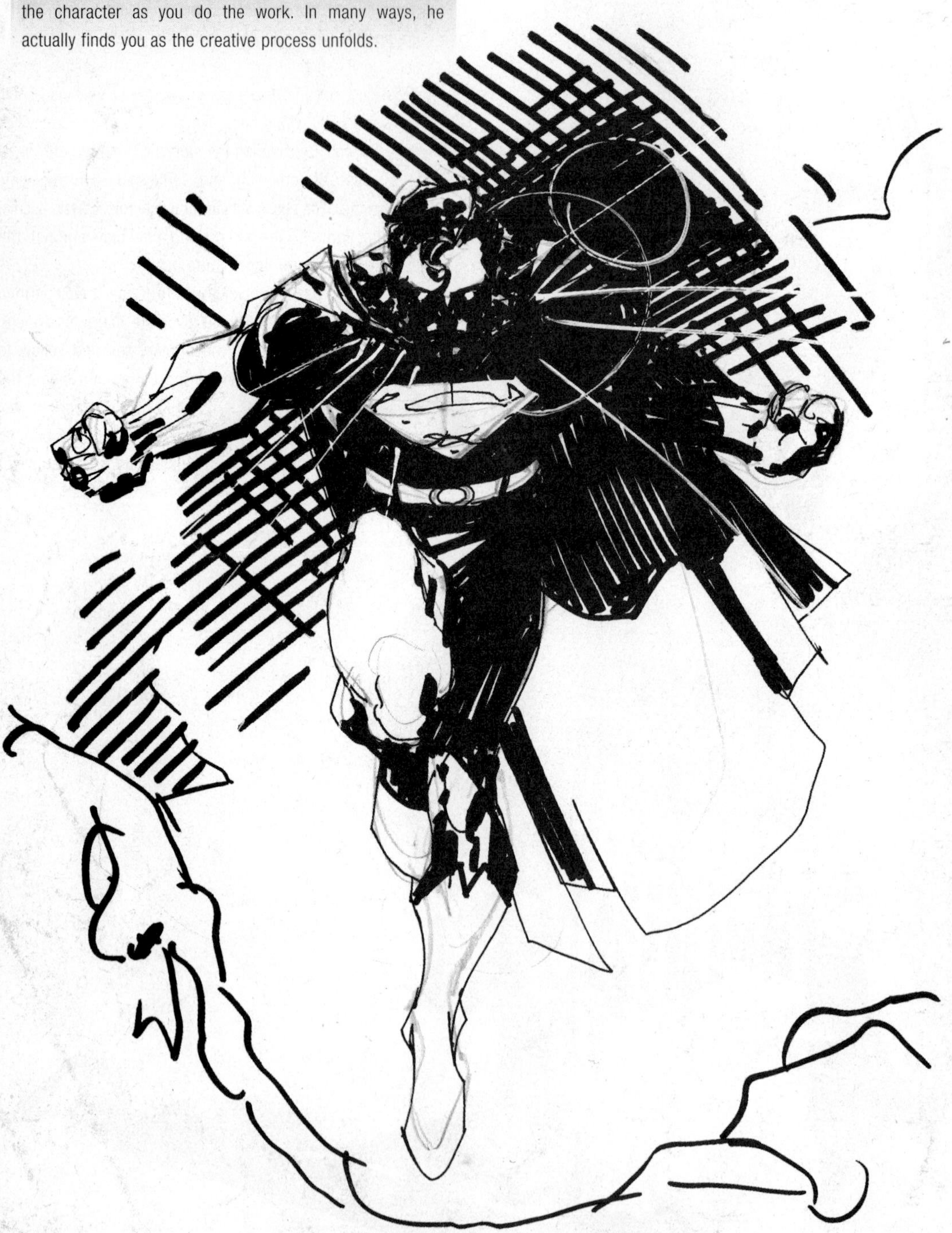

# BIOS

**BRIAN AZZARELLO** has been writing comics professionally since the mid-1990's. He is the writer and co-creator with Eduardo Risso of the acclaimed Vertigo monthly series 100 BULLETS, which won the 2002 Harvey Award as well as the 2002 and 2004 Eisner Award for best continuing series. Azzarello's other writing credits for DC Comics include BATMAN and JONNY DOUBLE (both with Risso), GANGLAND, BATMAN/DEATHBLOW, LEX LUTHOR: MAN OF STEEL, and an Eisner-nominated run on HELLBLAZER. He has also written *Cage* and *Banner* for Marvel Comics. Brian has been cited as one of *Wizard* magazine's top ten writers and has been profiled and/or reviewed in *Entertainment Weekly, GEAR, The Chicago Tribune,* and countless other publications. He lives in Chicago with his wife, artist Jill Thompson, and still does not have a website.

**JIM LEE** was born in Seoul, South Korea in 1964. He graduated from Princeton University with a degree in psychology but decided to try his hand at comic-book art — his childhood fantasy. He found work at Marvel Comics, where his work quickly proved so popular that the company created a new X-Men title just to show-case it. In 1992, Lee formed his own comics company, WildStorm Studios, which became one of the founding components of Image Comics. There, he launched the best-selling WILDC.A.T.S and helped to create many other characters. He also helped to discover and train a phalanx of writers, artists, and colorists. With its steady success, WildStorm as a business grew so demanding that Lee found he no longer had any time to draw, leading to his decision to sell the company to DC Comics. He remains WildStorm's creative director but now concentrates on his first love, art. He lives in La Jolla, California with his wife and three daughters.

**SCOTT WILLIAMS** has partnered with Jim Lee for more than ten years, and he was voted Favorite Inker for five years in a row (1990-94) in the Comics Buyer's Guide Fan Awards. His inking work can be found in BATMAN: HUSH, DANGER GIRL, GEN13, JUST IMAGINE STAN LEE..., WONDER WOMAN, WILDCATS/X-MEN, *X-Men: Mutant Genesis,* and *X-Men: X-Tinction Agenda.*

**ALEX SINCLAIR** has previously worked on KURT BUSIEK'S ASTRO CITY, TOP 10, HARLEY QUINN, and, with Jim Lee and Scott Williams, on WILDC.A.T.S, GEN13, DIVINE RIGHT; and BATMAN: HUSH. Sinclair lives in San Diego with his sidekick Rebecca and their four hench-girls: Grace, Blythe, Meredith, and Harley. He would love to fight crime, but the weather's too nice. Instead, Sinclair became an editor at WildStorm in the spring of 2003.

**ROB LEIGH** is a graduate of the The Joe Kubert School of Cartoon & Graphic Art. His lettering first received critical notice in 1972, when he was sent home with a note for writing a four-letter word on the blackboard of Miss Tuschmann's second-grade class. In addition to lettering, Rob has inked many titles for DC. He lives in northern New Jersey with his wife, Vaughan, and homicidal cat, Barley.

**NICK J. NAPOLITANO** is also a graduate of the Joe Kubert School. Nick has worked for DC Comics, in one capacity or another, for nearly 13 years. Having pencilled, inked, lettered, edited, etc., he has finally settled down to manage DC's In-House Lettering Department, where he spends his quiet days surrounded by eccentric artists and frantic editors (he wouldn't trade it for anything). He lives on Long Island with his wife, Christine, his dog, Buffy, and about 30-40 of his goombata.

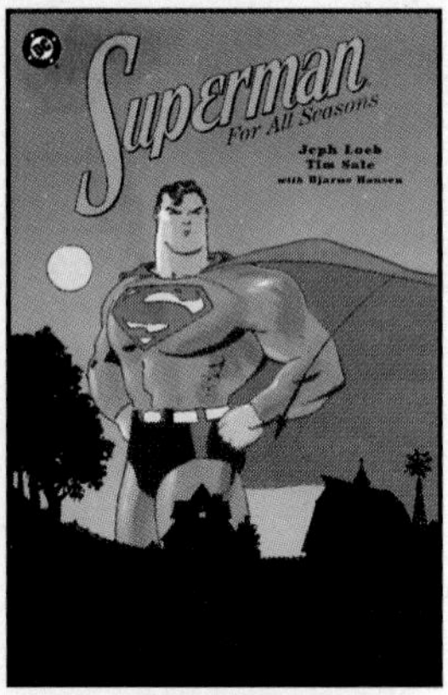
Superman
For All Seasons
Jeph Loeb
Tim Sale

SUPERMAN
FOR ALL SEASONS

Jeph Loeb/Tim Sale

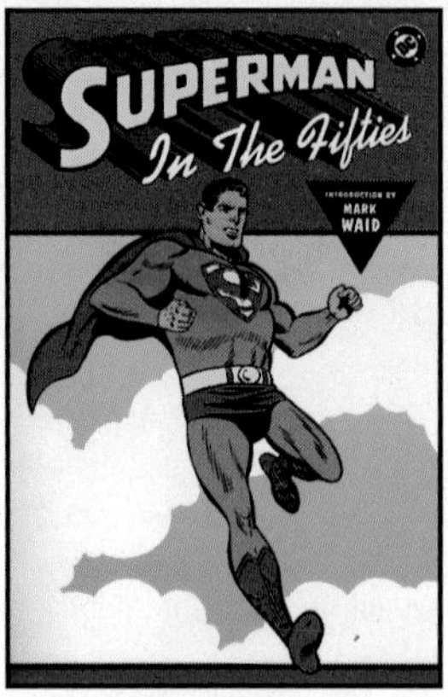
SUPERMAN
In The Fifties
INTRODUCTION BY
MARK
WAID

SUPERMAN IN THE FIFTIES
SUPERMAN IN THE SIXIES
SUPERMAN IN THE
SEVENTIES

various

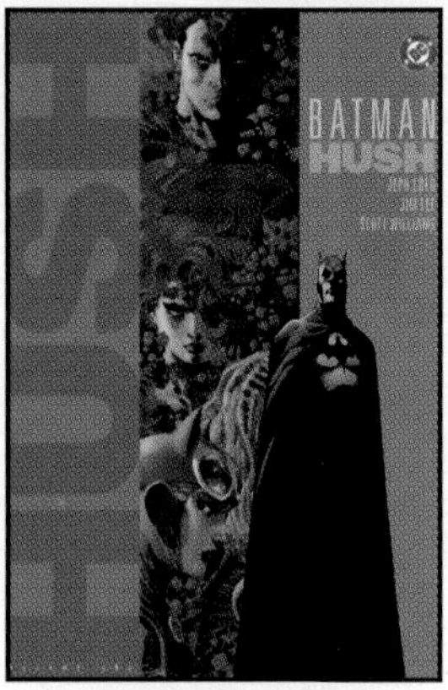
BATMAN
HUSH

BATMAN: HUSH
VOLUMES 1 & 2

Jeph Loeb/Jim Lee/Scott Williams

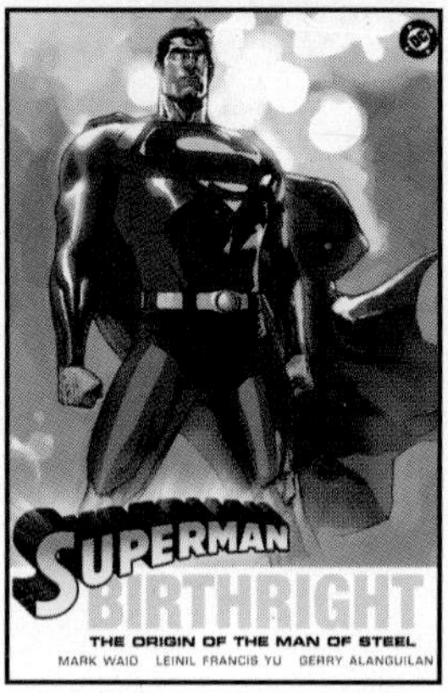
SUPERMAN
BIRTHRIGHT
THE ORIGIN OF THE MAN OF STEEL
MARK WAID LEINIL FRANCIS YU GERRY ALANGUILAN

SUPERMAN: BIRTHRIGHT

Mark Waid/Leinil Francis Yu/
Gerry Alanguilan

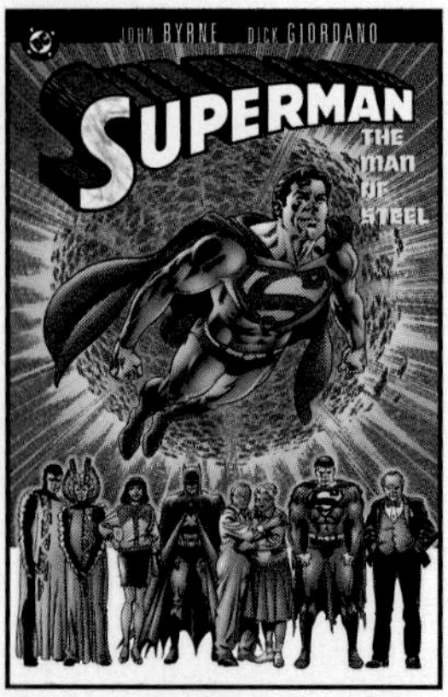
JOHN BYRNE DICK GIORDANO
SUPERMAN
THE
MAN
OF
STEEL

SUPERMAN: MAN OF STEEL
VOLUMES 1 - 3

John Byrne/Marv Wolfman/
Jerry Ordway

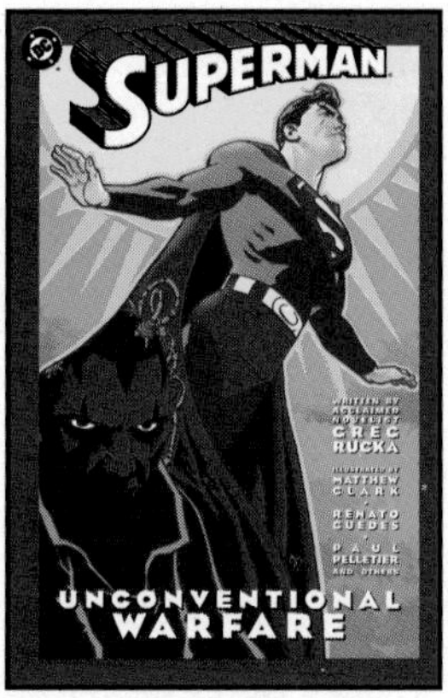
SUPERMAN
GREG
RUCKA
UNCONVENTIONAL
WARFARE

SUPERMAN:
UNCONVENTIONAL WARFARE

Greg Rucka/various

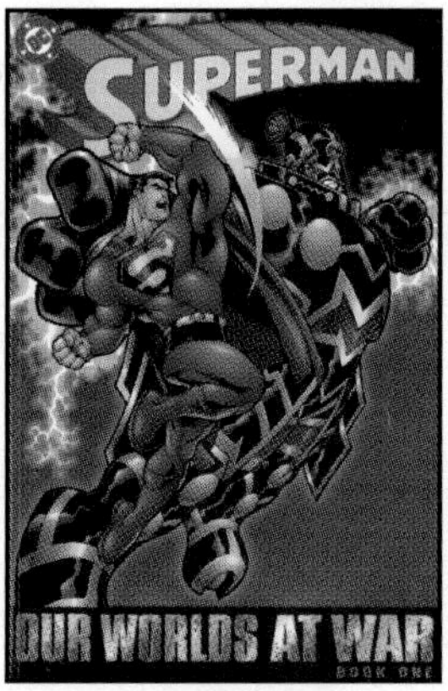
SUPERMAN
OUR WORLDS AT WAR
BOOK ONE

SUPERMAN:
OUR WORLDS AT WAR
VOLUMES 1 & 2

various

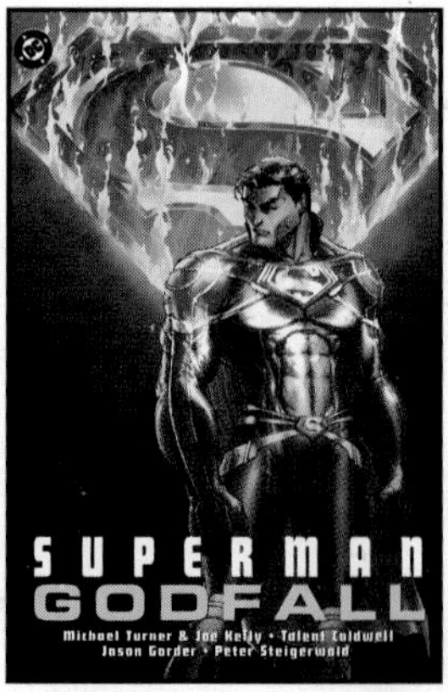
SUPERMAN
GODFALL

SUPERMAN: GODFALL

Michael Turner/Joe Kelly/Talent Caldwell/
Jason Gorder/Peter Steigerwald

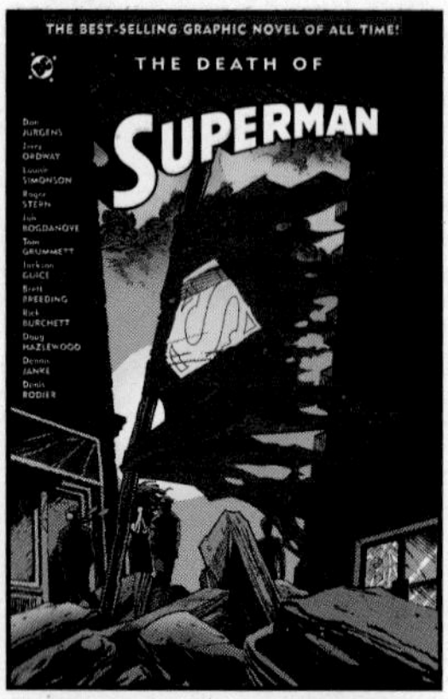
THE BEST-SELLING GRAPHIC NOVEL OF ALL TIME!
THE DEATH OF
SUPERMAN

DEATH OF SUPERMAN

various

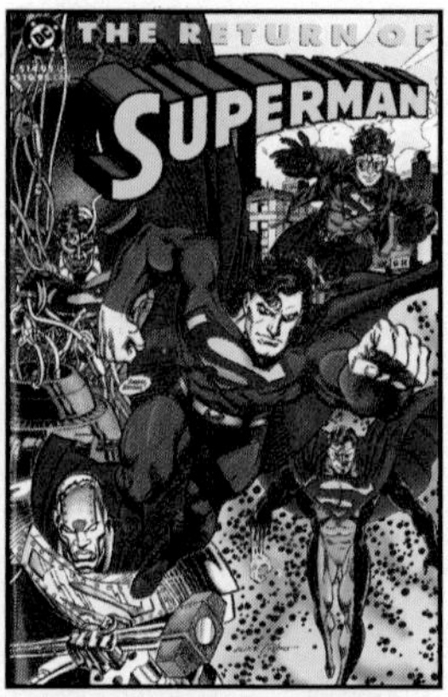
THE RETURN OF
SUPERMAN

RETURN OF SUPERMAN

various

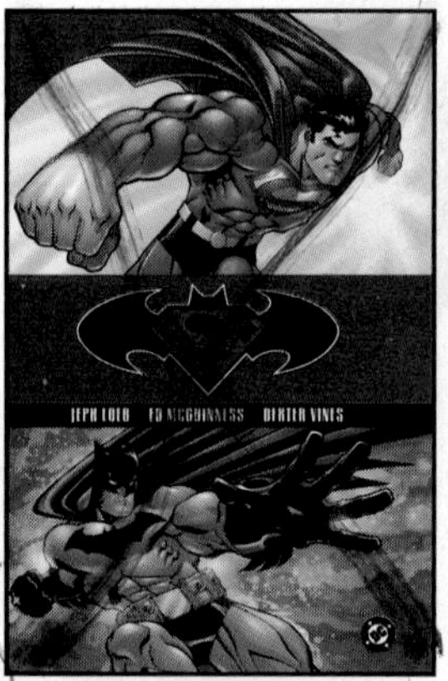
JEPH LOEB ED MCGUINNESS DEXTER VINES

SUPERMAN/BATMAN:
PUBLIC ENEMIES

Jeph Loeb/Ed McGuinness/
Dexter Vines

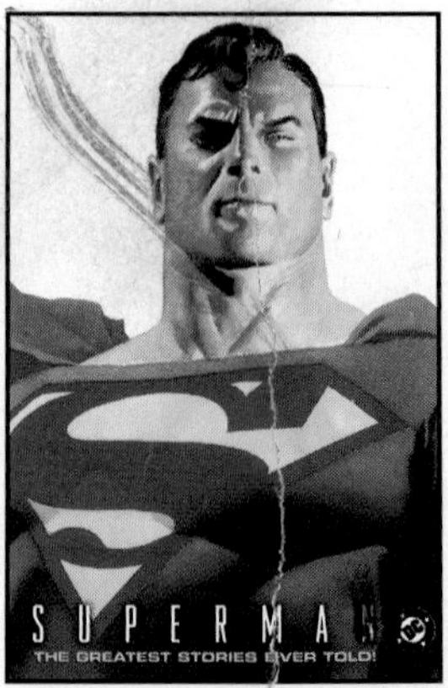
THE GREATEST STORIES EVER TOLD!

SUPERMAN:
THE GREATEST STORIES
EVER TOLD!

various